STARTING
AND
RUNNING
YOUR OWN
MARTIAL ARTS
SCHOOL

DEDICATION

To our husbands,

Drew Vactor and Gary Peterson.

Their support, patience, and good humor
made this book possible.

STARTING

AND

RUNNING

YOUR OWN

MARTIAL ARTS
SCHOOL

by

Karen Levitz Vactor

and

Susan Lynn Peterson, Ph.D.

TUTTLE PUBLISHING
Tokyo • Rutland, Vermont • Singapore

First published in 2002 by Tuttle Publishing, an imprint of Periplus Editions (HK) Ltd., with editorial offices at 364 Innovation Drive, North Clarendon, Vermont 05759.

Library of Congress Cataloging-in-Publication Data

Vactor, Karen Levitz
    Starting and running your own martial arts school / Karen Levitz Vactor and
    Susan Lynn Peterson.—1st ed.
        p. cm.
    Includes index.
        I. Martial arts schools. I. Peterson, Susan Lynn, 1957-II. Title.

GVI102.V22.2002
796.8—dc21   2002024285

ISBN-10: 0-8048-3428-8
ISBN-13: 978-0-8048-3428-5

Distributed by:

North America,
Latin America and Europe
Tuttle Publishing
364 Innovation Drive
North Clarendon, VT 05759-9436
Tel: (802) 773-8930
Fax: (802) 773-6993
Email: info@tuttlepublishing.com
Web site: www.tuttlepublishing.com

Asia Pacific
Berkeley Books Pte. Ltd.
130 Joo Seng Road
#06-01/03 Olivine Building
Singapore 368357
Tel: (65) 6280-1130
Fax: (65) 6280-6290
Email: inquiries@periplus.com.sg
Web site: www.periplus.com

Japan
Tuttle Publishing
Yaekari Building, 3F
5-4-12 Ōsaki, Shinagawa-ku
Tokyo 141-0032
Tel: (03) 5437-0171
Fax: (03) 5437-0755
Email: tuttle-sales@gol.com

09 07 06   10 9 8 7 6 5 4 3

Printed in Canada
Design by Sheila Selden Design

TUTTLE PUBLISHING ® is a registered trademark of Tuttle Publishing, a division of Periplus Editions (HK) Ltd.

TABLE of CONTENTS

SECTION TWO: OPERATING
A SUCCESSFUL MARTIAL ARTS SCHOOL   **115**

CHAPTER TEN:
SIGN UP NEW STUDENTS   **116**

ACKNOWLEDGMENTS

Many people have touched our lives and helped us grow in knowledge and spirit along the way. Some are close friends, others just passed through our lives leaving a significant impression behind.

Some of these people have been specifically helpful to this project, and we wish to thank them here.

We both would like to thank our husbands, Drew Vactor and Gary Peterson. Drew's business insights and editing help were invaluable in the final stage of the project. His willingness to put off work on his own book allowed us the time we needed to finish ours. Gary's flexibility makes a writer's life possible. And his suggestions for the source of the title were, if not plausible, at least a source of much-needed comic relief. Their patience, good humor, and support made it possible for us to complete this book.

We appreciate the support and encouragement we received from Hanshi George Anderson, Shihan Johnny Linebarger, Shihan Patrick Hickey, Shihan Pam Hickey, Sensei Lend McCaster, Sensei Thomas Linebarger, Sr., Sensei Melvin Dilts, and Sensei Judith Robinson.

Karen especially wants to thank her father, Sam Levitz, pioneer of the warehouse-showroom style of selling furniture, who introduced her to the wonderful world of retail at a young age. He taught her patiently and well, generously sharing his insight along with his fatherly wisdom. A warm thank you to her mother, Lee Levitz, who instilled in her a sense of wonder and adventurism that guides her daily, and who taught her to always believe in herself.

Susan especially wants to thank the writers of the CompuServe Writers Forum. Their insights on everything from semicolons to publishing contracts, book titles to creative health have been invaluable. She also wants to thank her parents, Donald and Shirley Johnson, for their continued support.

Our thanks also to:
Bette Martin, our photographer and good friend. Donald C. Brandenburgh, our literary agent. Charlotte Wood, owner of Talking Book World, Tucson, for her insights into the SBA loan process. Melinda Williams for her insights into balance sheets and accounting. Dayna Macy of Nolo Press, and Ardella Ramey of Oasis Press, who provided research materials.

How to Use This Book

Who Is This Book For?

Do you dream of opening your own martial arts school some day? Are you now in the process of planning and building a school? Do you have a school but struggle to run it efficiently and pay the bills? Do you have a successful school but want to learn ways of streamlining day-to-day management so you can spend more time training and having fun?

Then *Starting and Running Your Own Martial Arts School* is for you.

Starting and Running Your Own Martial Arts School is for experienced martial artists who dream about owning a successful school. It's a thorough, practical introduction to the tasks and obligations involved in opening a martial arts business. Written in language that doesn't take a business degree to understand, *Starting and Running Your Own Martial Arts School* shows martial artists what they can do to ensure the success of their school before they put their hard-earned cash and reputation on the line.

Starting and Running Your Own Martial Arts School also offers guidance for martial artists opening a new school. It provides step-by-step information on what to do, when to do it, and why. Based on years of practical experience, *Starting and Running Your Own Martial Arts School* helps new school owners establish successful habits while their school is still in its infancy. It helps them start right so they don't have to undo mistakes or relearn habits as their school grows.

Starting and Running Your Own Martial Arts School offers assistance to martial artists whose schools are struggling. It contains a troubleshooting guide to help school owners pinpoint their school's symptoms and diagnose its problems. It gives them simple steps they can take to help turn their school around. It provides practical, proven ideas to put their school back on the road to success.

Finally, *Starting and Running Your Own Martial Arts School* contains insights for those who have a healthy school but who are always on the lookout for ways of making it better. It offers experienced counsel on choosing advertising methods that work. It shows school owners how to sign up a higher percentage of people who walk through their door. It helps them reduce their drop-out rates. *Starting and Running Your Own*

Martial Arts School is packed with real-life information and ideas that school owners can use today to make their school even more successful.

Starting and Running Your Own Martial Arts School lets ordinary martial artists in on trade secrets usually reserved for business school graduates. It turns complex business information into simple, practical solutions to everyday business challenges. *Starting and Running Your Own Martial Arts School* takes the mystery out of business.

How Do You Use This Book?

Starting and Running Your Own Martial Arts School is a practical guide. Pull ideas and information from it. Use it to help you focus your dreams. Use it to spark new ideas and breathe new life into your existing school. Most of all, use it to spur action.

Before you start reading, get a three-ring notebook and a package of paper. Every time you get an idea for building or improving your school, write it down on a page entitled "Ideas."

You don't need to read this book from cover to cover. Read the first chapter to help you nail down your marketing identity. Then, dip in any place you need information or ideas.

As you work through the book, dream a little. Decide where you would like to be in a month, a year, five years. Then turn each dream and idea into a goal. Write your goals down. Compile a list of short-term goals, another of one-year goals, and still another of five-year goals.

Then determine what you need to do to make your goals a reality. Label another page "To Do List." Go through your goals and break them down into specific tasks. Decide when you want to do these tasks. Give yourself deadlines. Put each task into your calendar. Then get to work. Start building your future today.

STARTING
A
SUCCESSFUL
MARTIAL
ARTS
SCHOOL

CHAPTER ONE:

BUILD A SUCCESSFUL MARKETING IDENTITY

Your marketing identity is the face your business presents to the public. It contains the benefits you have to offer to a prospective student. It reflects your image, the way you project the things you believe in. It contains the things that best distinguish you from your competition. Your marketing identity is the foundation for all your advertising, for the way you approach prospective students, even for the way you decorate your school. It is your single most important marketing tool.

Focus on Your Image

Rule number one of marketing: people buy on emotion, on instinct. That doesn't mean all consumers are irrational. It just means that if people are going to spend hard-earned money on something, they are going to want to feel good about doing so. How often have you purchased something on a whim, just for the fun of it? How often have you relied, at least in part, on instinct or "street smarts" to tell you if what you were looking at was a good deal or a fraud? Your potential students do the same thing.

Your School's Image

When developing a marketing identity you must first ask yourself what image you want to project. What image do you want for your school? When prospective students talk to you for the first time—when they hang up the phone or walk out the door—how do they feel? Is that how you want them to feel about you? How can you get them to know in their gut that studying with you is the right thing to do?

Before you dismiss image as some artificial advertising fiction, think about the teachers you have studied with. Were they people of integrity? Did they care about the well-being of their students? Whether you answered yes or no, how could you tell? You could tell by the way they conducted themselves, the way they managed their school. You could tell by the way their "walk matched their talk." That, in its simplest form, is image.

If you believe in honor and integrity, the individual decisions you make about your business must reflect that honor and integrity. If children are important to you, you should show that in your day-to-day dealings with them. If you value strength tempered by self-control, if that is what you teach your students, ask yourself whether you project that value in your daily dealings with people. Looking at image is a reality check: Do your "walk and talk" reflect the things that are valuable to you?

If you are both the teacher and the owner of your school, about 60 percent of your school's image will be a reflection of your personality. The other 40 percent, however, will come from choices you make for your business. These choices will eventually give your business a personality of its own. Just as your personality comes through in your choice of clothes, the way you wear your hair, the way you speak to others, your business personality comes through in the way it looks and feels to others.

When examining your image, consider what target market you wish to attract. Your target market is the people you want to serve. Who is likely to want to study with you? To define your target market, think in terms of age, gender, marital status, and disposable income. These characteristics are called the "demographics" of your target market. Think about your preferences, but also think about the kind of people your art has attracted in the past. Talk to other martial arts school owners in your city about whom they teach. If your style has a national organization, check with them on their demographics. If your style has very few children (or adults), very few people in urban (or rural) areas, very few people with incomes over (or under) a certain level, there may be good reasons for those demographics. If you plan to attract a target market different from what your art usually attracts, make sure you have good reasons to support that choice.

A word on choosing children as your target market: if you want to teach children, your target market will be the children, yes. But it will also be the parents of those children. Specifically, your target market will be young adults with children and the disposable income necessary to enroll them in your school.

Your target market should be defined by the image you choose. If your target market is young children, you probably don't want to present yourself as a school for serious hand-to-hand combat. If your target market includes mostly soldiers from a nearby army base, teaching playground self-defense is silly.

In your idea notebook, describe your school's image—the way you want to come across to students and prospective students. Who is your target market? Do you want to come across as a school where the whole family is welcome? Or do you teach mostly children? Or perhaps are you directing your services at just adults, or just a certain group of adults? Look at the choices you have made for your school. Do you want to create an image of stability and permanence, or do you want to look lean, mean, and highly mobile? Do you want a large school with a dozen teachers, a midsized school with you and an assistant teacher, or a handful of students who become like a family to each other? Are you a place where people can work out at their own level and have fun, or are you a training ground for serious martial artists relentless in their pursuit of excellence? If a reporter were to do a feature article about your school, what would you like to read in it? Finish this sentence: "(Name of your school) is a school that _____." Get as detailed as you can. Remember that the more detailed you can get now, the easier it will be to use the information in your marketing identity later.

When it comes to image, there are no right or wrong answers. You are free to choose the image you wish. But the image you choose will have consequences. It will affect the kind and number of students you bring in. It will also affect your financial success. That being said, your school is your school. You choose your image, and you reap from the results of your choice, both positive and negative.

Your Own Personal Image

The next question, once you've pinpointed your business's image, is "What is your professional image?" How do you want to come across to current and potential students? Are you a mentor, a professor, a kindergarten teacher, a drill sergeant, or something else? What is your outlook on life, your views about education, your opinion about the role of the martial arts in society? How do you dress? How do you carry yourself? Are you a full-time, professional teacher? Do you do some other work by day and teach martial arts instruction in the evening? Is your art a way of life you share with a handful of students? If a reporter were to do a feature article about you, what would you like to read in it?

In your notebook, describe the image you yourself want to project. Get as detailed as you can. Again, the more detailed you can get now, the easier it will be to use the information in your marketing identity later.

The Image You Project

Now go back and read your notes on image, both for yourself and your school, and ask yourself another question. What tangible things do you do to project that image? This stage of the process is a reality check. You cannot afford to have an image that exists only on paper, only in your own mind. Look at what you have on paper and compare it to what exists in the real world of your school.

Take a look at your school and yourself. What do you do (or what will you do) to make your image real? For example, do you consider yourself a family school, a school for both adults and children? Then examine your dressing rooms, your equipment, your pro shop, every corner of your school. What do you have for children? Can they reach what they need to reach? Is your waiting area child-safe? Do you and your assistants know how to talk to children? Do you have activities for parents and children to do together? Perhaps you see yourself a winning tournament coach. Then look at your tournament program. Do you have training equipment for your athletes who choose to compete? Do you look for sponsors to help pay tournament expenses? Are you with your athlete at the tournaments? Do you avail yourself of programs that will make you a better coach?

Look, also, at your current students, especially your senior students. Many school owners have defined their target market as adults, both men and women, young to middle-aged. But when they look at their senior students, they are almost all young men or children. Look at your program, the physical demands, the atmosphere you create within your school. Is it suitable for your target market? Are you doing what is necessary to capture and keep the students you want?

Go back to the things you've written about your image. For each part of your image, ask yourself, "Am I projecting this now?" If the answer is "yes," add it to a page in your notebook and title it "Current Image." If you're not projecting the image right now, can you change a few things and make this part of your image a reality in a month or less? If so, add it to a "Short-Term Image Goals" list. Make a note, too, about what you need to change to make this part of your image real. If the image is still more dream than reality, that's OK. Those dreams can inspire your long-term goals. Add that part of your image to a "Long-Term Image Goals" list.

Remember these lists aren't just lists, they're your goals, the rudder for your school. Keep them in front of you. Figure out how you're going to meet them and when you're going to do so. Dream big dreams. Then, work as much as you dream.

PEOPLE WHO DON'T PAY ATTENTION TO IMAGE

COME ACROSS AS PEOPLE WHO

AREN'T PAYING ATTENTION.

THAT IN ITSELF IS AN IMAGE.

BUT NOT A GOOD ONE.

Examine Your Features—What Do You Have?

Now that you have a clearer idea of your school's image, let's look at its features, what you and your school have to offer. Image is the impression you want to make on your students and prospective students. Features are the specific things you have to offer them.

On a list entitled "Features," list the noteworthy features of your school. Think about equipment, physical space, resources, your own training and skills—in short, physical, objective characteristics. If you use Olympic-regulation equipment or nationally recognized teaching methods, those are features. So are well-lighted dressing rooms, a training area with good lighting and ventilation, a pro shop, your own credentials and associations, and your employees and their credentials. Walk around the school and look. List all the positive features.

Then recognize that a student will choose a school for more than just its features. A student will choose a school for the benefits those features offer.

Determine Your Benefits—What's in It for Them?

Let's say you're a member of a national association of martial artists. A new student walks through the door. You tell him, as a part of your introduction to the school, that you and your school are a part of this great organization. He nods with a blank look on his face.

Let's say, by contrast, that you listen to your prospective student, find out what's important to him. If he has dreams of seeing himself standing on a dais with a gold medal around his neck, you show him how your affiliation will offer him tournament opportunities. Or if he is worried about having to start from scratch should he move to another city, you show him how your organization offers recognition of his rank throughout the country. What you have done is shown what a feature of your school can do for that prospective student. You have demonstrated its benefit. Benefits are how features tap into the basic needs and motivations of your students. Benefits satisfy the wants and desires of prospective students.

A brief word on people and what makes them do what they do and buy what they buy: One of the most commonly used hierarchies of motives was developed by the American psychologist Abraham Maslow.

> **Level six:** curiosity and
>
> the need to understand
>
> **Level five:** self-fulfillment
>
> **Level four:** competence, prestige, and esteem
>
> **Level three:** love, sex, and feelings of belonging
>
> **Level two:** security and safety
>
> **Level one:** physiological needs: food, shelter, oxygen, water

He maintained that people have six kinds of basic needs. The most fundamental of those needs are the physical ones: food, shelter, oxygen. If these fundamental, primitive needs are met, then people are freed to meet their second level of need: safety and security. Once people feel safe and secure, then they seek out the third level, and so on through the six levels.

How does this work for you? Remember: people's hearts motivate them to buy as much as or more than their heads do. Typically they are motivated by the lower-level needs more strongly than upper-level ones. What benefits can you offer to tap into one or more of your potential students' basic needs?

Let's say that one of your features is a spring-loaded training deck. This allows your students to train without putting undue stress on their joints. In short, it helps keep them safe. Safety is one of the basic human needs (level two). A pro shop is a feature. If students can get your opinion before purchasing gear, they will feel that they know enough to make a wise selection. That increases their feelings of competence (level four). Moreover, they will be more likely to have gear that matches the gear of the other students, increasing their feelings of belonging (level three).

Go back to your features list. Pick out your top ten features—the features that are your strongest, that are most likely to distinguish you from your competition. List how each feature will benefit your students. Write down as many benefits as you can think of.

Each feature should have several benefits, and those benefits may be different for different students. For example, a spring-loaded, padded floor may appeal to an adult student because it saves wear and tear on arthritic hips: it makes them feel safe. Parents of young students will like the idea that it takes the pressure off the growth plates of their child's joints: it appeals to maternal and paternal instincts. And the three-year-olds might just enjoy jumping up and down on it: it makes their time with you more fun. For prospective adult students, your benefits must appeal to adults. For elementary school students, the benefits must appeal to the parents. For teenagers, the benefits must appeal to both the parents and the teenager.

Let's go back and summarize. When figuring out what you have to offer, ask yourself four questions:

1. What image do I want to project?
2. What tangible things project that image?
3. What are the features of my school?
4. What benefits do those features offer the prospective student?

Once you have answers for these questions, once you have a clear view of who and what you are, you can pull together the necessary information to build a marketing identity.

Develop Your Marketing Identity

Go through your lists—image, features, and benefits—and pick out the five to ten most important points. Choose aspects of your image you can project convincingly. Include the feature-benefit combinations that are likely to be most important to your prospective students.

Remember: this is your marketing identity. It is an identity that will convince prospective students that your school is the right place for them to study. What can you offer them that no one else can? What feature-benefits are so attractive that they would be tough to say "no" to? What part of your image says, "Come study with me, I can make your life a better one."

Turn these five to ten points into a single paragraph that expresses the best of who you are. Once you have the information in place, rewrite the paragraph to make it personal. It should sound as though you are talking to a potential student: friendly, personal, informative. This paragraph is your marketing identity.

What do you do with a marketing identity? You build your business communications on it. It is the basis for your brochure and all the rest of your advertising. It is a part of your business plan and loan applications. It helps you choose a location. It helps you sign up new students. It helps keep you focused when serving your current students. What do you do with a marketing identity? Let's just say that marketing your school successfully without one would be tough. A marketing identity expresses who you are and why people should choose you and your school.

Choose a Name That Reflects Your Image

Large corporations spend big bucks choosing names that make people want to buy their products. You probably don't have that kind of money to throw at a market research campaign. Nonetheless, you must choose your school name carefully. What you name your school does make a difference.

Choose a name that fits with your image. If you were a parent looking for a place for your shy seven-year-old to study self-defense, would you choose a place called Bloody Tiger Gym? If you were a young adult looking for a traditional martial arts teacher, would you even darken the door of Little Dragons Karate School and Day Care Center? Your name should capture your image.

Your school name should be partly descriptive, partly inventive. The descriptive part tells what you do as a business. It identifies you quickly to potential customers. For example, let's say you want to call your school "Eastern Treasures." In your mind, put that name on a storefront sign. Now drive by and look at it as though you were unfamiliar with the business. What do you see? A martial arts school? An import shop? A jewelry store? If the sign, however, were to say "Eastern Treasures Wushu Academy" you would know what happens inside. Part of your business name must state what you do.

The other part of your business name should be inventive. If your name is purely descriptive, you cannot protect it from others who might want to use it. So for example if you call your martial arts school

"Shorin-ryu Karate," and if another school down the street opens a school that teaches the same style, they too could call their business "Shorin-ryu Karate." Why? Because "Shorin-ryu" is the name of a style of karate. Like the names of specific objects, the name of a specific martial art or specific martial arts style cannot be protected as a trademark or service mark (unless of course the art is something entirely new and invented by you). A better name would be "Golden Leopard Shorin-ryu Karate."

How about a name like "Dave Smith's Taekwondo Academy"? A business name that incorporates your own name can be legally protected. You should, however, think of the wider consequences of using your own name. If your school doesn't succeed, will you want your name associated with a failed business? If it does succeed, but you want to open another business of a very different kind, could there be image problems if the one business is associated with the other? What if the business is successful beyond your wildest dream? If someone comes to you to buy the business, including the name, would you sell? Would you want someone else controlling a school bearing your name? Using your own name as a part of your business name has its disadvantages. If, however, your name is highly recognizable or a central part of your school's image, using it can be a savvy marketing decision. If using your own name as a part of your business's name will draw in business from your target market, you may decide the advantages outweigh the disadvantages.

Choose a school name after you've put together a marketing identity. Naming a school before you've determined its identity is like naming a baby before you know whether it's a boy or a girl. Your school name must project your school image.

Your marketing identity affects everything you present to the public: your business name, your brochure, your posters, your selling approach, your tour for prospective students, and all of your mass-media advertising. It states who you are, what benefits you give to your students, and why you are different from your competition. It helps you to focus your strengths and minimize your weaknesses.

Later we'll show you how to build on your marketing identity to create your mission statement and to secure financing for your school. We'll show you how to turn your marketing identity into effective advertising, and how to use it to bring in and sign up new students. You'll also need a clear picture of your marketing identity to choose the right location for your school. You'll need it to help you set the right fees for your services. In short, if you don't have a clear marketing identity before you begin putting the pieces of your business together, you can waste a lot of time and effort. Spend some time putting one together now.

CHAPTER TWO:

FINANCE YOUR NEW SCHOOL

Starting a new business is not cheap. With the privileges of being your own boss, you will also be taking on the financial risks of being your own boss. Small business statistics show that those risks are great. But they can be minimized by careful advance planning.

The tool you use to do this advance planning is called a business plan. Putting together a business plan involves making accurate estimates of income and expenses, profit and loss. It involves setting financial and personal goals for the business. It involves choosing a legal form for your business, setting up a preliminary marketing strategy, assessing your competition, and charting a path for the next several years of your business life. A business plan can help you obtain start-up financing. It can help you see where your own business skills may be lacking. It becomes a framework for future action. But most importantly, it can help you get a realistic picture of the financial risks and rewards inherent in owning your own martial arts school.

Start with Estimates

The first step in putting together a start-up business plan is making estimates. Estimate how much money you will need for start-up costs. Calculate your break-even point. Then make some financial plans for your first two years in business.

Start-Up Capital

Start-up capital is the money you need to set up your business. To put it another way, start-up capital is the money you will need to spend before you can open your doors to do business.

Unfortunately, no simple formula can tell you how much start-up capital you will need. The only way to come up with that figure is to list all your expenses. As a start, consider these costs:

START-UP COSTS

First and last months' rent
Triple net expenses
Utility deposits
Licenses and permits
Insurance
Legal fees
Accountant's fees
Other professional fees
Decorating and remodeling
Office equipment
Computer and software
Fixtures
Furniture
Display cases and racks
Training equipment
Installation costs for fixtures and
    equipment
Office supplies
Printing costs
Janitorial supplies
Other supplies
Signs
Initial inventory for your pro shop
Advertisement of your opening
Operating cash
Unforeseen expenses (add 10 percent)

If you're making these estimates only to satisfy your own curiosity, you can make educated guesses. If, however, you are trying to calculate start-up costs for a loan application, guessing can get you into big trouble. Many lenders, especially those associated with the Small Business Administration (SBA) program expect you to know precisely what you will need to purchase and what it will cost to do so. If you're building anything at all on these numbers, even if it's just the assurance that you can make a school work financially, don't cheat yourself. Do the research. Make estimates you can rely on.

Remember, too, that these expenses are only the ones you can anticipate. Starting a new business usually takes more money than you expect. Allow yourself a buffer for unforeseen expenses.

Break-Even Point

Another crucial step in planning for the financial health of a new business is calculating your break-even point. Your break-even point is how much income you need monthly to pay all of your bills including payroll.

Monthly Break-Even

To calculate your break-even point, begin by adding all your obligatory expenses.

TYPICAL MONTHLY EXPENSES

Rent and other expenses mandated by your lease
Insurance
Employee wages
Payments on loans
Advertising
Office supplies
Other supplies
Postage
Printing expenses
Utilities (approximately a third of your rent, ballpark estimate)
FICA or SE taxes
Other payroll taxes
Sales taxes
Taxes you are required to pay according
    to the terms of your lease
Maintenance
Miscellaneous costs of doing business (for example, costs of
    uniforms for yourself and your employees, membership dues
    for professional organizations, franchise fees, etc.)

Some expenses, such as FICA and SE taxes, are annual expenses. Others, such as insurance premiums, may need to be paid semiannually or quarterly. If an expense comes due annually, divide that annual expense by twelve to calculate monthly break-even. If an expense comes due quarterly, divide by three. In other words, calculate expenses on a per-month basis.

Some people like to add their own monthly salary into this equation. Others figure it separately. If, just to stay afloat, you must get some money out of the business for yourself, add a minimum salary into your calculations. If, at least at first, you have other sources of income to meet your personal needs, calculate your salary separately.

Always estimate expenses a little on the high side if you want to avoid unpleasant surprises. The sum of your expenses is the minimum amount of money you will need to take in each month. It is your "break-even point."

Number of Students Needed to Break Even

Another way to keep track of your break-even point is to think of it in terms of how many students you need to pay the bills. That number, of course, depends on how much you expect each student to spend. Besides tuition, several other expenses come into play in this calculation. How many seminars or tournaments will each student be participating in? After expenses, what could you expect to earn per student on these

---

CALCULATING MONTHLY PER-STUDENT INCOME

For each student:

	Annual tuition fees
Plus	Annual retail sales from their retail purchases
Plus	Annual income from seminars, promotions, and tournaments
Minus	Annual per student expenses (cost of emblems, books, certificates you give them for the above fees, calculated on a per-student basis)
Divided by	12
Equals	Monthly per-student income

---

events? Will you have a formal ranking or certification program? If so will you charge for each promotion? How much do you expect to earn from promotion fees? Do you plan to have a retail area? If so, how much can you expect each student to spend on uniforms and gear each year? How much of that income can you keep as profit?

Add each of these additional sources of income to your yearly tuition to get your annual per student income. Then subtract any per-student expenses you might have. For example, you may get $200 per student in testing and promotion fees each year, but spend $50 of that on certificates, registration with the state or national organization, or emblems-of-rank belts, patches, or a plaque on your school wall. Subtract these annual per-student expenses from your annual income. Then divide the remainder by twelve to get your monthly per-student income.

To calculate the number of students you will need to break even, divide your total monthly expenses (your break-even point) by your monthly per-student income. For example, let's say you need $3,000 each month to break even. Your monthly per-student income is $100. You need thirty students just to break even. Those first thirty students pay the bills. Every student beyond thirty (your break-even number) adds to your profit.

If you eventually also want to make a salary for yourself, you'll need to figure that into your calculations, as well. Divide the monthly salary you would like to be making by your monthly per-student income, and that will tell you how many more students you will need to pay yourself. Add the two numbers to get your target enrollment number.

CALCULATING TARGET ENROLLMENT

	Monthly expenses
Divided by	Monthly per-student income
Equals	Number of students needed to break even
	Desired monthly salary
Divided by	Monthly per-student income
Equals	Number of students needed to pay your salary
	Students needed to break even
Plus	Students needed to pay your salary
Equals	Target enrollment

Be aware, however, that "target enrollment" is not the number of students you will need to sign up. Target enrollment is the number of paying students you need every month to pay your bills and yourself. To keep your school at its target enrollment, you'll need to sign up not only enough students to pay the bills; you'll also need to sign up new students to compensate for those who drop out. Remember, too, that we're talking about paying students, not training students. If they don't pay, they aren't a part of your target enrollment.

A word about the future: While you're figuring out expenses, also look at "optional" expenses. For example, you may eventually want to be able to hire an employee. You may want to expand your school. Consider, too, your own continuing education: you may want to set aside money for seminars and teacher-training classes. Sure, at the beginning, you will probably be glad if the business makes enough to support itself. Eventually, though, you may want to run not just a self-supporting business but a thriving one. To figure out how many students you would need to support additional expenses, you can use the same formula. Monthly expenses for your optional projects divided by monthly per-student income equals number of students needed to support the optional projects.

Calculating your break-even point and additional expenses in terms of target enrollment makes those expenses "real" in a way numbers can't: "I need thirty students to break even. No more than twenty of my regular students have been training this month. I need to check to see if I can repair the problem before next month's bills come due." "To hire a part-time employee to manage the office, I need ten more paying students." "To afford the expenses at a new location I need another twenty-five students." In other words, if you think of your break-even point in terms of number of students, you can look at your monthly sign-up, attendance, and payment records and get an immediate, intuitive sense of whether you are getting closer to your financial goals.

Your First Two Years

In the early months, while you are still building your student base and trying to reach your target enrollment, you will need outside funding to meet your monthly expenses. As a rough estimate, assume that for the first six months you will be paying nearly all your monthly expenses out of pocket. That means before you open your doors you need to know where you will get those first six months' operating expenses.

Assume that after those six months are over, you will still have to pay out of pocket for some of your operating expenses for up to two years. Why? Statistically, you will not be making a regular profit for two years. Sure, you will have profitable months before then. But you may need two years to figure out what your annual business cycle will be. You will probably need two years to learn to anticipate slow months. And you will probably need two years to save enough reserves to weather them. In short, it normally takes two years before you are out of the building stage of your business and into the maintaining stage. Of course, you might hit a steady target enrollment before then. Some businesses are self-supporting in a year or less. But though you can hope to be out of the building stage in a year, though you can work toward that goal, you should plan to have backup funds available for two years.

How do you handle the financial demands of those first two years? One way is to get a business loan for just start-up costs. You then set up a revolving credit line with a bank or private lender for initial operating expenses. You can draw money from the credit line as you need it, and repay the debt as you have extra profit. Another option is "bootstrapping." You borrow the start-up costs and keep your day job to meet your living expenses, maybe even to help pay some monthly business expenses, while you're growing the business. Whichever option you choose, make sure you know where you will get the money for those early operating expenses. You don't want to get desperate and eat up your family's nest egg.

Discover Sources of Money Available to You

You will probably finance your business from two sources: equity and debt. Equity funding is the owner's cash contribution to the business. It can include personal funds and also funds invested by family and friends. Equity funding is money that remains in the business indefinitely. Unlike a loan, it has no set pay-back schedule.

If you don't have enough money to start a business on your own, you can turn to various kinds of lending institutions. Generally, you will need to be willing and able to invest most of the initial equity in your business. Lending institutions are typically reluctant to provide more than half the start-up funds for a small business. Any loan you get from a lending institution will have a predefined repayment schedule. Under that schedule you must repay specified amounts of principal and interest within a specified amount of time.

Commercial Loans

Commercial loans are the most common kind of small business loan. They come from your local bank, savings and loan, or credit union. The terms and requirements of these different institutions vary widely. If you're interested in a commercial loan, familiarize yourself with basic lending terminology and read the pamphlets various lending institutions have available. Then make an appointment with a loan officer. Show up on time, professionally dressed for the business world (not the martial arts world), and present your well-thought-out and professional-looking business plan. After you sell the lender on the potential of your business and your ability to run it, they can help you get started on the loan application process.

Government Loans

Another possible source of funding is government loans. Government loans come in two kinds: guaranteed loans and direct loans. Guaranteed loans are loans made by commercial lending institutions backed by a government loan loss guarantee. In other words, the government program functions something like a cosigner. Direct loans are loans made by the government, typically to members of a specific group or for specific purposes.

The SBA loan program offers guaranteed loans. The SBA has a congressionally mandated program whose purpose is helping small businesses gain financing. Most SBA loans are made through the 7(a) Loan Guaranty Program. These government-guaranteed loans are made by banks and other lending institutions. The average SBA loan is for 50 to 75 percent of the start-up costs of a small business, typically around $175,000. The average maturity is about eight years. The SBA also offers a "MicroLoan" program, in which the amount borrowed is less than $10,000 and the repayment period is less than six years. Sometimes (but not always) these loans have a higher interest rate than what the bank offers. Usually, however, they have fewer qualification requirements than the bank's conventional loans. If you don't qualify for a loan directly from a bank, you may be able to qualify for an SBA loan.

Be aware, however, that the SBA loan program is a government program and, as such, has government-style quirks. For example, if you borrow money from your uncle Fred, he will probably write you a check and you can spend the money as you see fit. If you borrow money from Uncle Sam, however, the process is not that straightforward. Most SBA loans don't make payments directly to you. They pay the people you are buying goods and services from. If you want to use the money to buy, for example, a desk, you have two choices. You can go out and buy the desk, submit the receipts, and have the lending institution reimburse you. Or you can go out and get an invoice for the cost of the desk, and the lending institution will pay the store directly.

Furthermore, an SBA lending institution will earmark percentages of the money for specific categories. If you estimated in your application that you will need $3,000 for inventory and $5,000 for fixtures, don't expect the SBA to allow you to spend $2,000 for inventory and $6,000 for fixtures. Also, you need to make sure that when you say "inventory" and "fixtures" you mean the same thing the SBA program means when they use the terms. The government is not thinking, as you are, about how you will use these things; they're thinking about how they could sell them and get their money back should you default.

One special SBA program is the Minority Prequalification Loan Program. If your business is at least 51 percent owned and managed by a member of an ethnic minority, the SBA will find you an intermediary to help you put together a loan application and find a lender.

The government also offers direct loans to special groups. For example, the SBA has a loan program for disabled veterans and for Vietnam veterans. The Handicapped Assistance Loan Program offers start-up loans to business owners when either the owner is disabled or disabled individuals work 75 percent (or more) of the staff hours. Special loan programs for women or minority-owned businesses are also available.

If you think you might be eligible for a direct loan, check with the SBA or your state lending agencies. SBA offices are listed in the telephone directory under "U.S. Government," or you can call the Small Business Answer Desk at 1-800-8-ASK-SBA.

Private Family Loans

In your investigation of commercial and government loan programs, don't neglect one of the most common sources for loans: friends and family. Many, perhaps most, new businesses are funded by family members. Often, the best place to borrow money is from relatives. But sometimes, the worst place to borrow money is from relatives. On the one hand, who is more likely to appreciate your vision or to want to see you succeed than your family? On the other, if your business doesn't succeed, you will lose not only your money but that of the family member who invested in you. Think through the long-term implications of borrowing from family.

If you decide to use a relative's or friend's money, treat the loan as an "arm's-length transaction," the same as you would if it were from a bank. Give them your business plan. Decide the amount of interest and the payback schedule. Make sure the arrangement is in writing. Then stick to the terms as though your future family relations depended on it.

Sometimes a family member who cannot give you cash will be willing to cosign a commercial loan. Again, be sure you don't stick them with your bad management. A cosigner is equally responsible for the loan repayment. If you can't repay your debt, they must.

Apply for a Loan

One of the best ways to boost your chances for getting a bank loan is to do some groundwork before you apply. Learn about banking procedures, policies, and constraints. Put together a business plan that anticipates what the loan officer will need from you. Banks typically have an application form they want you to fill out. But applying for a loan involves more than just filling in all the blanks. Put some time and effort into your business plan. Doing so will help you stand out from other loan applicants.

Compile the evidence you need to present yourself as a good credit risk. What does a good risk look like?

1. You are someone of good character. You are willing to work hard. You have a proven reputation as a responsible citizen.
2. You have what it takes to run the business. Your credit report shows you have a good track record when it comes to handling money. You have the business skills—acquired through education, practical experience, or both—that you need to make the business a success.
3. You have quite a bit of your own money invested. By investing your own money, you show that you are likely to work to build your investment and theirs.
4. You have collateral to support your primary repayment source.

If any of these statements aren't true, you may need to find an alternate source of funding. If all of them are true, make sure you have the evidence to show your lender.

A word on credit reports: Expect your lender to check yours. Before you apply for a loan, before your lender points out credit trouble, order a copy and address any problems that might be on it. The largest supplier of consumer and business credit reports is Experian (formerly TRW Information Systems). If you wish to purchase a copy of your credit report using a credit card, you can call them 1-888-EXPERIAN. They can get you a copy in about a week. They also have mail-order forms available on their Web site. If you need help reading your credit report, or if you need to repair poor credit, the Experian Web site (www.experian.com) has information to get you started.

When you've thought through the questions your loan officer might ask and put together your loan application in a neat, easy-to-read format, it's time to present it. Make an appointment. Dress professionally. Show up on time. Allocate enough time that you don't need to be looking at your watch during the interview. Present your request clearly and honestly.

Ask questions if you don't understand something.

Expect your lender to ask for three sources of repayment: standard repayment, collateral, and a personal guarantee. You probably plan to repay your loan with the proceeds of your business. Expect to prove that you can do so. Expect also to be asked for collateral. Loans in which assets are pledged as collateral are called "secured loans." If yours is a secured loan, and you aren't able to pay off the loan, the bank takes over ownership of the asset you've pledged. Small business loans are often secured loans. If you don't have collateral, you may find that getting a loan is more difficult. Don't necessarily assume, however, that it's impossible.

Besides collateral, your lender may also ask for some form of personal guarantee from you, the owner of the business. In other words, if you cannot repay the loan from the proceeds of your business, you must repay it from personal funds.

You may ask, "Do they really need three sources of repayment?" Perhaps not from a mere bookkeeping point of view. What they really need, what they secure by asking for three forms of repayment, is the assurance that you are motivated to repay your loan. You have to admit that the thought that they could tap into your assets or even your personal bank account is a powerful motivator. By allowing them three sources of repayment, you prove that you are both able and highly committed to repay your loan.

When applying for a loan, you will, of course, want to be as persuasive as possible. But never do so at the expense of the truth. Do not inflate your assets or your projections. If anything, underestimate your projections. Why? Not only is it unethical to overstate your financial status, it's illegal.

On the flip side, the federal government has protected your right to apply for credit. The Equal Credit Opportunity Act (ECOA) says no one may deny you credit based on sex, marital status, race, national origin, religion, age, or receipt of public assistance income. Neither can the bank refuse to lend you money based on the personal traits of potential customers. The ECOA doesn't guarantee that you will get a loan, only that you will not be discriminated against in the loan process. If you want more information, contact the Federal Trade Commission.

A little advance planning can save you a lot of financial worry over the years. First, make careful, realistic estimates, always allowing enough buffer for emergencies and unforseen expenses. Break down your budget in terms of number of students needed and target enrollment. Work up a detailed business plan, and develop both short-term and long-term goals. Then find the most appropriate financial partner available to you. If you learn the basics of financing a small business before you start spending money, you can build your school on a solid financial foundation right from the start.

CHAPTER THREE:

LAY THE BUSINESS GROUNDWORK

Assemble Your Team of Advisors

Running a small business means doing a variety of jobs. The life of you
business requires you to make professional decisions about everything from
finance to dealing with the government, from insurance coverage to advertis
ing. How do you do it all well? You get help.

You need to have a relationship with an accountant, an attorney, and
a banker, before you need them. These business professionals have
specialties. You will want yours to be familiar with the needs of a small
service business.

Don't be afraid to interview several accountants, attorneys, and
bankers before choosing one. Make sure your advisors have experience
with the kinds of things you need them to do. Make sure, also, that they have
the same philosophy of business you do. For example, if you want to pursue
every possible income tax deduction, you don't want an extremely conserva-
tive accountant. If you are running a small business, you don't want an
attorney who works only for multinational conglomerates and considers your
small businesses a waste of time. Find advisors who share your values and
understand your business priorities. Look at who they have as clients. Does
your business fit in with their client list? Then, listen to them when they
answer your questions. Do they talk with you in terms you can understand?

If you have students who are attorneys or accountants, you may want to engage their services for your business. Be sure to pay them or offer like-valued services in exchange for their help. If students feel that you are taking advantage of them, you could lose them, both as students and as advisors. Moreover, be sure these students can get away from their business when they're studying with you. One main reason working adults sign up with a martial arts school is to spend some time each week forgetting their job. Make sure your students who work for you do so during their work time, not during their recreation time.

Accountant

At a minimum, have your accountant do your business income taxes. The IRS tax code makes it difficult and very time-consuming for untrained individuals to do their own business taxes. Having your accountant do your taxes can not only save you time and aggravation but also save you money.

A good accountant can be a valuable consultant not only at tax time but whenever you need insight into financial matters. For example, ask your accountant for a list of the licenses and tax forms you will need to open and run your business. Accountants deal with such things as a part of their job. They should be able to make sure you haven't forgotten something crucial.

By the way, if you can't read a financial statement, don't hesitate to ask your accountant for help. Reading a financial statement is a matter of understanding ratios. Your accountant can teach you which ones are necessary for you to get a good idea of how healthy your business is. (See chapter 12 for more information on financial statements and ratios.)

How do you find a good accountant? Ask business associates, your banker, your attorney. Look for someone who is a member of a state or national professional accounting association. Most of these associations require their members to subscribe to a code of ethics. They also require continuing education, which is crucial for an accountant who wishes to keep up with new accounting methods and the ever-changing tax code.

Accountants typically have a price list for various services. It's a good idea to get that list before you begin a relationship. In fact, get the list before you begin making financial estimates for your prospective business. Budget enough money to hire a good accountant right from the beginning.

Attorney

Do you need an attorney? Yes. It's an attorney's job to know where the legal land mines are. Especially if you've never owned a small business before, attorney's fees will probably be a small price for peace of mind. An attorney's function is not just to get you out of legal trouble. A good attorney can help you avoid legal problems before they happen.

For most of your needs, you want a basic business attorney, in other words, a corporate attorney who knows small businesses. Describe your business needs to the attorney. If your needs lie outside her specialization, ask for a referral to the correct specialist. Many attorneys work in large practices with experts in several different specialties under one roof. These large firms give you the advantage of multiple resources when you need them. Always have one main attorney representing your interests, though.

When you go in for the initial interview with an attorney, in fact any time you go in for a consultation, have a list of questions. Time with an attorney is not cheap. Do some advance planning. Use your attorney's time wisely. Doing so is using your own money wisely.

Banker

Of course you will want a checking account with a bank. But more than that, you should have a good business relationship with a bank. A good bank can handle your accounts, provide you with a line of credit, handle your credit card transactions, and even give you valuable business information.

Make an appointment with the manager or account representative of several banks in your area. Tell them you're opening a martial arts school in the neighborhood and are interviewing banks. Compare overall service, fees, and whether they offer the specific services you need. In your interview with a banker, you are doing three things: First, you are getting enough information about fees and services to make an informed decision about where you want to bank. Second, you are feeling out where you might be able to get a loan and what would be required in doing so. And finally, you are getting a feel for the "personality" of each bank and the people who run it. Based on these three kinds of information, you make your choice of bank.

If you develop a good, long-term relationship with your banker, you can get important business advice from her. Ask your banker to give you her definition of a healthy business. Ask her to describe the telltale signs of a business that's getting into financial trouble. Remember that bankers make a career of determining which businesses are good credit risks and which aren't. Ask them what ratios they like to see on small business balance sheets. Forge a relationship with not only a bank but also the people who run the bank: the branch manager, a loan officer, the person in charge of credit card services. Greet them by name when you come in to make a deposit. Make them your allies.

Other Consultants

The SBA supports several organizations whose purpose is to foster small business growth. Throughout the United States, this federal government agency has local offices whose sole purpose is helping small business owners.

For example, the SBA's Small Business Development Centers offer free counseling, training, and technical assistance to small business owners. These centers are staffed by a mix of government and private sector consultants, mentors, and teachers. Their purpose is to direct you to experienced professionals who can teach you how to put together a business plan, find financing, or set up a profitable business. SBA consultants are available to small business owners who can't afford to pay a private consultant to help them begin or expand their first small business. The SBA has at least one Small Business Development Center in each state. SBA offices are in the telephone directory under "U.S. Government," you can check their Web site at www.sba.gov, or you can call the Small Business Answer Desk at 1-800-8-ASK-SBA.

Another service of the Small Business Administration is the network of Business Information Centers. These centers are high-tech laboratories that have computer workstations, videos, and other technical resources for start-up small businesses. Counselors can help you use these resources to set up your business or to improve your existing business. The Business Information Centers are less widespread than the Small Business Development Centers, but more than thirty are scattered throughout the country. Check your telephone directory under "U.S. Government" to see if there is one in your city.

For a novice business owner, one of the most valuable SBA resources is SCORE, the Service Corps of Retired Executives (www.score.org). These experienced volunteers work with the SBA to provide free counseling on most facets of starting and managing a small business. The SCORE program can help you find and supplement the areas where you are weak. For example, if you have experience in bookkeeping and accounting but have never done any management, SCORE can recommend a mentor with management experience. Be aware, however, that SCORE is a mentoring program. It's not their job to run your business or to do your work for you. They can give you experienced advice, but only you can chart the course of your business.

Set Up the Legal Form of Your Business

Once you've assembled your team of professionals, it is time to enlist their help and make some important decisions. Before you put together your business plan, before you start applying for loans, you need to choose the legal form of your business.

BUSINESS STRUCTURE OPTIONS

Sole Proprietorship

General Partnership

Limited Partnership

Limited Liability Company

C Corporation

Subchapter S Corporation

The legal form of your business determines the way the IRS and the legal system see you and your business. Your choice will have tax and liability repercussions. In most states, you have five main options: sole proprietorship, partnership (general or limited), limited liability company, C corporation, or subchapter S corporation.

A sole proprietorship is owned an operated by a single individual (or that individual and a spouse). The business is financed by that individual or by loans in the individual's name. Profits and losses are treated as personal income. The individual is personally responsible for paying any debts and liabilities against the business with his personal assets as well as those of the business.

A partnership is a business co-owned by two or more people. In a general partnership, the partners pool their time and abilities in the day-to-day operation of the business. Any member of the partnership can conduct business as an agent of the partnership. As in the sole proprietorship, profits and losses are treated as personal income, and all partners are personally responsible for any debts and liabilities against the business. A limited partnership gives only general partners the authority to conduct business. Limited partners are not involved in the day-to-day operation of the business and are liable for debts against the partnership only to the limit of their investment. Commonly, if one partner should die, a partnership must be dissolved.

A limited liability company is similar to a partnership or sole proprietorship, but the owners are not personally liable for business debts. Profits and losses are treated as personal income.

A C corporation is a separate legal entity. In other words, a C corporation in the eyes of the law exists as a separate "individual," independent from its owners. A corporation is formed when papers are filed, usually with the state in which the corporation operates. The owners of a corporation are known as stockholders. They receive a return on their investment in the corporation as stock dividends. The stockholders of a corporation are not personally responsible for debts and claims against the business (unless they have guaranteed something personally). Stockholders are at risk only for the amount of money they have invested. And the corporation pays its own corporate income taxes.

Although a C corporation offers business owners more legal protection than either a sole proprietorship or partnership, it is more complicated and expensive to set up. Some states require an attorney to file the articles of incorporation. And many C corporations find that an accountant is necessary to manage the tax and other financial implications of incorporation.

A Subchapter S corporation, like a C corporation, is a separate legal entity. The owners of an S corporation have the same legal protection as other corporate owners. An S corporation, however, is not taxed as a corporation. Shareholders in an S corporation report their share of the S corporation's profits as personal income when they file their personal income tax returns. Usually, an S corporation is a simpler financial and legal entity than a C corporation.

Learn as much as you can about the business structure options available to you. Consult with your accountant. Then take your questions and decisions to your attorney. The attorney will do the legal work necessary to set up your legal business structure.

Can you set up the legal form of your business yourself? Yes. In many states, you can file the paperwork yourself without going through an attorney. If you've done it before, or if you know someone you trust who has done it before, you may find the process is not too difficult. If, however, you make a single mistake, that mistake can cost you a great deal of time and money. If you plan to file by yourself, consider the possibility of pulling the paperwork together on your own and then paying an attorney to look it over before you file.

The choice of legal form for your business is not necessarily a permanent decision. As the business grows and changes, you may change forms later. But the decision you make will have legal, liability, and tax consequences from the very beginning. Educate yourself and consult with your advisors before making your choice.

Put Together a Professional Business Plan

It takes time and energy to put together a successful business plan. You may look at this outline and dismiss the process as too much work. Doing so would be an unwise decision. A business plan offers five very important benefits.

Why Put Together a Business Plan?

First, a business plan charts a course for your business. Think about the process a new student embarks on when she first begins practicing your art. You, as the teacher, know the progression of skills the student will need to develop. You possess the analytical and intuitive skills you need to assess and guide her development. Now think of your business. Can you see right now, in advance, the steps it will need to go through to develop and grow? Do you know what specific things you have to do to guide and spur that growth? A business plan helps you think like a business owner, to develop the analytical and intuitive skills you need to develop a profitable school. It is the "big picture" you need to have when deciding the course of your business.

Second, you will need a business plan if you want a business loan, whether from a bank or a private lender such as a family member. You will need to persuade your investor that you know how to make your business a success. Your business plan is your most important tool in convincing lenders that you know your business, that you can make money, and that you can and will repay a loan.

Third, it provides focus anytime you need to express your goals to a professional such as an attorney or accountant. You must know where your business is going before you can get effective help in getting it there.

Fourth, it allows you to see before you start spending money whether your business ideas are likely to succeed. It's easy to dream great dreams. It's harder to finance those dreams. Do you know how much money it will take to keep your dream school afloat? Do you know how many students you will need to support it? Do you know where your students will come from? Do you know how you will be advertising to them? If you make specific plans and run the numbers before you start spending money, you can decide whether your dream is likely to become a reality. Furthermore, in spending time with your business plan, you'll see if you have the skills and temperament you'll need to run your business well. Did you hate putting together financial projections and marketing plans? Did you find yourself procrastinating when it came time to put together cash flow projections and balance sheets? Then maybe you want to be a martial arts teacher, not a martial arts business owner.

Fifth, a business plan helps you keep track of your goals and what it will take to meet those goals. How will you know you've "arrived" as a business if you didn't know where you were going in the first place?

The Layer Approach

One way to put together a business plan is in layers. Especially if you're still in the process of growing your martial arts school from scratch, you will need to compile a layer of foundational information first. You can fill in the details as you are able to do the necessary research.

The first layer is the dream stage. Go through each point and sketch a qualitative picture of what you would like to see for each point. In other words, don't spend a lot of time thinking about the numbers at this stage. Without doing any serious research, get a rough picture of what you would like your school to look like.

The second layer is the planning stage. Do some preliminary research, and get estimates. Check out the martial arts schools in town to see what they look like and what they charge. Research your market, and decide who it is you want to teach. Investigate how much an appropriate facility will cost you, how much your monthly expenses will be. Set a tentative tuition rate and calculate your break-even point. Go through each point in the business plan, and do some research. In stage two of the process, you will say things like, "to reach my target market, children and young families, I will locate my school on the north side of town between 5th and 15th Avenue. In that neighborhood I can get a space that will meet my needs for $3,000–$4,000 per month." This layer of your business plan is for you, no one else. It's a tool you use to educate yourself about what it takes to make your dream a reality.

In the third layer you nail down your estimates and do a reality check. At this stage you need to be certain in your own mind that you have an accurate picture of what it will take to start and run your business. At this stage you want to know exactly how much money you will need to start up. You need to have a specific space picked out, and you need to know exactly what that space will cost you. You will know, to within 10 or 15 percent, what all your monthly and annual expenses will be. You will have well-researched financial projections for income and profitability. You will have a clear idea of what will be involved in advertising to your target market. In other words, the third layer is a detailed and accurate projection of what your business will look like. Put these projections together as though the life of your future business depended on them. It does.

The fourth layer is for other people to see. These are the plans you show your lender, the SBA, your attorney, your business advisors. By this time, you must be willing to stand by your numbers. If you tell the SBA you will need $8,000 for inventory for a pro shop, don't expect to change your mind a couple of months later and say you want $10,000. At this point in your business plan, other people need to be able to rely on your estimates.

The fifth layer comes into play after you have started your business. Your business plan at this point in its development includes not only projections but also real statistics about cash flow, actual expenses, actual income, and other figures. This is the plan you need to steer, adjust course, grow a new aspect of the business. Revisit your business plan every six months. Have goals—financial and otherwise—that you want to meet within six months, a year, five years. If you put them in front of you in writing, you will be more likely to make them a reality.

Anatomy of a Business Plan

What information goes into a business plan? Frankly, far more information than can be covered in any detail in a single chapter. If you want to create an effective business plan, you will need to find some more help. The SCORE program specializes in just such help. Books and computer programs are also widely available.

ANATOMY OF A BUSINESS PLAN

Title page
Table of contents
1. (Request for funds)
2. Overview of the business
3. Management profile
4. Marketing plan
5. Financial information
6. Personal and business goals

Double-Check Your Plan

A business plan is not something you can put together an hour or two before meeting a loan officer for an interview. For it to be convincing, you need have specific, accurate information, and you need to make your plan persuasive. Look at it from the perspective of the person who will be reading it. Does it help the lender see your business like you see it? Does it say "good risk" to your prospective lender?

Make the plan look neat and professional. Be descriptive and complete, but edit sections until most are two pages or shorter. Then, before you bring your business plan to the lending agency, have a friend or business associate, preferably one with business background, look at it. Listen to suggestions with an empty cup and try to incorporate those things that will strengthen your presentation.

Running a martial arts school requires more than just teaching skills. To run a successful school, you must learn to think like a small business owner. Assemble a team of advisors. Then start working on your business plan. Doing so will greatly increase your chances for success.

Chapter Four:

Find a Location That Will Work for You

Choosing a location is one of the most crucial decisions you will make. The location, the layout, and the appearance of your school can bring in—or chase off—customers. Given that your rent will be one of your largest fixed expenses, doesn't it make sense to find a space that will work for you not against you?

Find a Space That Will Work for You
Choose a Good Location

Where you locate your school depends in large part on your marketing identity, especially on your image and target market. If you've chosen an upscale image—providing the best instruction for those who are willing to pay for it—you need to start your business in a neighborhood where the prospective students are wealthy enough to pay your tuition and fees. If your image is a place for singles to meet, it doesn't make sense to put your school in a neighborhood with mostly young married people. Is your target market children? Put your school in a family neighborhood near schools or playgrounds.

How do you find out whether the neighborhood you're considering matches your target market? The information you need is called demographics, and it is the product of various censuses. One of the best sources for detailed demographics is your real estate agent. Real estate agents make it their business to know about the various neighborhoods they serve. Frequently, they offer a brochure containing maps and demographic information for each space they represent.

If you aren't using a real estate agent, check the U.S. Census Bureau publications. The Census Bureau conducts a census of the entire population of the United States every ten years. They publish the results, broken down by zip code, in their census books, which are available in your local public library. Statistics are also available on the Census Bureau Web site at www.census.gov.

Often overlooked sources of demographics include real estate ads in the local newspaper. These can give you an idea of what houses are worth in the neighborhood. The local chamber of commerce or economic development office often has not only demographic and economic information for your area but also projections for population growth and economic development. Local shop owners can tell you about their clientele.

How big of an area should you research? That depends on your trading zone. Your trading zone is the geographical area from which you draw most of your business. The size of your trading zone depends on a number of things: what transportation people use in your area, how far they usually travel for goods and services, whether your area is urban or rural, whether it is densely or sparsely populated.

You can use at least three methods to estimate the size of your trading zone. If you are on friendly terms with another martial arts school owner in your city, ask him if you can interview the school's students. Ask those students how long it takes them to get from their home or work to their martial arts school. Look at how far most of them travel. A few students, of course, are willing to travel great distances to study with a good martial arts teacher. Assume that those students will find you wherever you are located. In your interview, determine how far the majority of students are willing to travel.

If interviewing current martial arts students isn't an option for you, talk to people in the neighborhood you are considering for your school. Ask them how long it takes them to travel to their grocery store, health club, bank, any place they go two or three times each week. If you are in a rural area where people commonly drive thirty minutes to a grocery store, your trading zone will be larger than if you are in an urban area where people walk to services. Get a feel for the travel habits of people in your neighborhood.

A third method for estimating the size of your trading zone is to begin with the estimate that your students will travel no more than seven to ten minutes by car from their home to your school. That is a ballpark estimate for a typical suburban American school. Ask yourself if your students would have good reason to travel farther. For example, is the nearest martial arts school more than fourteen minutes away from you? Do people travel more than seven minutes several times a week to get to the other stores in your complex? Do you live in an area where people expect to spend a half hour in their car to get anywhere?

Let's say you've estimated your trading zone to be about seven minutes. How far away is seven minutes? That, too, depends on your area, the roads, and the traffic. Get in a car with a local map and a stopwatch. Drive the main roads that lead to your school, and mark off a seven-minute radius.

Then go back to your demographic sources. Within that seven-minute radius, look at average age, average income, disposable income, number of children. If you aren't on a widely used public transportation line, look at the number of vehicles. The question you need to ask yourself is, "If I put my school here, could my target market get to it in seven minutes or less?" If not, either your location or your target market will have to change.

Beyond demographics, you will also need to check your competition before settling on a location. How close is the nearest martial arts school? Too many schools in a small area may decrease the number of students likely to sign up with you. While you're checking schools in the area, look not just at martial arts school but at other sport schools—gymnastics, dance, swimming schools—aimed at your target market. They too are competing for the time and money of your potential clientele.

Find a Real Estate Agent

Once you've picked out a neighborhood, choose a real estate agent to help you find a space. Real estate agents serve two very important functions. Of course, they help you find a space that meets your needs. But they also can help sell the landlord on the idea of having you as a tenant. A real estate agent can be an important link between you and your landlord. But never forget that, though they serve you, they represent the landlord, the person who's paying them.

Understand what you need before you engage the services of a real estate agent. Draw up a description of your business, including your marketing identity, a detailed description of your target market, and any special requirements you will have (high ceilings, ample ventilation, or floor space without pillars). A good real estate agent listens to you, finds out what kind of a space you want or need, and then helps you lease it. If your real estate agent skips the first two of those three steps, find another real estate agent. Although real estate agents' fees don't come out of your pocket, an agent can cost you if you let them talk you into a property that isn't consistent with your image or your budget.

Look at several possible spaces. Even if you believe you've found the perfect space the first time you look at one, look at others. Contrasting several spaces will help you see what your first choice does and doesn't have. It will also give you information you can use later in bargaining with your landlord.

Choose the Best Space

Once you've found a space you think might work for you, draw up a description of your business to give to the landlord or property manager. Include your marketing identity and the reasons your school will benefit their center. Also include reasons why your business is a stable one: cite contracts, long-term training schedules, other factors that increase student loyalty. Describe your target market, how they come to your school several times each week, how they get out of their car and walk past the other shops in the complex to get to your school. Talk about how students' parents can be good customers for the center, how they bring their children to class and then often go to do errands or shop nearby. Describe how your cost per student decreases as your student population increases. In other words, make your landlord want you to move in. Doing so will put you in a better bargaining position when it's time to negotiate the lease.

Once you and your real estate agent find a possible location, decide if it suits your purposes. Be sure your prospective landlord knows up front what you have in mind for the space. Then before making a commitment, be sure to check out zoning and legal requirements. Some cities have very specific zoning regulation limiting where retail and service businesses can be located. If you are looking at space in a shopping center, make sure your school will fit in with the overall image of the center. If your image is family oriented, you don't want to be fifty feet from a biker bar or adult video store. If, however, yours is a kick-butt, kill-or-be-killed image, that location may work just fine for you. Consider how much walk-by traffic the center is likely to generate. Consider how many of the center's customers will be in your target market. Consider how many of the store owners and employees will be in your target market.

Look, too, at access to the property. Can vehicles and pedestrians get to you easily? How is the traffic? Will your students be able to find parking during the hours you plan to be open? If people in your area use mass transit, how close are you to the train or bus stop? Is the walk to your school safe?

Then make sure the space is one that will draw people in. The key to drawing people is visibility, and the key to visibility is walk-by traffic. Do people walk past the windows? Driving by doesn't count. People need to be moving past your school slowly enough to look in the windows, register what you are doing inside. Look at the other stores in the complex or the neighborhood. Ideally you want to be between locations people visit frequently—grocery stores, video stores, fast food restaurants. Granted, you will pay extra for a place with good walk-by traffic. But good walk-by traffic will bring people into your school. It may pay for itself and then some.

Look, too, at the size of the windows on the front of the space. A school with a closed-in atmosphere is forbidding. No sign or fancy window treatment will draw people in quite so effectively as the sight of people having a good time in an open, bright, clean facility. The front of your building, what people can see through the windows, should be able to reflect your image.

Find out about the size and kind of signs available to you. If you are looking at space in a shopping center, look at all the other signs in that center. It is not mere coincidence that they are all the same size, same color, same image. The shopping center will probably have restrictions on your signage. City or local government may also have restrictions for your area. Even if they don't have restrictions, taxes on the kind of sign you're thinking about may be prohibitive.

Once you've determined that the location works for you, check to make sure the space meets your needs. Look at the construction of the building. If the building is old and in poor repair, it will cost you. Look at the size of the space, not just the floor space but the ceiling height. A ceiling height that works fine for an empty-hand style may be too low if your style teaches long weapons. Trace the outline of the space on some graph paper. Carefully draw to scale not just your training floor but your office, dressing areas, restrooms, storage space, waiting area. Are there any pillars in the space? Draw them in as well. Draw in your furniture, your training equipment, your traffic patterns, your entrance and exits. Will your students have room to train freely in the remaining space? If you need more space a few months or years down the line, does the center have room for you to expand?

Think five senses: Can the ventilation handle a large number of warm bodies? Do you have adequate heating and cooling? Is the light adequate? While you hold classes, where will the sun be in relation to your windows? What is the air quality like? Is the noise level acceptable? Spend some time with the site, especially during the hours you will be holding classes. Picture yourself training there to see how it feels.

Figure Out How Much It Will Cost You

It's crucial you find out exactly how much a space will cost you before you start making commitments and financial projections.

Notice, we didn't say how much the rent will cost you. We said how much the space will cost you.

The landlord will probably quote your rent in annual price per square foot. A simple formula can calculate how much that means in monthly rent.

CALCULATING MONTHLY RENT
FROM ANNUAL PER-SQUARE-FOOT COST

	Price per square foot
Multiplied by	Square footage
Equals	Annual cost
	Annual cost
Divided by	12
Equals	Monthly rent

The rent, however, is not the total price for the space. In a triple net lease—one of the most common commercial leases—rent is only one of three expenses you must pay monthly. The other two are rental tax and triple net.

Rental tax may be assessed by your state or city. This tax is much like a sales tax—the government charges a percentage of the rent a landlord collects. The landlord passes that charge directly through to you. The rental rate tax varies widely from place to place. Ask your landlord how much it is in your area so you can fit it into your financial projections.

Triple net is the other expense you must pay with your rent each month. In some places, triple net is called "net, net, net." In others, it is called "common area expenses" or "common area maintenance," "CAM" for short. Triple net includes three expenses. The first expense is maintenance. This maintenance includes your share of the cost of managing the complex and of maintaining the parking lot, roof, signs, elevators, landscaping, and other shared resources. The second expense of triple net is your share of real estate taxes. The third is your share of any insurance your landlord keeps on the property.

Triple net is typically expressed in price per square foot just as rent is. Your landlord charges it annually but impounds it monthly. At the beginning of the year, your landlord makes an estimate of annual expenses. They divide that amount between the merchants in the complex (usually based on percentage of square footage). Then they divide your share by twelve so they can bill you monthly. At the end of the year, they check the actual triple net costs against the projections and either bill you for the balance due or refund the amount you overpaid.

Besides rent, taxes, and triple net, the terms of your lease may require you to take out your own property and fire insurance. Although you pay the cost of that insurance to the insurance company, it is still as much a cost of renting the space as rent is. Check additional insurance requirements as a part of your investigation into what the space will cost you.

CALCULATING YOUR MONTHLY COSTS

	Rent
Plus	Triple net
Plus	Rental taxes
Plus	Required insurance
Equals	The cost of your space

Compare your rent with other comparable properties in the area. A real estate agent can help. Make sure what you will be paying is comparable to other similar spaces. Differences in price may reflect some crucial differences between complexes. Larger spaces and spaces with longer leases usually have lower square-foot prices. Older buildings and buildings in bad neighborhoods usually have lower overall prices. But some complexes are just a good deal. Either way, comparing prices helps you determine whether a space is worth what you are going to pay for it.

Negotiate a Lease You Can Live With

Once you've picked out a space, it's time to get the lease nailed down. Unlike many apartment leases, commercial leases typically have some "wiggle room." In other words, a certain amount of negotiation over rent, improvement to the space, payment schedules, and other provisions is not only possible, it's expected. In fact, most commercial lease contracts are initially biased toward the landlord. It's your job to protect your interests—not to make the contract biased toward you, but to bring it back to center, where it is fair to both parties.

What do you do if you want to lease a commercial space and you aren't a very good negotiator? First, make yourself comfortable with the issues involved in your lease. Read as much as you can about commercial leases. Talk to commercial real estate agents and brokers while you're looking at sites to learn as much as you can from them. Once you have the lease in hand, take it to a real estate attorney. She can look over the contract for you to make sure it protects your interests. Then read the lease yourself. Make sure you understand everything—every word, every provision—in the contract. Know what you are getting into before you begin negotiating.

If you still aren't comfortable with the actual process of negotiation, you can get help. Commercial real estate agents are used to negotiating contracts. But remember, your real estate agent gets a percentage of the rent they negotiate. Their commission is paid by the landlord. During the negotiation process, real estate agents are generally very professional, but they do walk the fine line between keeping you happy and keeping their commission high. If you're uncomfortable using your real estate agent as a go-between in the negotiation, you may be able to get a friend with real estate or negotiation experience to help you. Or you may want to hire your accountant, a broker, or a real estate attorney to represent your interests. They cost money, of course. But if they know the business, they can often get you a better lease than you could get yourself. However, once you've signed the contract and paid any outside consultants you've hired, you are on your own. Your representative doesn't live with the results of the negotiation; you do. It is your responsibility to weigh all your options and then to live with your choices.

Basic Negotiation Principles

When negotiating a contract remember two things. First, in the world of contracts, if it isn't on paper, it isn't "real." Your landlord is not legally bound by anything they say, only by what they write down and sign. Second, you are not negotiating only with the person across the table. Your landlord may be a very pleasant person, a person of their word, a person you can trust. But you are not only making the contract with them. You must assume that the contract will be referred to and used by others: by the landlord's business partners, his attorney, anyone the landlord might sell the property to, the courts that may have to be involved should there be a dispute or bankruptcy. The contract must be able to exist as a stand-alone document, a document that protects your rights no matter what should happen or who should get involved later.

Tradeoffs and compromises are the name of the game in contract negotiations. Think about what you bring to the table before you sit down. One bargaining chip you have is the business you will bring to the center. Think about what your landlord wants. They want stable, professional tenants who can fulfill the terms of their contract and pay their rent on time. They want tenants who fit in with the image of their shopping center. They want steady business that will make their center

THE PROCESS OF LEASING A SPACE

1. Find a space that suits your needs.
2. Contact the real estate agent or landlord.
3. Find out the asking price and current triple net.
4. Make an offer on a price-per-square-foot basis, including triple net costs, if applicable.
5. The landlord makes a counteroffer.
6. The two of you agree on the price.
7. Get the standard lease from the landlord.
8. Read it, make notes, and mark up a photocopy.
9. Take the lease and your notes to a real estate attorney.
10. When you're sure you understand every thing and have noted every change you want, present your proposed modifications to the landlord.
11. The landlord tells you what he or she will accept, what isn't acceptable.
12. The two of you find middle ground.
13. Get a corrected lease and show it to your attorney.
14. Renegotiate fine points, if any, brought up by your attorney.
15. Sign the lease.
16. The lease takes effect when it is returned to you, signed by your landlord.

thrive. If you can prove you provide these things, it puts you in a good negotiating position.

Another bargaining chip you may bring to the table is a willingness to make improvements to your space yourself. The landlord will expect to make certain improvements to the space before you move in. If you are willing to move into the space as is, to make the TIs ("tenant improvements") yourself, you can trade the cost of the improvements for rent-free time or a reduction in your monthly rent. Conversely, if you don't have a contractor's resources, if you want the landlord to help you make the space ready to do business, you may have to begin paying full rent immediately. Or you and your landlord may be able to find some specific middle ground.

The art involved in playing the tradeoff game is that the landlord typically won't tell you up front how much he has budgeted to make improvements. Negotiation becomes a little like playing poker without knowing how many chips you have in front of you. Go ahead and guess a little (but not outrageously) high. Your landlord will have no problem telling you if you are unrealistic.

A general principle: bargain in good faith. Don't ask for the moon. Don't ask for a lot of things you don't want, expecting to use them later as bargaining chips. Go ahead and ask for everything you want. But expect to make concessions to keep the deal fair for both you and your landlord. Be reasonable, but don't settle for anything less than what you need.

Remember, your goal is to negotiate the best deal you can with your landlord. It is not to beat the landlord into the ground. This is negotiation, a controlled sparring match, not war. Your goal is to establish a fair, equitable long-term relationship between you and the person who owns the building you will be working in for several years to come. Be good to your landlord. Be assertive, but treat the landlord fairly during negotiations. Then, after you move in, be the landlord's eyes and ears on site. Watch out for the landlord's interests, and he may do the same for you.

Plateau-Level Bargaining

During the contract negotiations, you will be doing plateau-level bargaining. Here's what that means: You put together all the things you must have and a few things you would like to have but can do without. Your landlord does the same. The two of you sit down and negotiate to an agreement. At that moment you're done. If the day after reaching the agreement you declare that you want something you didn't mention during the negotiation, you have less of a chance of getting it. Perhaps more importantly, if you present your requests out of turn, your position of power will be greatly reduced.

Plateau-level bargaining expects you to put everything on the table during the negotiations. It expects you to be willing—though of course you don't have to be eager—to make concessions. You need to be clear about what is important to you and what is essential. And you need to listen to what is important to the landlord. In places, your landlord will not budge. Everyone has their deal breakers. Know what yours are. Listen to find out what your landlord's are. Then negotiate within those bounds. At the end of the negotiations, you are finished. You walk away with clauses in the contract that further your interests, and so does your landlord.

What Is a "Fair" Contract?

Ideally, you want a contract that is fair for both parties. Of course, the contract will be designed to protect the interests of the landlord. It's his space you're renting, and he will want legal and financial protection for that ownership. You need to make sure the contract is fair to you. You need to make sure you are liable only for normal costs of doing business and for things you can control.

If the contract has a clause that is blatantly unfair, and the landlord will not budge on that clause, you may need to walk away. You may need to begin the leasing process all over again with your second-choice space. You are, after all, trying to establish an amicable long-term relationship. The contract negotiation will be your first clue about whether that is possible.

Hazards to Avoid in the Contract

How can you tell if what you've been offered is a good contract? That's a complex question. The best way to know is to consult a real estate attorney. A couple of general principles, however, can help you avoid some of the worst pitfalls.

First, you want to make sure you can do what you need to do in your space. Your contract will probably contain a "permitted uses" clause. This is a clause that says you warrant that you will conduct business in strict compliance with normal business practice. A martial arts school, however, is not a normal business. How many "normal businesses" involve people shouting so loud the windows rattle? You will be moving around, running, jumping, falling more than most service businesses. You may be selling state-regulated weapons in your pro shop. Be sure the contract allows you to conduct all the activities associated with a martial arts school. Include a clause that you will conduct your business in strict compliance with uses that can reasonably be expected in a martial arts school. Describe the use of your space correctly—martial arts school, martial arts club, martial arts academy and retail store. But describe it loosely enough to allow for growth. In other words, don't say "a children's karate school" if you may later teach adults, teach some other martial art, or operate a pro shop.

Your contract may include a clause limiting noise you can make. Alternately, it may say you are responsible for sound insulation should the noise from your studio disturb other lessees. You may be able to add a proviso that the clause applies to sounds other than those reasonably expected in a martial arts school.

Watch, too, for a clause saying that anything you attach to the floors or walls becomes the landlord's property. If you put floor coverings, walls, or special lighting fixtures into the space, they become the property of the landlord (unless you are allowed by your lease to remove them, returning the space to its original condition when you leave). That kind of provision is standard in commercial contracts, and it is an acceptable provision for most martial arts schools. Chances are good, however, that you will also have to anchor some of your equipment—bag racks, decking, equipment racks—to the walls or floor.

Having that equipment become the property of the landlord is unacceptable. Know what equipment you will need to anchor to the property, and write each piece into the contract as exceptions. Also add a provision that all trade equipment, those things you need to conduct your particular business, remains your property.

You will, however, need to agree to leave the space in the condition you found it in except for normal wear. If you plan to anchor equipment to the floor, you will need to know how to restore the floor to the original condition. Also you need to figure that the landlord will probably want right of approval over any alterations of the space you make.

A second general principle is that you want to eliminate extraneous costs that the landlord assesses but doesn't do anything for. For example, if the landlord has to arrange for maintenance on something that is your responsibility—air conditioning, heating, any other maintenance expense that the contract says you must pay—make sure the costs are billed at net. If the costs are billed at net, you pay only the cost of getting a repair person out to do the job—materials and labor—without the building manager's overcharge.

Finally, if you want to make sure your lease is a good contract, check it with a good real estate attorney. It's their business to know a good contract when they see one.

Lay Out Your School

Once the lease is signed, it's time to turn your space into a school. Perhaps one of the most exciting tasks involved in setting up a school is physically laying out the place. Watching the space take shape makes the dream real. The temptation is to hurry the process, to start building before you've thought your plans through. But if you plan on paper now, you won't have to rebuild later.

Plan Your Space

You probably already have some initial sketches of your space from when you were deciding whether it would meet your needs. Now it's time to turn those preliminary ideas into building plans.

Take a tape measure to your space and draw it on graph paper. Make several copies so you can try different layouts.

On your plan, lay out your main working areas: your training floor, office, waiting area, retail space, rest rooms, and dressing rooms. Check them to see if they're the proper size. This is especially true of your training area. A space always looks much bigger before you bring in the equipment. When you're planning your layout on paper, be sure to draw in the equipment to scale. Then look at the traffic patterns between equipment. Can the space handle the number of students you plan to have? Do they have room to do normal moving and training? If you have any questions about whether all your students will fit in your space, you may want to cut out circles representing students and place them on your plan.

When laying out your dressing rooms, do so on paper first. Then, go in and tape off the area (including any fixed lockers or benches) on the floor. Taping any floorplan onto the floor gives you a chance to see your plan in live space. Taping off the dressing room floorplan is especially crucial. If possible, put the number of people you expect to use the dressing room at any given time inside the taped area. "Enough space" on paper is one thing. "Enough space" when you're undressed and digging through a gym bag with several other people who are doing the same thing is quite another thing. Could the people inside your taped-off area move, change clothes, pack and unpack their bags comfortably? If you have a shower, can people get to the shower in privacy without going through a bottleneck? Overcrowded dressing rooms will chase away students. Know that you have enough room before you start building walls.

Then think about the various people who will be at your school. Where will parents wait? Where will younger brothers and sisters wait, and what will they be playing with while they wait? Where will prospective students sit while they are checking out your classes? Where will the people waiting for the next class stand or sit? Can students and spectators get to the restrooms easily?

Next look at the things you plan to bring in. Where will you store them? Where will you store equipment you aren't using at the moment?

Where will you store inventory for your pro shop? Where will you store office supplies, student records, books and manuals? Where will you put your party supplies and holiday decorations? Where will students stow their gear, both gear they bring with them when they train and gear they leave overnight at the school (if you allow them to do so)? Where will you keep your cleaning supplies, your toolbox, your first aid equipment, your emergency gear? If you are in a climate that requires coats, raincoats, umbrellas, boots, where will they go?

Once you have a layout, check your traffic patterns, indoor foot traffic, that is. One of the most important things about laying out a commercial space is the flow of people. Can people get in and out easily? Look at where students will park and how they will go from the parking lot to the training floor and dressing rooms. When they go through the usual activities, do they encounter any bottlenecks? Think about areas where the traffic flow will stop-water coolers, the business office, dressing areas, the places where people will meet friends and stop to talk. Will those stops in traffic create an obstacle for the people who are still moving?

Then look at sight lines. Can you see people coming through your front door from the training area and the business office? Can parents see their children train from the waiting area? Are the dressing areas private, or can people moving through the traffic patterns see inside them when the doors are open?

Consider, too, that you want to make it as easy as possible for students to do business with you. If possible, put the business office and pro shop just off the major traffic pattern. If students walk by a new uniform every day, it will be on their mind when they finally get the money to pay for it. Similarly, the place where they pay their tuition needs to be convenient and visible. The trick is to keep the office and pro shop visible without having them be disturbed by training (and without having people training distracted by things going on in the office and pro shop).

Go through your floorplan and think about how it appeals to the senses of your customers. Sight: Is the lighting adequate, not glaring? Are the dressing rooms and restrooms well lit and private? Are the colors you choose energizing but not harsh? Smell: Do you have adequate ventilation, especially on the training floor and in the dressing areas? Does every enclosed area have its own ventilation duct? Can you open doors and get a good cross-ventilation? Sound: If you need a quiet area to talk to students privately, do you have one? Do you have a place where you and prospective students can talk without having to shout over training noise? Touch: Can you keep the dressing rooms and training floor warm enough or cool enough? Taste: Do you have good drinking water available to the students? Do you want to sell snacks, sports drinks, energy bars? If so are they convenient for the students to buy after class?

Comply with the ADA

Another thing you need to consider when laying out your school is compliance with the ADA, the Americans with Disabilities Act. You will be required to make your school wheelchair accessible. You will be required to have accessible parking spaces for people with disabilities. You may need ramps, grab rails, curb cutouts, signs in Braille, easy-to-open doors. As you might expect from the government, you will be required to obtain detailed and specific guidelines, and you will be expected to comply with them.

"But," you say, "none of my students are likely to be disabled. I teach an art that's physically very demanding." That may be true. But quite apart from the myriad of things disabled people can do, have you considered the families of your students? Would you put a barrier between them and watching their loved one train? Check with the U.S. Department of Justice, Civil Rights Division, for ADA requirements before you start building.

Comply with Your Lease

Another thing you need to consider before you start building is the provisions of your lease. You may be installing equipment, anchoring it to the floors and walls. But your contract will probably dictate that you restore those floors and walls to their original condition when you leave. Know how you will do so before you start drilling and hammering. Also make sure to check your contract to see if the landlord has right of approval over any alterations to the space you might want to make.

Convey Your Image

Once you have the walls and fixtures in place, it's time to consider furniture, carpeting, wall paint, decorations, and pictures. When choosing these things, especially for the office and waiting area, consider your image. If you consider yourself a family school, look at other places that draw families—doctors' and dentists' offices, family restaurants. If you're interested in drawing singles, look at places that cater mostly to singles. If you want to draw in children, design your place to appeal to children, and the people who pay the children's tuition—their parents.

Maybe the details of a commercial lease sound like too much hassle to you. Maybe you'd rather be on a month-to-month handshake agreement. If so, consider that you are going to spend lots of time and money building your business, its image, and its good name. If you have a well-negotiated lease, you and your landlord know what to expect from each other. You know how long you are going to be at your location. And as long as you continue to pay the rent on time and meet the other obligations of the lease, you don't have to worry about being asked to leave. Potential students will know how to find you. Current students won't be dropping out because of your frequent moves. You can spend the time, money, and effort to set up a space that meets your needs, because your lease protects your right to train in that space. It is worth the effort to negotiate a solid lease so you can get on with the business of teaching without worrying about the roof over your head.

CHAPTER FIVE:
TAKE CARE OF RED TAPE

Your marketing identity is in place. You've secured financing. You've
signed the lease. You've begun to outfit your space. What is left to do
before you can open your door to students?

Investigate Government Requirements

One of the first things you will need to do is to investigate what it
will take to keep the government satisfied. Specific requirements will
depend on the size and nature of your school, whether you plan to sell
equipment, and where you are located. Federal, state, and local
agencies will all want to regulate various aspects of your business and,
of course, will want their cut of your profit. Pay the government their
due first. Always. You can pay the government the easy way (on time
with the proper forms), or you can pay them the hard way (with
interest and late penalties). Either way, you will have to pay them.

Investigating government requirements will take time, so start
the process early. Your accountant and attorney can help you out. So
can friends and colleagues who have set up similar businesses. SCORE
and SBA small business advisors offer experienced help. After all is said
and done, however, if you miss a requirement, it's your problem, so
be thorough.

City and County Requirements

Many cities require various licenses and certificates before you can open your doors. You will probably need a business license. Fees for business licenses are usually based on the kind of business, its projected income, and its number of employees. The city or county might also require you to have a certificate of occupancy. This certificate is a license the city issues when it has made sure you meet all the zoning laws and building codes. Some cities also require you have a city sales tax license if you plan to sell equipment.

State Requirements

The state you do business in may also require you to register your business. Usually the Division/Department/Bureau of Revenue/Taxation—different states have different names for the department—will not only register your business, they will also give you a retail license and a withholding number if you have employees. While you're at the state offices, also get the forms you need to collect sales tax. You will be required to file forms for state sales tax on either a monthly or quarterly basis (depending on the laws in your state). If you will only be teaching, not selling equipment, you may not need a retail license. You should, however, check to see if your state requires business registration.

Federal Requirements

The United States federal government requires that your business have a federal tax number (the employer identification number or EIN). If your business is a sole proprietorship and doesn't have any employees, you may use your Social Security number. Obtain a copy of IRS Form SS-4, "Application for Employer Identification Number," for more information. The instructions will tell you whether you must file for the number and how to do so. If you are going to have employees, you also need to educate yourself about withholding and federal unemployment tax.

IRS Publication 334, "Tax Guide for a Small Business," can give you more information about other federal requirements. The IRS's STEP (Small Business Tax Education Program) service can also help you understand and meet your tax obligation. IRS Publication 910, "Free Tax Services," details what educational services they offer.

Ferret Out Information

Expect to spend some time at the government offices learning about and meeting your requirements. Ask questions, listen, follow up on leads. Read whatever government pamphlets you can get a hold of. Then don't be surprised if you still miss a requirement. The government bureaucratic maze is difficult to navigate. The surest way to do so is to find a good guide. A good business attorney or accountant can help familiarize you with the requirements, and she can take you a long way toward meeting those requirements. Yet you will probably still have to spend a day or more walking through government offices, getting licenses, permits, and approvals.

A couple of cautions: Investigate your business category before signing up for your small business license. Your school may fit under several categories—private school, retail outlet, health club, sports facility. Yet the costs of licenses and whether you have to pay sales tax on services differ from category to category in some states.

Also, investigate your city's policy on signs. Some cities tax business signage. The amount of the tax is usually proportional to the size of the sign. Even small, decorative signs painted on your front window could cost you money. Check the policy and costs before hiring the sign painter.

A book of this nature can't begin to go into detail about all government business regulations and requirements. Bottom line? Educate yourself. If you're unfamiliar with business tax laws and other government requirements for business, ask your accountant. If you get a letter from a government agency, read it. Even if you are "positive" you know what's in it, read it anyway. Government agencies have some very firm ideas about what they want from you, but those ideas can change. If you get a form from a government agency, make sure you know if they want you to return it. Even if you don't owe taxes or fees, check to see if they want the form back. You can sometimes be penalized for failing to send in a form even though every blank contains a zero. In general, if you don't comply with the government's requirements on their terms, they have ways of making your life complicated.

Register Your School's Name

You probably already have a good idea what you want to call your school. Now is the time to make that choice official. (See chapter 1 for more information on choosing a name.)

First, you will need to find out if the same name, or a confusingly similar name is already in use by another business. Look through the Yellow Pages for your town. Do any other schools have a name similar enough that a potential customer could get confused? If not, check with the secretary of state's office in your state and the county clerk's office in your county. Have them run a search on the name you've chosen.

If the name is unused, you may record it with state and/or county offices. In some states, you will not be able to open bank accounts in your business name until you've registered it. Neither can you protect your business name from use by another business until you register it.

Place Your Order with the Printer

Place your printing order before you open. This order may seem a small thing, but it's more important than it first appears. Your stationery, business card, and brochure are the face you present to much of the world. Look at chapter 7 for more information on choosing a slogan, logo, and business card format. Design a brochure and have it printed, too.

You will need your brochure and business card before you start bringing in students. You will need your letterhead before you can open an account with wholesalers.

Select Insurance

Before you open your school, you should have a comprehensive insurance plan. Your city or county may require certain kinds of insurance. Your lease may require others. Even if outside agencies do not require you to purchase insurance, you will probably want at least basic coverage for your own peace of mind. Your insurance policy should cover three things: the building itself, the equipment and merchandise inside the building, and medical or general liability for the people inside the building.

Property Insurance

Your lease will probably require you to maintain fire insurance at specific limits. The reason for the requirement is that if a fire begins in your space and spreads to other spaces in the complex, you can be held liable. Buy a policy that covers damage to the property caused by fire, explosion, flooding, or smoke. You will need at least a million dollars of property insurance, more if you can afford it. If that seems like a lot of coverage, consider what it's going to cost you if you accidentally burn the entire complex down. If you don't carry enough insurance to cover the replacement costs, you will have to pay the remainder out of your pocket.

Personal Property Insurance

Personal property insurance covers the contents of your space—your equipment, furniture, computer and software, anything you keep at your business. Like the renters' insurance that apartment dwellers have on the contents of their apartments, personal property insurance covers replacement of the things you keep inside your space, not the space itself.

Business Interruption Insurance

Should anything happen—fire, serious illness, or other catastrophe—to prevent you from doing business, business interruption insurance pays the bills. Depending on the limits of the policy, it can cover your salary, your expenses, even the salaries of your key people, until you can get up and running again. If you rely on your school as your main or only source of income, you should consider business interruption insurance. If yours is a small operation, if you have other sources of income, or if you can afford to shut down for a few months, you may be able to get by without it.

Medical Liability Insurance

This insurance protects your business from financial loss due to claims of bodily injury connected with the business. A few companies specialize in liability insurance for martial arts businesses. Your insurance agent can sometimes help you find these companies. If your agent doesn't know an appropriate company for your art, check with your national organization, trade magazines, or with another martial arts school owner.

Policies vary widely. Some require your students to wear specific training equipment. Others do not. Some have a high deductible. Others, for higher premiums, offer a lower deductible. Shop around. Find the balance of deductible, coverage, and premiums that meets your needs.

General Liability Insurance

If medical liability covers you against claims of bodily injury, general liability covers you against other claims. If someone's property is damaged or lost, if you are charged with false advertising or defamation of character—in short if someone has a claim against you that doesn't involve bodily injury to a student—a general liability policy is what you need to cover you. This coverage is also what you need if someone other than a student is hurt on your premises. Depending on your policy, your medical liability may not cover injury to, for example, a parent who slips in the rest room or a prospective student injured while you are giving them a tour of your school. If your medical liability policy does not cover these kinds of claims, you'll want to make sure your general liability policy does.

Other Insurance

List the insurance your lease requires you to have. Investigate whether you are required by law to have corporate insurance. Decide what kinds of insurance you need for your own financial security and peace of mind. Then take your list to an insurance agent.

Shop around. You don't have to get all your insurance from the same company or the same agent. But you do want to make sure all your insurance companies are highly rated. Various agencies evaluate the financial ability of insurance companies to pay. Others evaluate their track record in paying prior claims. Information from these agencies— Standard and Poor's, Weiss Research, A.M. Best, Moody's—is typically available at your public library. Your insurance agent will also have it. Pay serious attention to the rating of the insurance company you choose. It doesn't matter how cheap the insurance is if the company doesn't pay you when you need them.

Being self-insured is also possible. In other words, you agree to pay for any claim, no matter how small or large, out of your own pocket. The advantage to being self-insured, of course, is that you aren't paying insurance premiums. The disadvantage is that if you are faced with a large claim, you could lose not just your business, but everything you own.

Unemployment Insurance

In most states if you have employees, you must have unemployment insurance. In some states, the agency that issues this insurance is a private, independent company, governed by state law. The premium for unemployment insurance is based on the amount of your payroll and your experience rating.

The purpose of unemployment insurance is to allow your employees to receive unemployment compensation benefits if you lay them off. If, however, you fire an employee for just cause, for example for stealing from you, he is not entitled to unemployment compensation. If an employee quits, he isn't entitled to it. If an employee didn't work for you for very long, he isn't entitled to it. If however, you have to lay off a regular employee, he can collect unemployment to help him out until he finds another job.

Here's how state unemployment works: You lay off a regular employee. Your employee files with the state for unemployment. The government lets you, the former employer, know he has filed. If you have good reason for letting the employee go—if he was fired for just cause, if he was a temporary employee, or if he quit rather than being laid off—you may contest his claim. If you contest the claim, the unemployment agency will make a decision, sometimes with, sometimes without, a hearing. If the agency finds in your favor, your former employee doesn't get the payments, and your account isn't charged. If you do not contest, or if the agency finds for your former employee, he gets unemployment payments. Any time a former employee gets unemployment payments, your experience rating goes up and with it your premiums.

A word of caution: don't confuse state unemployment insurance with federal unemployment tax, also known as FUTA. You have to pay FUTA at least annually, more often if your payroll is large enough. Be aware that the federal government may not find you to give you your FUTA forms. You must find the forms yourself and pay the tax. The amount is only a small percentage of your payroll. If, however, you don't pay it on time, the penalties and interest can amount to real money. Sometimes even if you don't have an employee, you still have to pay FUTA. Why? Because you yourself are considered an employee.

Be forewarned that the laws regarding unemployment are not always intuitively understandable. Talk to your accountant about the state and the federal requirements as they apply to your business.

Workers' Compensation Insurance

This insurance covers employee injury and loss of wages resulting from accidents on the job. Some states require any business with more than a certain number of employees to have workers' compensation insurance. If someone is hurt and goes to the doctor, either immediately or in the near future, you need to file a worker's compensation injury report. The injured person also needs to take specific forms to the doctor.

Like unemployment insurance, workers' compensation is typically offered through private agencies, and it is closely regulated by the state. It, too, is payroll driven. You tell the agency what your payroll is. They send you a bill. Talk to your insurance agent. She can usually tell you how to get the necessary workers' compensation insurance.

Chapter Six:

Get Ready to Take In Students

Before you open your doors to students, you need to have a few more things in place. You'll need a complete fee schedule written down and available to prospective students. You'll need a student contract or agreement. And you'll need to have various policies and procedures in place.

Set Up a Fee Schedule

How much you charge for your services is going to depend on several factors: your costs, your competition, your personal financial goals, and your marketing identity including your target market, your image, and the benefits you offer. This chart on the following page lists the steps necessary to set up your fees.

First, look at your goals. How much income do you need to meet those goals? Look again at your break-even estimates, your per-student income estimates, and your personal financial goals. (See chapter 2 for information on making these estimates.) Based on these figures, come up with a tentative tuition and fee schedule. Calculate how many students you will need to break even. Then calculate how many more students you will need (beyond break-even) to pay your salary. Add the two. The resulting number is your target enrollment. Now look at your

SETTING YOUR FEES

1. Calculate your break-even point.
2. Develop a tentative fee schedule.
3. Calculate break-even in terms of number of students needed to break even.
4. Decide what kind of salary you need. Calculate the number of students you need to pay your salary, and add that number to your students-needed-to-break-even figure.
5. Assess whether your facility and schedule can handle that number of students.
6. Compare your tentative fee schedule to your competition's fees.
7. Look at your fee schedule in light of the disposable income of your target market.
8. Look at your fee schedule in light of your image and benefits.
9. Decide if you want to offer family or student discounts.
10. Adjust your fee schedule with all these factors in mind.
11. Write down your fee schedule and make it available to prospective students.

space. Can your space and schedule accommodate that many people? If not, you may need to raise your tuition or fees.

Another factor to consider when setting your fees is your competition. Call around. See what other schools in your community are charging. You will probably want to price your school comparably. Bear in mind, however, that your competition consists of more than just other martial arts schools. If you are a Taekwondo academy whose target market is children, you will be competing not only with other Taekwondo academies but also with dance schools, karate studios, gymnastics programs, and other sports programs that cater to that age group. See what these programs are charging as well. In other words, know your market competition not just your martial arts competition.

Of course, you may want to price your services below your competition. Bear in mind, however, that you will have to find the difference in income somewhere. Perhaps you can find a cheap location.

But a cheap location is usually cheap for a reason. Perhaps you hope to meet your financial goals by bringing in a large number of students. Remember, however, the number of students you teach will be limited by your facility and your own time and energy. Pricing below competition is a plausible marketing strategy, but it is a difficult strategy to sustain.

Pricing above competition is also possible. But it only works when you offer something special, something your customers believe is worth the extra charge. It's not enough that you throw extra features their way. They have to see the added benefits.

Monthly tuition need not be your only source of income. You may also have other fees, private lessons, and retail sales. You may want to institute registration or sign-up fees, ranking or promotion fees, seminars or tournaments, sales of equipment, or scholarships or grants from outside sources. Be sure to factor those income sources into the equation while you are setting up your pricing schedule.

Know your target market. Some people may prefer a single flat rate to being assessed a small fee for everything they do in the school. Others feel a pay-per-program system lets them know what they're paying for.

While you are setting prices, consider whether you want to set special prices for families or groups. Consider what a family with two, three, or four members would have to pay to enroll in your program. Could a family in your target market afford that price? You might consider a deduction for additional family members, or you might consider a flat family rate. If families train together, your school becomes more than an activity; it becomes a shared family interest. Families who train together are often very stable students. Encourage them.

As for spreading out the payments, you ought to know that "financing plans" are a nightmare. You might be tempted to say that tuition for the year is due up front at the beginning of the year but that you will allow the students to establish a line of credit and pay off the debt over time. If you do so, the federal government and the "truth in lending" laws are very specific about what is needed: You must give the customer disclosure forms and inform them about annual percentage rate of interest. Unless you live to tangle with government paperwork, don't get involved in calling anything a "financing plan" or "handling charge."

An alternative to allowing students to finance their annual tuition is to have a set monthly rate and then give a reduced rate to students who pay off the whole year's tuition in advance. Most people, however, will probably want to pay their bill as monthly tuition (or dues). They don't have the money to pay you for a year's agreement up front. They get paid weekly or monthly. Each month they pay their light bill, their gas bill, and you. It's simple, straightforward, something they're used to.

Collecting everyone's tuition on the first of the month will probably be easiest. That, however, is not always possible in a service business. Some people get paid on a weekly or twice-monthly basis. Like you, they probably have rent due on the first of the month. Bearing that in mind, you might want to ask students if paying you on the first or the fifteen of each month is better for them. Try not to let students pay each month on the date they enrolled. Having thirty separate payment dates for a hundred different students makes your record keeping more difficult. It also makes it more difficult to remind those students who may be behind on their payments. Rather, group all payments on the first (or the first and the fifteenth). That way you can schedule extra help on those days or plan for a longer day to collect dues yourself.

Finally, it's normal also to offer a lower "grand opening" price when you first open. For the first couple of months, bring in students at a reduced tuition rate, or reduce their enrollment fee. When the time for your special prices run out, bring the next student in at your regular fee. Having a grand opening price helps you build your student base quickly. It also gives prospective students a good reason not to put off enrollment until "tomorrow."

Deciding on your fees is a matter of balancing your financial goals, the limitations of your time and space, and money your potential students are willing to pay for the services you offer. Consider your fees carefully before you open your doors. Once you have students committed to paying a set amount each month, you will find it very difficult to raise your rates.

Set Up a Contract That Protects Your Interests

A contract is merely an agreement to do business—you agree to teach a student and they agree to pay you. It doesn't have to be a frightening document. But it should be something both you and your student take seriously.

Contracts are not essential. But they do have advantages for you. They help you protect your legal interests. They help you gather the information and permissions you need. And they help you plan financially and for a student's training as a martial artist.

A contract also has advantages for your students. It helps them think of their training as a long-term part of their life. It gives them another reason to stay in training when things get difficult. And it guarantees them a specific tuition rate during the term of their contract.

Contract Contents

Your contract, or a separate enrollment and release form, should collect basic information you will need during your student's study with you. This information includes name, address, phone number, and any physical/medical challenges. It should also include emergency contact information and a statement that gives you and your staff permission to act on their behalf in an emergency. In the case of minors, include a statement that allows you to act on the parent or guardian's behalf should the child be injured and the parent or guardian be unreachable.

Your contract should also include a statement of how much the student agrees to pay you and when that payment is due. Some schools prefer to have a yearly fee, which the student agrees to pay in full at the beginning of the year. If the student prefers, they can pay the yearly fee off on a monthly basis at a higher rate. If you choose to do something like this, be careful. By adding an additional fee, finance charge, or handling charge to monthly payments, you have moved under the jurisdiction of federal truth in lending laws. These laws require you to conform to specific lending practices and disclose your annual percentage rate of interest. Unless you enjoy learning about and complying with a maze of federal government requirements, avoid anything that looks like a finance charge. An alternative might be to charge one rate for people who pay on a month-to-month basis and a discounted rate for anyone who pays the entire year (or six months, or two years) tuition up front.

Whatever your terms, they should be clearly spelled out. Should a question of payment or responsibility arise later, the contract is your legal protection. Yes, you need to protect yourself. But you also need to be fair to your student. Beginning a relationship based on a document that is unfair to your student is a very bad precedent. For example, if you plan to use your contract to force a student to pay four years' tuition, even if they quit after six months, consider how that reflects on your image. Beyond that, consider how it reflects on your own personal honor.

Contracts usually have a seventy-two-hour provision for cancellation. You may also wish to add a clause that either you or the student can cancel the contract with written notification and for good reason after the seventy-two-hour period is up. This cancellation clause is for both your and your students' benefit. You need to have the option of dismissing a student who refuses to comply with the rules and policies of your school. Your students need to be able to get out of the contract if they should move, develop health problems, or be transferred to a work shift that makes training with you impossible. But since part of the purpose of the contract is to encourage commitment, you don't want to make it too easy to get out of. Try to strike a balance in your cancellation clause wording.

Release Statements

As part of the contract, or perhaps as a separate document, you should have a liability release statement. The purpose of the release statement is to release you, your company, your employees, and your landlord from responsibility should a student be injured on your premises, either during one of your classes or at any function sponsored by your organization.

In its most basic form, the release should include a statement that the student understands the inherent dangers in the activity and assumes all risks. The release says the student will hold you, your teachers, your students, your organization(s), and your landlord harmless should the student be injured or any property of his be lost or damaged. You might also want to consider the following:

1. A statement that gives you permission to administer first aid or to call for emergency assistance should a student be injured. This statement should also include the acknowledgement that the student, parent, or legal guardian recognizes that any treatment received from you will be first aid only and that they will hold you harmless for any consequence of that first aid.
2. A statement that the student, parent, or legal guardian will bear all costs associated with emergency treatment.
3. A statement that says the student agrees to abide by the school's rules and regulations and to conduct him or herself within the limits of safety.

If a student, parent, or legal guardian signs a release statement, does that mean you are no longer accountable should students hurt themselves? Not necessarily. A release never gives you the right to be negligent. Neither does it absolve you from your responsibility for the safety of your students. A release does, however, give your prospective students a chance to consider the part they play in keeping themselves safe. It may be a help in deterring frivolous suits. But it will not prevent them. Whether your release statement would hold up in court, however, is an issue for you to discuss with a qualified sports attorney.

Your release should be short, never more than a page. Write it in normal, everyday language, not legalese. Print it in clear, readable print.

Make signing a release statement mandatory for anyone who trains with you. Make a clear, written, unwavering policy. Anyone who steps on deck to train, anyone who picks up a piece of training equipment, anyone who tries out a class must provide you with a signed release form.

Visitors who are only joining you for one class must sign it. Minors may not train until their parent or guardian signs it. Make no exceptions.

Photo Release Statements

Another clause you might want to include in your release form is a photo release. This statement says that the school has the right to use photos taken during school activities for publicity or promotion purposes. The clause also states that the student waives compensation for these photos. Some students may not wish to sign a photo waiver. They may need to avoid publicity or they may just be shy. If so, allow them to cross out the clause and initial it. Their doing so puts the ball in your court. It is now your responsibility to see that no pictures of them are taken.

Make It Legal

Most fundamentally, your contract and release statement need to be legal documents, something you can enforce if you must. Go ahead and look at contracts from other schools. Go ahead and draw up something that meets your needs and represents your interests. But have the document reviewed by an attorney familiar with sports law before you start using it.

Take Credit Cards

Do you want to be able to take credit cards? On the one hand, accepting payment by credit card is a hassle and an added expense. The company will charge you a percentage of every credit card purchase you run through their system. You will need to rent or purchase a capture machine (the magnetic strip reader that sends the credit card information off for payment). And you will need to spend the time to learn to use it. On the other hand, credit cards are a convenience many of your students have come to expect. Taking credit cards will typically promote bigger payments and increase your business.

If you choose to take credit cards, how do you get set up to do so? The easiest, most straightforward way is to talk to your banker. Most banks can set you up with the paperwork, the instructions, and the credit card capture machine.

Credit card brokers also offer the same service. They will come in, offer to set you up, give you a great rate, in short will try to persuade you that doing business with them is the only reasonable choice. If, however, a credit card broker offers you a "great deal," ask yourself how they're making their money. Usually they make it by waiting a day or two to deposit the money into your account. In the intervening time, they use your money to make interest for them. By contrast, if you deal with a bank, when you take a credit card payment and clear it, the money is usually deposited in your account that night or the next morning. What's the difference? Think about the beginning of your month when tuition is coming in and your rent is due. Can you afford to wait for your money?

Another thing to consider when you're choosing a credit card service is whether that service requires you to own and maintain your own credit card capture machine. If you do your credit card business with a bank and rent your capture machine through them, they will typically maintain both hardware and software themselves. If you deal with a credit card broker, they will usually sell you the machine outright or will rent it to you with an option to purchase. That means that if the credit card company requires a software or hardware upgrade, you will need to pay for that upgrade.

When deciding who to do your credit card business with, think not just about whether the broker can save you a penny here and there. Think also about the cost in time and aggravation. Which service will allow you to collect your money quickly and easily so you can get back to teaching? Find out the details of the terms offered by your bank and by brokers. Read their information carefully. Be very clear about all of the charges. This is a world of hidden and surprise charges that can make an impact on your profitability if you don't pay attention. Then judge the service on its merits, not its hype.

If you do accept credit cards, make sure you have signs in your business office and your retail sales area that say which cards you accept. You're paying for the opportunity to take credit cards, you might as well advertise that you offer the benefit.

Select Training Equipment

Selecting training equipment is a matter of anticipating what you will need for your classes. If you have been training for several years, you probably have a good idea what your ideal equipment setup looks like. Do bear in mind, however, that equipment that will be used in a school must be sturdier than equipment used only in personal training. Buy quality.

If you plan to have a pro shop eventually, get your retail licenses and establish an account with a supplier before you start buying equipment for your school. As a retailer, you can get wholesale prices and volume discounts that can save you a significant amount of money when you're outfitting your school.

Hire Employees

If you're thinking about hiring an employee, write up a job description before advertising the job. What do you want your employee to do? Will they teach? Will they do just janitorial work or just bookkeeping? Or do you want an all-around assistant who, like you, is willing to do whatever needs to be done at the time? Don't just hire "help." Hire someone to do specific tasks.

Wages and Taxes

How much do you pay your employee? The answer to that depends not only on fair market value but also on government wage laws. If you aren't sure which government wage laws apply to you, check the Department of Labor requirements before hiring anyone. The "blue pages" in your phone book should have a listing for the Department of Labor's local Wage and Hour Division. They can give you the information you'll need.

While you're checking out government requirements, check the IRS and the Social Security Administration for tax requirements for small businesses employing employees. Look into unemployment insurance and FUTA. See chapter 5 for more information on insurance and taxes.

Who Do You Hire?

A word about employing family members: if you do so, you must be professional. Unless your family member is a co-owner, you must pay them a salary just as you would a stranger. You and your employee must evaluate on-the-job performance based not on the relationship you have at home but on what is best for the business. If you cannot give or take criticism from the family members, you probably shouldn't be working with them. The same goes for close friends. Going into business with a friend is not about how close you are as friends. It's about whether you can work together, make tough choices together, take criticism for the benefit of the business from each other. If you can't without ruining your relationship, don't do business together.

A word about employing one of your senior students: again, you must be able to separate the two roles. A good athlete is not necessarily a good employee. Even if she is your best student, you will need to decide whether she can handle herself professionally as an office manager or teacher before you hire her as an employee. Get the same background information from your students that you would get from any other employee. Hold them to the same professional standards. If you can't correct your office manager for fear of alienating your student, you don't have the relationship you need to make your business run smoothly.

General Guidelines

Management is an art. As with any art, you will not begin practicing it with all your skills fully formed. A few basic guidelines, however, will take you a long way.

First, be clear about what you expect from your employee. Develop a job description that lists tasks and when you expect them to be done.

Second, do not allow your employee to be moody. Do not allow yourself to be moody. When you are at work, you are there to work. If student needs must be met, they must be met regardless of whether your employee or you are having a bad day. Focus on the task.

Third, don't take advantage of your employees. Treat them well. Treat them fairly. Treat them as you'd want to be treated if you were doing their job. If you don't, you may find they discover a myriad of small ways of getting back at you. A disgruntled employee can manufacture dozens of ways to sabotage your business.

Good, contented employees, however, can make your job very easy. They know what's going on at the "front lines" and can help you spot problems before they become too large. They can shoulder many of the tasks around the school, leaving you to do what you do best. Listen to them. They are your best ally in getting things done and keeping students happy.

Prepare for Emergencies

Plan to keep your students accident free. Train them in the kinds of techniques that will prevent accidents. But prepare yourself and your school in case an accident does happen.

Have a good emergency first aid kit readily available to the training floor. A good commercial kit will have the things you need. Know what's in your kit, and know how to use it. Then keep it for emergencies.

For injuries that aren't emergencies, like the scrapes and bruises that sometimes happen during normal training, keep separate supplies. Figure out what you need—tape, adhesive bandages, ice packs, antiseptics—and keep them in a drawer separate from your emergency first aid kit. That keeps your kit full for serious emergencies, while giving you easy access to the items you may need on a more regular basis.

Also near the training floor, keep a spray bottle containing disinfectant. Use it to clean up any blood or bodily fluids that might get on the training floor. Although commercial disinfectant solutions are available, an effective, inexpensive solution contains one part bleach in ten parts water.

Train yourself in first aid and injury management. Train your assistants as well. Take a first aid and CPR class. Get certified and keep your certification current. Get a good first aid book. Then don't just read it; study it. Know how to treat common martial arts injuries. Then make a list of any injuries you may possibly need to deal with. Consult your first aid book, and come up with an emergency management plan for each kind of injury. Know which of your students and parents have emergency training. Keep your address and phone number near the phone so anyone calling 911 can give it to emergency services.

Then look at your other emergency equipment. Do you have fire extinguishers charged and readily available? Do you have ceiling sprinklers and smoke alarms in your storage rooms? Do you have emergency lighting? Do you have flashlights charged and readily available? Do you have an escape plan in the event of fire? Do you keep your emergency exits unlocked during business hours? If you live in an earthquake- or tornado-prone area, do you know what you would do if one struck during class hours?

Think through emergencies, both large and small, before they happen. Write down your emergency management plan listing how to handle each kind of emergency. Make up emergency report forms to record information about accidents. Bind both in a separate, clearly marked folder. Review it regularly, and have your employees do so as well. Keep a copy in your business office where anyone who wants to see it can. Should you be faced with an emergency, your students will look to you for leadership. Be prepared.

IN CASE OF AN ACCIDENT

If you should have an accident at your school—whether that accident happens to an employee, student, observer, or stranger—you should write down the following information as soon as possible after the accident:

1. Name of the injured person
2. Date and time
3. What happened
4. What caused the accident
5. What the apparent extent of the injury was
6. Who saw it happen (attach a brief statement from each)
7. What you did

Sign and date each statement.

Opening a school involves accomplishing a lot of little details. It's easy to be carried away with the novelty of buying new equipment, building a training floor, hanging your certificates. But don't get so carried away that you neglect the less glamorous tasks. Take care of government requirements, legal requirements, and insurance requirements up front. Neglecting them can cause you grief later.

CHAPTER SEVEN:

ASSEMBLE YOUR ADVERTISING TOOLS

If you want to establish a successful advertising program, you must first do some advance planning and pull your tools together. These tools can make the difference between a program that works and one that merely uses up time and money.

HOW TO BECOME AN EFFECTIVE ADVERTISER

1. Put together a marketing identity.
2. Use the marketing identity to develop a logo and slogan.
3. Use the logo and slogan to develop business cards, brochures, a sign, and other marketing tools.
4. Learn to use elements of your marketing identity in flyers and other advertisements.
5. Put together an advertising plan.
6. Develop an advertising calendar and follow it.

Marketing Identity

The foundation of all your advertising is your marketing identity. Your marketing identity is a clear statement of who you are as a business. It contains your image. It contains the features and related benefits you have to offer a student. It contains a statement of what you have that your competition doesn't. It is, in short, a clear picture of how you want your business to come across to the public. (Check out chapter 1 for more information. Then put together a marketing identity before you start assembling the rest of your marketing tools.)

From your marketing identity you develop two basic building blocks you will use in your advertisements: your logo and your slogan. Your logo and slogan are used on your business cards, stationery, and sign. You combine your logo and slogan with information from your marketing identity to produce brochures, and flyers. Once you've learned to put together a basic flyer, you can then use those same skills to produce Yellow Pages display ads, newspaper ads, door hangers, even coupons.

Your Slogan

A slogan is a short statement—eight image-rich words or less. You use your slogan every time you put the name of your business in print. The purpose of a slogan is to link a central facet of your image with the name of your business.

Think about the slogans you've heard over the years: "Have it your way." "It's more than a cruise. It's the love boat." "Kills bugs dead." "The rock." They all create an emotionally charged image in your mind, and they all are connected inseparably to the name of a particular business or product.

How do you come up with a slogan? Look at your marketing identity. Pick out something central, something rich in imagery. Capture the imagination. Make an emotional, gut-level statement: "Where winners like you train." "Kick butt and don't look back." "Molding the youth of tomorrow." "Creating a future with the wisdom of the past." How do you want to come across? How do you want people to react when they hear your name? Whatever you choose, make sure you can back it up in reality.

One word of caution: choose your slogan carefully. It's going to go on your letterhead, your business cards, your Yellow Pages ad, all your printed material. Changing it, therefore, can get expensive. Besides, if you want to build an image in your customers' minds, it's going to take time and a lot of repetition. The slogan-of-the-year syndrome doesn't allow your image time to filter up to your customer's conscious mind. Pick something that will still be true several years down the line. Pick something you won't get tired of. Change it if it's no longer true. Change it if you're getting too much negative feedback and not enough positive feedback. But don't change without a lot of thought.

Finally, if you can't come up with a good slogan, don't use a slogan at all. Having your business name inseparably linked to something in poor taste or ineffective can be devastating.

Your Logo

Your logo is the name of your business rendered in a distinctive graphic image. Like the slogan, it captures something about your school and conveys it in an immediate, gut-level way. Put it on all your advertisements. It's one of the simplest ways to promote name recognition.

Think back to the last time you were picking up your favorite soft drink or breakfast cereal at the grocery store. Did you pick up each container and read the labels? Probably not. You probably scanned the shelves for a specific color, a specific shape, a specific logo.

That's what your logo does for you. It provides instant recognition and identification of your school.

How do you come up with one? If you have to ask that question, the answer is, "You pay a graphic artist and have it designed." Small changes in color or shape can radically alter the impact of a logo. Look around at other local, independent businesses. When you see a logo you like, ask the owners of that business who designed it. Do some research: Check prices. Look at various artists' portfolios.

When you've found someone you can work with, negotiate prices and service. Then bring them the name of your company, your slogan, and a clear statement of your marketing identity, including your image and your target market. Tell the artist what you want your logo to "say" both literally and nonverbally. They can then convey that image in a clear, simple, distinctive graphic. Once you're satisfied with the logo, be sure to get "camera-ready" copies in several sizes. If you use a computer, get a scanned copy in a format you can use.

Your Sign

The sign you put on the front of your building is one of the most important advertising tools you can use. Undoubtedly, once you see the price tag for a good, lighted business sign, you will be tempted to get by with something painted on the front window. Don't yield to that temptation. Your sign is your main locator. It's what attracts drive-by and walk-by business. It is the first hint of your image a potential customer gets. Even if someone has your address, it will probably be your sign they see first.

When planning for a sign, check first to see if you have any restrictions on your signage. Check with your city. They often have restrictions on size and how close to the road it can be. Then look at your lease and talk to your building manager to see if your complex has required guidelines. Don't have a sign made before checking with the proper authorities to see if you will be allowed to put it up.

Consider what you want your sign to do for you. Like any other advertisement, your sign has to be consistent with your image. It needs to be visible both to drive-by and walk-by traffic. If you teach classes in the evening, it needs to be visible in the dark. Take a walk or drive through your area during the time of day you will be teaching. Look at the signs. Notice how the blue and yellow signs are much more difficult to read at night than the red and white ones. Notice how simple fonts are easier to read than frilly script or highly complex logos. Notice which signs can be read from the street and which can be read from the sidewalk. Notice which signs grab your attention. If you see a sign you especially like, ask the business owner for the name of the company that made it.

Shop around for a sign maker. Get bids. Then compare sign makers by price and reputation. Get addresses for the signs a sign maker has made, and go look at them during the hours you plan to be open. Once you've chosen a sign maker, nail down prices. Does the price quoted include permits and installation? Does it include wiring and time clocks? Ask to see working drawings or plans before the sign is made. Then ask about maintenance. Your sign will be up for a long time, so you need a company that will be there when you need repair and service. The cheapest bid is not always the cheapest over time.

Then take a deep breath and pay what you need to for a sign that will meet your advertising needs. The money will be well spent when students find their way to your door with ease.

Business Cards

Your business card should be clean and professional. It should have your logo and slogan and your name, title, address, and phone number. If you have an e-mail address, a Web site URL, or a fax number, you may wish to include those as well. That's all. Don't use your business card to explain your business. The purpose of a business card is to make it easy for a prospective student to get in touch with you in the future. You should have your cards professionally printed in a generally accepted business format. If you want something to set you apart from the rest, use spot color, or use the back of the card to offer a free lesson. Don't, however, go with odd sizes or wild and barely readable type. Business cards don't have to be boring, but they must be readable.

Brochures

A brochure is a leaflet that introduces a prospective student to your school. It contains the most persuasive elements of your marketing identity. You give it to people who have inquired about classes at your school. You can also place it in a rack outside your front door to give more information to potential students walking by. Its purpose is to give a prospective student enough information that they will want to come in and sign up.

What does a prospective student need to know about your school? Look at your marketing identity. It's all there. Putting together a successful brochure is simply a matter of putting your marketing identity into brochure form.

OPTION ONE—FOR A FAMILY SCHOOL

Cover page: The name of your school and its address

Inside page one: What makes you different from your competition (image & benefits)

Inside page two: What you have for children (features & benefits)

Inside page three: What you have for adults (features & benefits)

Inside page four: General philosophy of what you teach (image)

Back cover page: Your credentials as an instructor

The most common brochure format is an 8-1/2" x 11" sheet of paper folded in thirds. Most office supply stores have paper designed for brochures. Graphic-design computer programs can help you do an attractive layout. Or you can bring your written information to a printer and have them lay it out for you. Your brochure can be full of action, packed with pictures and lively text. Or it can be simple, with a lot of white space, a few elegant and well-chosen words, and perhaps a graphic or photo. The choice depends on your image. Whatever the choice, however, your brochure needs to be attractive and professional.

Folding the brochure in thirds gives you six columns, which you can fill with six different topics. The way you use those six columns depends on who your target market is and what you have to say.

OPTION TWO—A SPECIALITY PROGRAM

Cover page: The name of your school and a slogan

Inside page one: Brief description of the program (features & benefits)

Inside page two: Brief description of your facilities (features & benefits)

Inside page three: What makes you different from the competition (image & benefits)

Inside page four: Your credentials as instructor

Back cover page: Your address, phone number, and a map to your location

If yours is a specialty program, marketing to only one age group, you might want to try option two.

Or you can develop your own order based on the information in your marketing identity. Develop each page by concentrating on one or two important feature-benefit statements in your marketing identity. Make a rough mockup—handwritten on folded notebook paper is fine. When you're sure the information flows from one page to the next, you can use the mockup to develop a more polished printed version.

Before you have copies of your brochure made, proofread it. Get a friend who's good with words to proofread it. Then proofread it again. A brochure littered with typos, misspelled words, and grammatical errors reflects badly on your school.

Most of all, make your brochure exciting and informative. Use good-quality artwork, pictures that reflect your image in an interesting way. Answer some of the general questions prospective students might have. Don't, however, tell them everything. Get prospective students interested, but leave a little mystery. A brochure can get people interested, but it can't sign them up. The purpose of a brochure is not to educate or entertain. The purpose is to pull them through your door for a face-to-face interview.

Flyers

A flyer is a one-page, one-subject announcement done in a catchy layout. A flyer is not a brochure. Its purpose isn't to tell the reader everything they need to know about your school. A flyer is specific, attention-grabbing, and gets people interested in a single event or single feature of your school. At the very least, a flyer does four things: It draws attention to itself. It captures people's interest. It gives them a reason to act immediately on that interest. And it gives them the information they need to do so.

Event Flyers

One would think that an event flyer would be an announcement of a particular event. That's true, but it's only part of the truth. More importantly, an event flyer is a tool to get people to contact you about a particular event. These six steps can help you put together a successful event flyer:

Step one:
Carefully plan the event you will be featuring. The first step in producing a compelling flyer is having a compelling event to advertise.

Step two:
Decide who the flyer will be going to. Tailor the overall look and the message of the flyer to your target market. If you're advertising a summer camp for children, make the flyer fun. Give it a good children's graphic to catch the attention of the parents and children who will be reading it. If the event is for adults, use a picture that is more appealing to adults.

Step three:
Compose your message. Again, think features and benefits. Offer something interesting, fun, unique. Make the message concise, but promise more information when people call. A good message includes an attention-getting headline in big, bold type followed by four to five sentences giving the details of your event. Cover six basics: who, what, where, when, why, and a call to action.

1. Who: Your logo or name in bold type.
2. What: The event you're featuring.
3. Where: The location of the event and your location, including phone number.
4. When: The time and date of the event
5. Why: A brief feature-benefit statement. Tell them why they shouldn't miss this event.
6. Call to Action: Ask for the sale. Ask them to call or attend.

Check the accuracy of the information. Make sure your address and phone number are clear and accurate. If you're unsure how to spell a word, look it up.

Step four:

Pay careful attention to the layout (how the words and pictures go on the page). The layout should be simple, attractive and eye-catching. Pictures, especially of people in action are great attention getters. Don't try to squeeze too much onto the page. This is definitely a place where "less is more." Imagine your flyer on a bulletin board covered with flyers of all shapes and descriptions. What can you do to make yours stand out in the crowd? Imagine handing it to someone at the mall. What about the flyer will compel a person to read it (and call you) rather than wadding it up and tossing it into the nearest trash can?

Flyers can be produced on brightly colored paper. The weight of the paper depends on where it will be going. If it will be a general handout to many people, use a normal bond. If it will be going on a bulletin board, use heavier paper.

Step five:

Look at the flyer as an advertisement. Be ruthless. Be objective. Try to judge your efforts as an unbiased outsider would.

Step six:

Put it up on the wall and check it from a distance. Then check it up close. Can you read the headline? Does it draw your attention? Does it look attractive and appealing? Is it clean, not jumbled?

Feature Flyers

You can also produce flyers that inform a specific target market about one aspect of your school. For instance you can gear a flyer toward children or women or people interested in fitness. Follow the steps for putting together an event flyer, but build the flyer around a theme rather than an event. Look at your list of features and benefits. Select the two most compelling feature-benefit statements for a particular target group. Use these two points to develop the headline and copy for the flyer.

Remember: These flyers represent you and your school. They are "silent salespeople" for you, and they will determine whether a prospective student will be interested enough to talk with you face to face. That prospective student is forming their opinion of you purely from these pieces of paper. Make them good.

> **NEVER BE IN SUCH A HURRY THAT YOU PRODUCE SOMETHING THAT IS "GOOD ENOUGH FOR NOW." YOUR NAME AND REPUTATION RIDE ON EVERYTHING YOU HAND OUT.**

Flyer Layout

How do you lay out an effective flyer? Some people go to art and trade schools for months, sometimes years, to learn the intricacies of layout. If you plan to use flyers as a central part of your advertising plan, you may want to talk to an advertising professional. Ask the graphic designer who did your logo to provide you with several general-purpose layouts. You then fill in the blanks when you wish to advertise a specific event.

For those who don't want to hire a professional graphic designer, personal computers offer an alternative. Most computer graphic design programs—PrintMaster Gold, Print Shop, Announcements, and many others—have predesigned layouts to help you get started. Add to them a few simple principles and almost anyone can be turning out clear, effective flyers with very little learning time.

Principle #1:

Your layout should catch the reader's attention with a headline or catchy graphic in the upper-left corner. It should then funnel the attention down through the rest of the flyer to the lower-right corner where the "action" material is. The action material is what you want the reader to do—call, come in and ask about a special offer, attend an event, or sign up for a program.

Principle #2:

Choose typefaces that are clear and legible. Script and funky lettering are difficult to read. Print headlines in sans serif type. Print the body of the ad in serif type.

SERIF VS. SANS SERIF

The difference: Serif type has strokes projecting from the main line of a letter. Sans serif has no extra strokes.

This is a serif typeface.

This is a sans serif typeface.

Principle #3:

Print headlines in all capital letters in a bold, clear typeface. Print subheadings in uppercase and lowercase in a smaller typeface.

Principle #4:

Make sure your reader can tell one paragraph from the next. Indent paragraphs, or double-space between paragraphs (or both).

Principle #5:

Highlight information sparingly. Don't use all upper case letters in the body. Use italics to highlight only the most important or interesting information. Remember: if you highlight everything, nothing stands out.

Principle #6:

Use no more than three, four at the most, typefaces (fonts) per flyer. Use a change in typeface when you need to set one kind of information off from another. Use a change in typeface to highlight something. Use changes in font size, boldness, or italic rather than switching to a fourth or fifth typeface. In other words, don't use multiple typefaces just to get fancy; use them to create clarity. Your logo, by the way, doesn't count as a typeface. It's considered a graphic—a picture, not a font.

A slogan, a logo, a sign, business cards, brochures, and flyers are the basic tools you will use to build an effective advertising program. If your tools are commonplace or unremarkable, your advertisements will be that much easier to ignore. But if your tools are well thought out and distinctive, they will serve you and your advertising program well.

Chapter Eight:

Create a Successful Mass Marketing Program

Marketing is placing the goods and services you have to offer into the marketplace. It includes market research and advertising. Advertising, then, is anything you do to put your name in front of a prospective student. It need not be complicated, and it need not be expensive. It does need, however, to be well thought out and conscientiously executed.

Mass Marketing 101

Mass marketing is one of two kinds of marketing you will be using to bring in new students to your school. The other is direct marketing. Mass marketing is far-reaching but somewhat impersonal. To do mass marketing, you hire someone else—a newspaper, radio station, television station, or coupon company—to get your message out. Mass marketing is what most people think of when they think of advertising. It includes newspaper advertisement, radio and television commercials, Yellow Pages listings, coupon books, card decks, local advertising circulars, and direct mailing. Direct marketing, on the other hand, is a person-to-person form of advertising. It includes door hangers, tell-a-friend programs, neighborhood canvasing, and other more personal methods of getting your message to the public.

The Pros and Cons

The advantage of mass marketing is that you can reach a large number of people in a short time. It does have several disadvantages, however. It can be expensive. It's a scatter-gun approach. A 2 percent response to a mass market ad is often considered very good. Moreover, it's a widespread and impersonal way to advertise a local and personal service.

The Key to Mass Marketing Success

Whether you choose mass marketing or direct marketing, however, your advertisement must reach that segment of your target market living within your trading area. In other words, for your ad to be successful it must find its way into the hands of those people likely to respond to it.

When considering what kind of mass market ad to choose, the rule of thumb is this: advertising a fitness facility to people who live beyond your trading area doesn't pay. People usually won't drive more than seven to ten minutes from their home or office for this kind of service. Advertising to people outside that seven- to ten-minute radius is typically a waste of money.

How, then, do you reach people within your trading area? You need to do some research. Identify which phone book is most used in your area, which newspaper has the most readers in your target market. Does your area have fitness magazines or newspapers? What free newspapers, magazines, and advertising circulars are distributed at the stores in your area? Go where your target market goes—to grocery stores, convenience stores, video stores, malls, movie theaters. What publications and advertising do you see there?

Ask around. Check with friends, neighbors, current students, anyone in your target market to see what they read. Interview local clerks, bookstore owners, and grocers to see who's buying local newspapers or magazines in your area. Look up the circulation figures and demographics of local publications at your local library. Or call the paper's circulation department. They'll know their figures.

Mass market advertising can be effective, but only if you do your homework. Don't rely on the newspaper or Yellow Pages sales people to make your advertising decisions. Their job is to sell you an ad—the bigger, more expensive, and more widely circulated the better. Your job is to sell your school, to place your ad where your target market will see it, and to attract as many new students as possible.

Mass Marketing Options

The kinds of mass marketing most commonly used by martial arts school owners include: a Yellow Pages ad, newspaper advertisement, coupon packages, direct mailings, a Web page, and television. Which you choose depends on your budget, your marketing identity, and your target market.

Yellow Pages Listing

Most likely, a Yellow Pages listing will be your most expensive advertisement. It will probably also be your most effective. We have all been taught to "let our fingers do the walking." (That, by the way, is an example of an effective slogan.) And most of us do.

The first time you hear the prices for a Yellow Pages listing, you will probably be a bit stunned, especially when you discover the charge is monthly. These listings don't come cheap. But they do work.

The Yellow Pages offer at least four kinds of listings. The most elaborate is the display ad. It has its own separate box and takes up anywhere from an eighth of a page to a full page. It can incorporate color, photos, graphics, and text. A less elaborate ad is the in-column listing. It's smaller, no wider than a column, and it cannot include a photo. It is usually limited to a specific number of lines. It can, however, broaden your listing with a logo, slogan, typeface changes, color, or brief text. A boldface listing is just your name, address, and phone number. The print, however, is a little larger or a little darker to make the listing more visible. A regular listing, which the telephone company includes as a part of your regular business telephone service, contains simply your name, address, and phone number in standard print. The phone company may offer other alternatives in your area, and those alternatives may differ from year to year. Check with your representative to see what they have available.

Which kind of ad should you choose? Part of the answer to that question depends on how much money you have. A display ad can be flashy and visible. It can incorporate a photo, which is useful if your face is widely recognized or if your appearance or that of your school is a large part of your image. But a display ad is expensive. If you choose to place a display ad, you should do two things.

First, have it professionally designed. Why spend all that money to place a full-year ad that says "amateur"? Don't rely on the Yellow Pages' graphic artists to create your ad. They don't know your business, and they don't really have the time or incentive to learn about it. Furthermore, if your ad is put together by the same graphic artist as most of the other ads, it will probably look just like most of the other ads. Hire your own graphic artist. Give him the information to design an ad that shows off your marketing image and makes you stand out from the competition.

Second, keep accurate records of how many new students call your school after finding you in the Yellow Pages. Try the display ad one year and an in-column listing the next. Then compare the cost against the effectiveness. More than one martial arts school owner has found a good in-column listing to be just as effective as a display ad.

If you can't afford either a display or in-column, at least use a bold-face listing. The small print of regular listings often gets lost among the larger ones.

Once you've chosen the size of your listing, what do you put in it? Look at the listings in your current local Yellow Pages. Then go back to your marketing image. What do you do that sets you apart from the rest? People who look in the Yellow Pages are already sold on martial arts in general. They need to be drawn to your school specifically. Don't waste your money saying you help your students get into shape. Everyone does that. What do you have that your competition doesn't? That—plus your logo, slogan, address, and phone number—is what you put in your Yellow Pages listing.

A few words of caution: Make sure your ad is clear and easy to read. Avoid reverse type ads—the ones that have light printing on a dark background. They're hard to read, and they're more likely to be ignored than other ads.

Remember that anything that you put in your listing you must live with for a year. It's not the place to advertise short-term specials or experimental programs. If you put something in your listing in January, you must be willing to stand by it in December.

Go with the business directory that has the largest number of listings and the widest circulation in the area you're marketing to. Most cities now have several telephone directories that list businesses. Many of these directories are either called "Yellow Pages" or are printed on yellow pages. Yet not all of them have wide circulation. Some that do reach every house aren't used regularly because they aren't complete. Know which Yellow Pages you are listing in before you place an ad.

Be aware of deadlines, and work well ahead of them. When the Yellow Pages' representative calls, make time to listen to her and the options offered to you. Ask for a time schedule and reserve your space early. Then get your ad to the designer early. Allow enough time to see a proof and make changes before you submit the ad. You will live with any mistakes for a full year. You don't want to submit a rushed job. You want to present your most professional image.

Newspaper Advertisements

Another kind of mass market advertising you might want to consider is a newspaper ad. Newspaper ads can be effective, or they can be an expensive disaster. What makes the difference is how well you reach your target market within your neighborhood.

Unless you live in a small city and are centrally located, you don't need an ad that will reach every home in the city. People an hour away by freeway aren't going to be interested. They may drive that far for a good deal on a car or a sofa, but they won't make the drive several times a week to attend your classes.

Find out if your city newspaper has a neighborhood section. Or advertise in a small local paper, fitness paper, or local magazine. Or maybe skip the newspapers and check the possibility of advertising in local business, church, school, apartment complex, or community newsletters. Check out how many publications are both in your target market and in your neighborhood. Of those publications, how many can you afford to place an ad in?

If you do decide to place an ad, bear in mind one very important principle: Repetition sells. If you are placing an institutional ad, an ad that increases recognition for your school but doesn't make a specific call to action, you will only get that recognition over the long run. A special offer ad, one that offers a great deal for a limited time, should get a quicker response. But even with a special offer ad, people must notice your ad before they can respond to it. Consider how many advertisements, even full-page advertisements, you noticed in today's newspaper. It's very easy for readers to overlook a one-time ad. It's better to place a powerful two-column by three-inch ad every day for a month than it is to take that same amount of money and do a single-day, full-page ad.

Once you've decided where to place the ad, how large you want it to be, and how long you will run it, you need to come up with a message. Newspaper, magazine, and newsletter ads can advertise either a specific event or a specific set of feature-benefits. Use the "Flyers" section in chapter 7 to help you focus your advertisement and write the text. Always include a strong reason for the reader to act immediately on what they've read. Include a sale, limited-time offer, or event that will be held shortly. If they can wait until next month to call, chances are good they will forget to call at all.

Pay attention to layout. Some newspapers will offer to lay the ad out for you. Allowing them to do so might yield an effective ad, or it might not. Even if the newspaper's layout artists are conscientious and expert at layout, they aren't experts at your business, your image, or what you want to convey.

You must take responsibility for the success of your own ad. Get some idea of space limitations. Then write the text yourself. Build it on your marketing image. Target it toward your target market. Write a catchy headline. Choose a graphic or photo that fits with your image. Include your logo and slogan. Put together all the parts of a preliminary ad. At this point, listen to the layout artist's suggestions. They will know how to tweak the graphics and the layout for greater effectiveness. They may also give you suggestions about making your text clearer. But always ask to see a proof, a near-final copy of the ad you can critique and change. Check the ad for accuracy and make the necessary changes on the proof.

Never forget that it's your money that's being spent. It's your image that's being placed before the public. You must be involved in the production process. And you must have absolute approval before the ad goes to print.

Press Releases

Newspaper advertisements aren't the only way of getting your name in the paper. You can be the purchaser of a newspaper ad, or you can be news. A press release is the way you let your local paper know that you are news. It only works, however, if you have something newsworthy to release.

What makes good news? Public service events are news—for example, a seminar being held to benefit a police officer injured in the line of duty. Human interest stories are news if they are unusual enough. A twenty-five-year-old woman earning her black belt isn't news. A seventy-five-year-old woman earning hers might just be. Large events—tournaments, seminars, anything that brings in a large number of out-of-town guests—can find their way into the newspaper or onto the evening news. Even smaller tournaments might be covered by the sports section of your local newspaper. The grand opening of your school might be considered news if you plan a special event. Famous people often catch the eye of a journalist looking for a story. Prestigious awards do, too. If you want to send a press release that features one of your students, check with the student first. Some students may not want the exposure.

Don't be shy about sending press releases. If the information is well written and informative, the media will appreciate your releases. They are looking for people to be their eyes and ears in the community, alerting them to newsworthy events. Why shouldn't those events be yours?

Write about the event in press release form. Include a descriptive heading, a "contact" name and phone number, and whether the information is for immediate release or for release after a particular date. Keep the length to one double-spaced page or less. Include the who, what, where, when, and why of the event just as you did for your flyers. Then, think about benefits. What's in this for the reader or listener? What's in it for the journalist or news broadcaster (think interesting film clips, photos, and headlines that sell papers)? If you need more details about how to put together a press release, a good copywriting manual can help.

Do a little research before you send it. Don't just send the release to "The Newspaper." Send it to a person. If the story is a feature (human interest) article, look on the paper's masthead and find out who the feature editor is. If it's a sports story, send it to the sports editor by name. If it's going to the local television station, check the evening news credits for an appropriate name. If you can't figure out from the masthead or credits who to send it to, call the switchboard and ask the operator for the name of an appropriate editor. A press release is less likely to get lost if it drops immediately onto the desk of someone who's interested. If your event is particularly newsworthy, for example you are bringing in a celebrity or holding a particularly large tournament, you may even want to call the editor or reporter to give them a heads-up before the press release arrives. Similarly, if your news concerns a specific date, or if it could be a candidate for live news coverage, call the editor far enough in advance to give them some planning time.

Coupon Packages

A common advertising medium for martial arts schools is coupon books and packages. If yours is a coupon-oriented area, coupons might bring in prospective students.

Before you put any money into this kind of advertisement, however, do some research. Ask the representative about how the coupons are delivered. Is delivery consistent with your image? Does the target market for the coupons overlap significantly with your target market? Then look at the coupons currently being produced by the company you've selected. Is the appearance of the coupons consistent with your image? Are they duplicated on plain paper, in one color, with minimal graphics? If so, they may not fit with your image, unless your image is being the most affordable school in town. Check with owners of other service businesses who have placed coupons in the book you're considering. Call them up, explain who you are, and ask if they're happy with the results of the coupon offer. Don't spend any money until you're sure these coupons can get your marketing identity to your target market.

What if advertising in a particular coupon book is free (for you). Some coupon distributors will charge the person using the coupon rather than the business who is advertising. Coupons are only free if they fit with your image. If they are shabbily done, or if they are sold using high-pressure tactics, they can cost you in image. Image and results must drive your advertisements, not just cost. But if a book is suitable for your business it can be an effective way for you to reach new students.

If you do decide to advertise using coupons, you must be aware of at least one legal requirement. For coupons, or any other advertisement, if you advertise a "sale" or a "special," the price must indeed be special. You must either offer your usual services at a special reduced price or offer something extra for the same price. You must be willing to provide exactly what the coupon says when your new student comes in.

When a new student comes in to redeem a coupon, congratulate them on how much money they saved. Everyone likes to think they're a smart shopper. Everyone likes a great deal.

Direct Mail

In many markets, direct mail is an effective way of getting your message out to a specific public. Direct mail involves buying a mailing list and sending written material through the mail. Direct mail companies offer mailing lists containing specific zip code, demographic, and other target market information. You can use these address lists to mail a flyer containing a special offer to people who might be interested in your program.

Direct mail is effective because it allows you to send your mailing to a specific demographic group, only to your target market. In short, using direct mailing can place your flyer in the hands of that segment of the population with the greatest possibility of becoming students. It is a far less scatter-gun method than citywide newspapers or general magazines. Nonetheless, an 8 to 10 percent return is considered excellent. In other words, if 10 percent of those who receive your mailing contact you, you have done better than most direct mailers. The number of those who actually sign up depends on your ability to go from initial contact to signing up a new student.

The success of direct mailing comes from three factors: the list, the offer, and the presentation. The most important factor is the list. If it contains a low percentage of people in your target market, your mailing will be ineffective. Imagine sending a flyer for your new senior citizen's self-defense program to residents of an apartment complex for college students and young working adults. Even if the flyer and the offer are great, the response will be low if the mailing list is not tailored to your needs.

The second most important factor in direct mailing is the offer. Consider your target market. What kind of offer will grab their attention, make them say, "Wow, that's a great deal" or "Wow, I've got to go do that"? The program, event, or special offer you are advertising must be compelling.

The third most important factor in direct mailing is the quality of the advertisement itself. Barely readable text on the back of a cheap postcard says "junk mail." Go back to the section on flyers. Make your direct mailing a good-quality advertisement.

To make direct mail work for you, make it an ongoing campaign, not just a one-time try. Change your message and the offer you are making each time you do a mailing. Offer a great deal each time. Ask for the sale—ask them to call you, ask them to bring in a coupon, ask them to attend an special event.

A Web Page

More and more people are turning to the Internet when they want information about a particular product or service. In fact, martial arts schools around the world have established a presence on the Web. To decide if you want to join them, consider the costs versus the benefits. In other words, make your Web site decisions just as you make all your advertising decisions. Your marketing identity and your advertising goals affect your Web site as much as they do all your other advertisements. Before you build and place your site, have a clear idea of who you want to use your site and how you want them to use it.

DESIGN AN EFFECTIVE WEB SITE

1. Integrate your site with your marketing identity.
2. Keep your backgrounds simple and your typeface clear.
3. Make it easy to get around your site.
4. Keep your download times short.
5. Throw away your "under construction" graphic. Don't make a page available until it contains something worthwhile.
6. Provide a way for potential customers to contact you. Include address, phone number, and e-mail address.
7. Submit your site URL to several search engines.
8. Make your site a search engine friendly one.
9. Advertise your site so your target market can find it. Put your URL on your business card, in your Yellow Pages ad, in any print ads you may place. Exchange banners with other local businesses.

Set your goals before you start building your site. Are you providing an online brochure for prospective students who are looking for a martial arts school in your area? Are you approaching people in your area who may never have thought about martial arts but who are interested in fitness? Do you want to post information that will keep your current students fired up? Are you planning an online pro shop? Are you trying to gain more nationwide name recognition for your school and your style? (If name recognition is your purpose, ask yourself if that is a financial decision or an ego one. Both have their place, but only one pays the rent.)

Writing a Web page is a lot like writing a brochure or flyer. You must decide what information your customer needs, incorporate features and benefits, lay out pages in a way that will catch and hold interest, and ask for the sale. But Web sites also have some specialized considerations.

Your Web site should not only be a good advertisement for your school, it should also be a good Web site. That means keeping your backgrounds simple and your typeface clear. It means having navigation links to help readers find their way around your site. It means balancing visual impact with reasonable download times. If all of this is new to you, you might want to consider picking up a book or taking a class in Web site design.

Once your Web site is in place, consider how you plan to publicize it. First, submit your site URL to several search engines. Advertise your site so your target market can find it. Put your URL on your business card, in your Yellow Pages ad, in any print ads you may place. If your target market is local people who might not have thought about taking martial arts training before now, exchange banners with other local businesses. If your target market is martial artists no matter where they live, find out where on the Web martial artists hang out, and make your URL visible there.

TV or Not TV?

Wouldn't it be cool to see yourself on television, advertising your school, exciting the imaginations of thousands of prospective students with your martial arts skills and brilliant rhetoric? Cool? Yes, it would be definitely cool, but realistic? Well, that's another story.

Bottom line: television is expensive. Before you start spending money, you need to know just how expensive. Of course, you can probably find some cheap time in the early morning hours or in the more remote regions of cable TV. But putting on an ad during a 3:00 a.m. talk show isn't going to do much to pull in young viewers. In fact, no one is going to be intrigued by a commercial they don't see. Placing a commercial is a science. It's a matter of airing your advertisement during the programs your target market watches. Hire a professional advertising agency to check on ratings and advertising costs for popular martial arts dramas, sports programs, or children's or young adult programming. Find out when the people in your target market will be watching before you buy air time.

Who will be the spokesperson for your school? Can you be the on-screen talent, or should you hire a professional? Some business owners are very successful spokespeople for their companies. Others do more harm than good when they get in front of a camera. The only way to tell which is true for you is to ask someone who knows what he's doing. Hire a professional to produce the commercial. Ask him to assess your on-air skills.

Then check out how much it will cost to produce a decent commercial. Figure out who you want to advertise to, what you want to say, what image you want to project, and how much money you have. Bring that information to an expert to find out what's involved in producing and airing a commercial that will work for you.

Add up all the expenses involved in producing and airing a TV advertisement. You will not become a household name with just one week's airing of your commercial—look at the cost for a month or more. Add to that the value of your time—how many hours will you have to invest in finding a decent producer and making and placing the commercial? When you have a figure, calculate how many students you would need to bring in to make that advertisement pay off. How will you monitor the effectiveness of your commercial? How will you know when you've brought in enough students to pay the costs of the commercial? Consider all the financial implications before making a decision.

Then get real, brutally real. Forget the prestige of being on TV. This is about business, not your movie career. The only question is, "Can you make it pay?"

You have many tempting options in mass marketing. The option you choose must be able to reach your target market, capture their imagination, and turn that imagination into action. An advertisement that does not bring students through your door is not successful, no matter how pretty it is or how good it makes you feel. The result of all of your advertising, including mass marketing, must be to bring in new students. Period.

CHAPTER NINE:

CREATE A SUCCESSFUL
DIRECT MARKETING PROGRAM

Mass marketing might work for you. If you teach a good program that attracts and keeps students, direct marketing will work. Direct marketing is not the same thing as direct mailing. Direct marketing is person-to-person advertising. It is one person recommending your school to another person. When a student invites a friend to attend a class, that is direct marketing. When you go out into the neighborhood and place information in your neighbors' hands, that is direct marketing.

For martial arts schools, direct marketing works better than mass marketing for two reasons: First, teaching martial arts is a personal business. You win students and keep students by letting them know you can meet their personal needs. You win and keep students by being the kind of person they want to study with. Second, people typically choose fitness facilities close to their home or work. Mass marketing can rarely target that specifically. Direct advertising can.

To begin to do direct marketing, ask yourself, "How can I get my message to people in my target market within my trading area?"

Marketing to Your Neighbors

Many martial arts schools are located in shopping centers. If customers shop regularly in your complex, the complex and your school

---

FIVE LOW-COST DIRECT MARKETING IDEAS

1. Offer a coupon for a free month of classes to a local charity auction.

2. Make up "free week" cards for your current students to pass out to friends.

3. Hold a charity event—a tournament or seminar—at your school. Send a press release announcing it to your local paper.

4. Hold a potluck or pizza party for current students, their families, and their friends. Have flyers available with a "Friend special": 20 percent off the first month when a family member or friend is "sponsored" by a current student.

5. Do public-service, self-defense courses, then offer a special first-month deal if students wish to continue taking regular classes.

---

are within a comfortable travel radius for them. How do you get your message out to them?

One technique is to join—or form—an informal merchants' association with the business owners in your center. Each of you might agree to place the other merchants' brochures in your shop. Or you might offer specials for customers referred by a neighboring business. Or you may even offer other merchants a cash bonus if they recommend someone who signs up. Alternately, you might want to market to your center's employees themselves. Make up and send out a flyer offering a discount to your center's merchants or their families. At the very least, introduce yourself to the other business owners in your center. Invite them into your space. Give them a tour and let them know what you do. Familiarize yourself with their businesses. You and they share a common goal—you both want to bring business to your complex.

Look at your neighbors outside your complex. Would they be interested in your services? If you are next to a church or a school, talk to them about the possibility of your doing a self-defense seminar or an after-school program.

Companies in the neighborhood are good places to find prospective students. Make a special offer to local companies. For example, if five or more members from the same company sign up, each of those members gets a 5 or 10 percent discount. Some companies may be willing to subsidize tuition for their workers because fit employees are healthier and more productive. Others may want you to do a short-term self-defense seminar for employees.

If your school is next to a large apartment complex, check with the apartment manager about hanging some door hangers. Offer a limited-time offer to anyone who brings the door hanger in when signing up. Or allow the apartment manager to offer a free month of classes with every new lease. You can even offer the manager or leasing agent a free month of training for every four students she signs up. If a new housing development is being built in the area, check with the salesperson about offering a similar deal.

When you located your school, you put it right in the middle of your target market. Those people are now your neighbors. Find creative ways to introduce yourself. Find ways to get them interested in your program.

Service and Leads Clubs

Service clubs such as the Rotary, Lions, Elks, Boys and Girls Clubs, and others, are valuable support systems for small business owners. They are also great places to spread word-of-mouth advertising.

Both service and leads clubs are groups of people from different businesses who meet once a week, usually over a meal. Their purpose is to allow high-level managers or business owners from noncompeting businesses to get together, to share news and business ideas, and to seek advice from each other.

The only difference between a leads club and a service club is that the leads club generally does not do any fund-raising or donate as a group to charitable causes, whereas the service club's main purpose is to support one or more charities. The "leads" exchanged by a leads club are bits of information that someone else in the club might be able to use as a source for new business. If you don't have a lead that week, usually you have a small fine to pay such as giving a buck to the party fund. If you continuously come up dry, however, you will be asked to leave.

These clubs are the modern-day equivalent of "the old boy network." They work quite well and, if the group is good enough, can almost act as an informal board of directors. Clubs usually charge a fee for membership. Other expenses are the cost of the meals, the cost to pay a professional administrator, and an extra cost for a blow-out party at the end of the year.

Find a club whose members are also small business owners. Most of these clubs require a recommendation from a current member to join. Check with your accountant or business acquaintances you enjoy being with; let them know you would be interested. You can't invite yourself, but you can make yourself available and desirable.

Attend meetings regularly. Offer to be a guest speaker. Have your logo and business name tastefully embroidered on a golf shirt you wear to meetings. Tell people what you do. Get known in the community for volunteer work, and your business network and word-of-mouth advertising will expand.

Student Referrals

The most effective kind of direct advertisement is student referrals. Referrals only work, however, if you deserve to be referred. Offer fun, informative classes. Be a good personal example. Keep a clean orderly, school. Make sure you meet your current students' need. If your current students are satisfied, they will recommend your school to others.

Encourage current students to bring in their friends for a trial class. When people hear from friends that your school is a great place to train, they are likely to listen. And when your students train with friends, they are more likely to stay in training.

Make up a business-card-sized card that your current students can carry in their wallet to give to friends who express interest in your program. The card should have your logo, address, and maybe a line where the referring student can write his name. It should also include a brief statement of the offer you are making: one free week of classes, $25 off the registration fee, a free uniform with the purchase of a month of classes. If the friend signs up, you may wish to give the referring student a gift or a free private lesson. For example, when the friend turns in the card, they get a one-month introductory program at a special price, and the current student gets a $5 credit at your pro shop. Or the friend gets a discount on the registration fee, and the student gets a free piece of equipment.

Another possible gift for a student who refers a friend is a coupon for a neighboring business. The ideal coupon would be something that doesn't cost a lot of money, but that would be appreciated by the student. Consider an ice cream shop, a pizza parlor, or a video arcade. Or you may wish to make a deal with a neighboring video rental store. You purchase several free-rental coupons from the video store. In exchange, the video store agrees to put your brochure in all of their martial arts movies. You have coupons to give your students, which makes them feel appreciated. They bring in prospective students, who are good for your business. The video store gets publicity. You get your brochures in the hands of people with an interest in martial arts. Everyone wins.

Always send the person referring a prospective student to you a note of thanks. Even if you see that student in class every night, mail them a thank-you note. By referring a friend, they have done you a valuable service. Make a special point of letting them know you're grateful.

One final, crucial word on referrals: They can be very effective. But they are only effective when you have your act together as a business. Return calls quickly. Send out brochures immediately to prospective students whose names you have been given. When those students come in, make an extra effort to make them feel welcome. In short, if you want to be worthy of referrals, you need to be a first-class, professional organization. If you aren't, it not only reflects badly on you, it reflects badly on the person who referred you as well. If, however, you treat referrals like the gold they are, they can be the most effective form of advertising you have.

Marketing on the Premises

Direct marketing is more than just bringing students to your door. It's also enrolling most of the interested people who do come through your door. Think about it: of the people who dropped by last week to check out your school, what percentage actually signed up? If you are like most schools, the percentage is fairly low. Marketing done on the premises of your school can increase that number.

P.O.P. Materials

"P.O.P." stands for "point of purchase." Point-of-purchase materials are the magazines and candy bars at the grocery store checkout counter. They are the signs that cover televisions for sale at the department store. P.O.P. materials are materials you keep on the premises to help you get your message into your prospective students' mind. They're silent sales triggers strategically placed where you are most likely to do your selling. They're big and bright and "in your face" enough that your customers will probably look at them just because they can't ignore them.

Think for a minute about the place in your school where you do business—the place you sign up students, the place you take in money, where you sell seminars or special events. What materials do you have here at the "point of purchase"? If you're not careful, these materials can be negative. Does your office have uniforms stacked on the desk, popcorn crumbs on the floor, or sparring gear left by one of the children piled in a corner? If so, what your P.O.P. materials are saying is that this school has a chronic lack of attention to detail.

You want your P.O.P. materials to reinforce a positive message to a potential student. Go back to your marketing identity. Let's say one of the biggest things you have to offer is a chance for children to excel in tournaments. Then put trophies or pictures of children with their medals or pictures of competing children in the office. Are your professional credentials a selling point? Hang your certificates on the wall. Do you pride yourself on being a family school? How about hanging photos of families training together, or of you or your adults working with the children? Is your biggest selling point the facilities? Maybe you need a window in the office, so your prospective students can see the training floor while they sign up.

Think about the number-one theme in your marketing identity. How can you place something catchy before your prospective students to remind them of that theme as they sit down to sign the agreement? You don't have to be overbearing or distracting, but don't be shy either. You believe in what you have to offer—let prospective students know you believe.

No matter what aspect of your marketing identity you keep at the point of purchase, you need to make that place look and feel businesslike. Students will be parting with their money in your office. You need to project an image that says "this is a competent, well-established business." At the sign-up desk, display VISA/MasterCard signs if you accept credit cards. Have your brochures and business cards easy to pick up. Don't clutter. Make your office attractive and totally positive. You want the prospective students to get interested and excited about what they see.

Don't forget, too, that your current students are also customers. At the entrance of your school, post colorful posters—computer-generated or printed, not handwritten—that list future events, recent winners of competitions, special programs you have for children. Do you have a seminar coming up? Don't just announce it; make up a catchy flyer and place it in a central location—on the mirror in the dressing room, by the water cooler, or on the front door. Opinions differ, but placing flyers in the training area is probably not the best idea. When students are in the training area, they need to be thinking about training, not about reading flyers.

Be careful, also, not to put up too much. You don't want your flyers to be competing with each other, and you don't want your school to look cluttered. Besides, you need to change flyers often to maintain their ability to grab students' attention.

The bottom line? The "point of purchase," the place you do business, can either help you do business or it can chase away business. Your walls should do more than hold up your roof. Make the walls of your school, especially in your business office, reflect your marketing identity.

Walk-Away Packet

A walk-away packet is the information you give prospective students to take with them after an initial visit. It might include your brochure, a price list, a schedule, information about special offers. It should be presented neatly, in a way that reflects positively on your image, perhaps even in a folder, envelope, or simple binding. It will definitely include anything you want them to remember when they are assessing your competition.

Think about it: your prospective student is sitting in her car. She has just visited you and two or three of your competitors. She is relying on her memory and whatever you have handed her to make her decision. She's thinking about not only what makes sense logically and financially but what feels right. What concrete information and what image do you want in front of her at a time like this? That's what goes into your walk-away pack.

Give this packet to every person who comes to ask about classes. Offer to mail it to everyone who calls. Put the information in that person's hands, and then follow up after she has had a chance to look at it. The purpose of the walk-away packet is to get prospective students to walk back in and sign up.

Your Annual Advertising Plan

Your advertising plan helps you put your money and time into the forms of advertising that will work for you. If you've looked through the direct and mass marketing alternatives in these chapters, you probably already have some ideas about the best way to get your message to your potential students. An advertising plan will help you turn those ideas into a reality.

The Choices

Developing an advertising plan starts with deciding who you want to reach. Who is your target market?

Then do some brainstorming—Where can you reach your target market? Where are you likely to find young adults? List the places they visit, the local publications they read—figure out where you could put your message so they could see it. Then get creative. Let's say you've found your target market at the video store. Can you work out a deal with a local video store owner? You buy some gift certificates to use in one of your promotional campaigns, and they put your brochure in their martial arts movie cases. Or let's say you've found them at a singles group at a local church, synagogue, or mosque. Perhaps you could do a one-day self-defense seminar for them.

List as many options as you can think of, then look at your advertising budget. For your first year or two, plan to use 8 to 10 percent of your receipts for advertising. After you get established, budget 3 to 5 percent. Look, too, at how much time you have budgeted. Call around and get estimated costs if you plan to do mass marketing. Put some feelers out if you are thinking about doing some direct marketing in your neighborhood. Decide which advertising options are likely to pay off for you. Then start the plan rolling.

The Timing

Once you've decided what kind of advertising you wish to use, it's time to think about when and how you are going accomplish that advertising. An advertising calendar helps you plan what you need to do and when you need to do it. Typically, you will have times of the year when you can bring in a lot of new business and times of the year when business is always slow. An advertising calendar allows you to bring in more students during the busy times, while using the slow times to plan.

First, you need to know what part of the year is a good time for you. (See chapter 15 for information about determining seasonal trends in your business.)

Let's say that every September and October you get an influx of new students from the local college. If you're a smart advertiser, you will find ways of capitalizing on that trend. How can you advertise to college students? You may wish to place an ad in the student paper. You may wish to give referral coupons through your current students who attend the college. You may wish to make up a flyer to post on bulletin boards, offering a limited-time special enrollment fee to new first-year students. Or you may want to do it all.

Then, start planning your schedule. Find out when school starts. If the fall semester begins September 10, you will probably have to have your ad in to the student paper by August 15 or before if you want to make the first issue. Call to double-check deadlines. That means you need to have the ad ready by early August. You need to get everything to the graphic artist by mid-July. You need to decide on the image and content you want for the ad in early July, and you need to start thinking about saving the money you need for the ad in May or June. Do you want referral cards to pass out by September 1? Then, you will need to check with your printer in July or August (or earlier) to see how long it takes to produce them. Do you want to put up bulletin board flyers in late August? Then you need to investigate permissions in July or early August.

In short, to develop an advertising calendar, you decide when you want to run an advertising campaign and then count back from that date to schedule all the details of the campaign. If you keep an advertising calendar that looks at least a year into the future, you can plan for financial demands. If you keep an advertising calendar, you can make sure you never miss an advertising opportunity because you missed a deadline.

Don't keep your advertising calendar in a file folder. Write it into your regular appointment calendar. Or make notes on pieces of paper and drop them into your accounts payable accordion file. Or post the calendar in a conspicuous place above your desk. Keep it in front of you. And keep to it.

When Is Advertising Worth It?

Why do you advertise? To bring in people who are interested in becoming students, to build your business, and to meet the financial goals you've set for yourself. How do you know if your advertising is successful? Ask the people who are coming through your doors.

If you will be spending any money at all on advertising, you need to keep records on how each prospective student heard about you. When prospective students call or walk through your front door, greet them, make them feel welcome, invite them to take a tour of your school, but sometime during the conversation, ask them how they heard about you. Then jot that information down in a specific file folder or notebook. That advertising record should tell you exactly how many people contacted you because of each of your ads.

When it comes time to decide whether to continue your television or print advertisement, when it comes time to choose the format of your next Yellow Pages listing, when it comes time to plan your advertising budget for the next year, you can make your decisions based on facts. You will know just how many students, just how much revenue each advertisement has brought you.

SIX PRINCIPLES
OF EFFECTIVE ADVERTISING

1. Build your advertising on your marketing identity.
2. Stay true to your image.
3. Aim your advertising at your target market.
4. When you try a new kind of advertising, give it a fair trial time.
5. If a type of advertising doesn't work, don't use it next time.
6. If a type of advertising does work, budget the time and money to use it consistently.

Remember: a good idea is only good if you act on it. It doesn't matter how brilliant your marketing ideas are if you don't put them into practice. But if you put the same thought and effort into your advertising that you put into your martial art, soon you will be doing highly effective marketing.

OPERATING
A
SUCCESSFUL
MARTIAL
ARTS
SCHOOL

CHAPTER TEN:

SIGN UP NEW STUDENTS

A good advertisement will bring students to you. Yet if they don't feel a connection between what they want and what you have to offer, they won't sign up. If too few of them sign up, you won't have a school. How do you help students make that connection? Of course you need to have something to offer. You need to have the features and benefits of your school in place. But then you must put those features and benefits to work through active listening and problem solving—matching what you have to what your prospect student needs.

Build Your Business One Person at a Time

When prospective students call or walk through the door for the first time, it's no accident. They want something. If they don't think you can give it to them, they won't come back.

It's easy enough to say that what they want is to learn what you know. Though that may be true, it's only part of the truth. They also want to know they'll have fun, they'll be safe, they won't look silly. They want to know they'll fit in, that they'll be able to keep up and learn what they need to learn.

Each student comes to you with her own reasons for studying the martial arts. The only way you can discover what the reasons are, the only way you can let a student know you can meet those needs, is to make personal contact. Listen. Make connections between what your potential student is saying and what you have to offer.

Make Personal Contact over the Phone

Many students contact you first over the phone. They can't see you. They can't see your school. They can't see your technique, your teaching skills, your past successes. Yet even so, they will be sizing you up. Listening only to the tone of your voice and what you say, they will be drawing conclusions about your school. You can lose a prospective student in less than thirty seconds of conversation.

Or you can gain one.

A call from a prospective student is very different from a personal call. During personal calls you can ramble. During a call from a potential student, however, you must have a goal, a mission. And you must work to accomplish that mission quickly, efficiently, and with a personal touch.

The number one mission for any phone call with a prospective student is to get the student in to see your school. If the students don't come in, you can't show them how your school can meet their needs. You can't finalize a business agreement. You can't collect a check.

This point bears repeating: the initial phone conversation with a prospective student is a tool to get him to come see you in person.

Prepare to Handle a Call

The phone rings, what do you do?

First, monitor who answers the phone. Never allow children to pick up calls. Even if you're busy with a class. Even if you've gone to lunch. Put on an answering machine if you must, but don't let a child be the first voice your prospective students hear. When they call, they should be greeted by someone who represents the school and is willing and able to do business.

Next, when you answer the phone, all of you must answer the phone. If part of your mind is still teaching a class or working on the books, the person on the other end of the line will sense it. You'll come across as distracted and unfocused. "Distracted and unfocused" is the last image you want as a martial arts instructor.

So when the phone rings, here's the drill:

On the first ring, register that the phone is ringing. Excuse yourself if someone else is in the office. Take a deep breath. Bring your whole mind to focus: You're going to be talking to a real person, not just a phone receiver. And you're going to meet a need for this person. If you've practiced the martial arts for any length of time, you know what this focus feels like. Everything else drops away, and it's just you and the task before you.

On the second ring, pick up a pen and your information sheet (more about that later). Smile, pick up the phone, and in a friendly, warm voice let the person on the other end know to whom they're speaking. You'll have to find a greeting that feels comfortable for you, but it should include the name of your school. Try something like, "Good afternoon. Westside Arnis Academy. This is Pat."

When you hear the person's voice, imagine the face on the other end of the line. Invent a generic face in your mind if you don't know what the person looks like. If you have a lousy imagination, look at yourself in the mirror and talk to that face. In short, do what you need to do to get past thinking of the person on the phone as a nameless, faceless voice. Remember: today's faceless voice may be tomorrow's student. Five years from now that voice, that person, may be an old, familiar part of your life.

Once you've established that the person on the other end of the line is a potential student, you have only one ultimate mission: to get that individual to come see you and your school in person.

Avoid Call Enders

Does this call sound familiar?

You: "Good afternoon. Championship Judo Center. This is Andy."
Prospective student: "How much do you charge for lessons?"
You: "Sixty dollars per month plus testing fees."
Prospective student: "OK. Thanks. Bye."

Nothing ends a call quite so quickly as immediately answering the question, "How much do you charge?" Yet it's one of the most common first questions people ask when they call a martial arts school. To keep the call going long enough for you to generate interest for your school, you need to use this and other "call ending" questions as springboards rather than as the "be-all and end-all" of the call.

> **HANDLING CALLS FROM PROSPECTIVE STUDENTS**
>
> 1. Smile
> 2. Steer the conversation away from call enders.
> 3. Practice active listening to find out what the prospective student is looking for.
> 4. Build their interest with benefits that will meet their needs.
> 5. Get the information you need and give them the information they need.

Sure, sometimes price is all the caller is interested in. If that's true, and if being the cheapest school in town is part of your marketing image, you could possibly answer the question without ending the sale. It's more likely, however, that the caller is interested in much more than price, but price is the only thing she can think to ask about without sounding stupid. Chances are good the prospective student doesn't know much about what makes one style different from another or one school different from another. But money—that's something people know. So they ask about price. When you answer their price question, however, they run out of "intelligent" questions and close out the call.

With that in mind, let's consider some responses that will keep the call from ending with a single answer. Some possibilities:

- "Our prices differ from program to program. If you tell me more about why you're thinking of studying the martial arts, I can suggest a suitable program."
- "Are you looking at classes for yourself or for your child?"
- "I think you'll find our prices very competitive, especially when you see what we have to offer. What are your goals in studying the martial arts?"
- "Is price the only deciding factor for you? If so, I can recommend some schools that are cheaper—but either way, I can guarantee you'll get what you pay for. If you'll come by our school this evening, I can show you why we're the best value in town."

Whatever response you come up with, you must do three things: First, acknowledge their question, but don't answer it right away. Answer it eventually, but only after you have a conversation going. Second, steer the conversation to enable you to get some more information about the caller and what his needs are. Ask a question that will keep the person talking, allowing you to get the information you need. Third, steer the conversation in a way that's consistent with your image. The last of the above responses would probably be too abrupt for a program that prides itself on taking in shy people and teaching them to be more assertive. It might be just right, however, for a school with a hard-driving, take-no-prisoners image.

Remember, though, that you're trying to steer the conversation so you can find out more about what your potential student wants from you and the martial arts. And, most important, you're trying to arrange a time for the person to come in to see your school.

Listen Actively

Practice active listening to find out what the prospective student is looking for. What is active listening? It's taking control of the conversation, not by talking incessantly but by encouraging the caller to give you the information you need. Active listening means breaking the ice, then structuring the conversation so both you and your prospective student can achieve your goals.

It doesn't matter if you have the best training equipment in the western hemisphere, if students don't perceive you as friendly, trustworthy, and having their best interests at heart, they won't sign up with you. You must make a connection with them. You must let them know you're listening and registering what they're saying.

Comment briefly on the things they say. For example, let's say a caller tells you she has a six-year-old daughter who's interested in your program. You might respond, "Six? We have a great class for six-year-olds. What is your daughter most interested in?" Or when the caller gives you her address, "That's near the park, isn't it? There are some beautiful old houses in that neighborhood." All you're trying to do is to make a quick connection between the caller's world and yours. Be careful not to get sidetracked, though. This is a business call, not a cocktail party. Prospective students aren't interested in your long, personal stories. Keep it short, keep it positive, but let them know you're listening and processing what they're saying. Help them picture you, connect with you, just as you are trying to picture and connect with them.

The second part of active listening is making sure both you and the students get the information you need. Answer their questions. Then, ask questions that will help you collect information. Give them the information they need. Ask for the information you need.

Build Curiosity through Benefits

What information do you need? One thing you need is enough information to be able to match what the student wants to what you offer.

Do you remember the last time you read or heard about a sale, or movie, or new product so good you rearranged your schedule to go check it out? That's what you're trying to do with your calls from prospective students. You're trying to build enthusiasm that will make the caller want to come in to see you. The key to doing that is, again, your marketing identity. Find out what the caller needs. Then offer her something from your marketing identity that meets that need.

Think about the reasons people get started in the martial arts. What kinds of things are your prospective students likely to say to you during that first phone call?

- "I want to get into shape."
- "This town has gotten so dangerous that I don't feel safe any more."
- "I saw Chuck Norris do this really cool move where he jumps up and then spins and kicks and then chokes this guy. Can you teach me to do that?"
- "My daughter's grades have been getting worse and worse, and she can't seem to focus. A friend said martial arts might help. Is that true?"
- "I thought it might be kind of fun."

- "This guy's been picking on me and I want to learn to kick his butt."
- "Work has gotten so stressful that I need to do something or I'm going to go crazy."
- "My son watches karate cartoons on TV and then runs around the house kicking the furniture, so I thought maybe he'd enjoy this."

You can probably add several more right now. As you field calls from potential students, still more reasons will present themselves.

Let's take an example: "Work has gotten so stressful that I need to do something or I'm going to go crazy." Your response: "We have many people who find our classes help them relax after work. Besides, we have one of the best heavy-bag racks in town. We can show you the safe way to work out with a heavy bag for those days when the stress builds until you feel like hitting something. Let's make an appointment for this evening. You can see the bag rack and the rest of our facilities in person. How does six o'clock sound?"

> **NEVER BE SO BUSY OFFERING YOUR PROSPECTIVE STUDENT WHAT YOU HAVE THAT YOU FAIL TO FIND OUT WHAT THEY WANT.**

Notice what you're doing: First you're acknowledging the need your caller expresses. Not everyone will be attracted to your school for the same reasons. You have to listen before you can start selling your program. Second, you're matching a benefit to that need. To make this match, you need to know what your most persuasive benefits are. You have to have a marketing identity, and you have to know it like you know your own name. You need to be able to help a prospective student build a mental image of your program meeting their needs. Third, you're making an appointment for a specific time so the caller can see your school and its benefits in person.

Remember that you are meeting the prospective student's needs. The call is not a chance for you to show off. It's about the caller—finding a program that suits him. On the other hand, a call from a potential student is no time for shyness. If you can (honestly) meet the caller's needs, say that. Believe in what you have to offer.

If the benefit you offer doesn't strike a chord with the caller, listen some more and then offer something else. But don't answer all the person's questions. Leave a little mystery. That, and a suggestion that it might be better if the prospective student came in to see for himself, gives the caller the incentive to come by in person. In other words, don't tell prospective students everything, but tell them enough to pique their interest.

Get Follow-Up Information

Not only do you need to get enough information to match your benefits to callers' needs, but you also need to get enough information to be able to follow up. A tool that can help you get this information is a caller information sheet.

Your caller information sheet can be an 8-1/2" x 11" sheet of paper or a 5" x 8" card. The 8-1/2" x 11" sheet gives you more room, so you'll never have to write in the margins. But the smaller card can be filed easily in your monthly to do file. Choose a format that will work with your organizational system.

Information Card

Date:_____ Time:_____By:_____ Call ❏ Message ❏ Walk-in ❏
Name of caller:_____
Classes for (prospective student):_____ Age:_____ Class:_____
Phone number:_____ for: _____
Address:_____
City:_____ Zip:_____
Program discussed:_____
Knows the location of the school ❏ Gave directions ❏
How did you hear about us? Walk by ❏ Yellow pages ❏ Advertisement in _____
Referred by _____ other _____
Primary interest: Fitness ❏ Self-defense ❏ Relieve stress ❏
Self-confidence ❏ Fun ❏ Meet people ❏
  other:_____
Appointment: _____
Notes:

The information sheet contains blanks and boxes for five main kinds of information. Most important, it has blanks for the vital information you must know to follow up: the caller's name, the prospective student's name and age, a telephone number, and an address. The sheet has a place to note the caller's main interests, so you can begin to think about what you will present to the person when he arrives. It has a place to compile some marketing research information. If you ask each of your callers where he heard about you, and note the answers, you can see if your new newspaper or Yellow Pages ad is paying off. The information sheet also has a space to note whether you mentioned a particular program or offer. If the student is interested only in summer camp, or if you agreed to bring the person in under a special registration price, note that here. The final space is for miscellaneous notes—for example, that the prospective student is a new college student who has recently moved to town, or that she cannot start classes for three months. These notes can also include anything that will help you remember your initial conversation when you meet the person or talk to her again on the phone. You want not just "business" notes but also any personal information that will allow you to relate to the person quickly and easily when she comes in.

Bear in mind that you'll be writing while in the middle of a phone conversation. Put as much of the information as you can into checklist form. You know you'll be asking, "What interests you most about studying the martial arts?" If you have a list of the most common answers on your information sheet, you can check the ones that apply. Of course you need to have a space for interests you haven't thought of, but often you will be able to check boxes rather than spend time scribbling.

Remember: your mission anytime you talk to a prospective student on the phone is get that person (or his parent) to come in to talk to you in person. Whenever possible make an appointment. A specific appointment at a specific time is much better than "why don't you come by later this week?" Offer the caller a choice of times, "Would you be available to come at 6 p.m. or 7 p.m.?" If neither of the times you offer is good for the caller, ask the person to suggest a time when he will be available. Set a specific time, a time when you aren't teaching, a time when you can devote your full attention to the prospective student. Ask for the caller's phone number. Tell the person that you'll call them if anything comes up and you can't make the appointment, and ask him to do the same.

Finally, let the caller know where your school is, even if the person thinks she knows. You don't want to go through the effort of a phone conversation, get the prospective student interested, and then have that person show up on your competitor's doorstep. Somewhere on the caller information sheet, make a note to remind yourself to give the student the information she needs: the name of your school, its address, and very quick directions. For example you might want to give cross streets: "We're on Speedway Boulevard between Pantano and Kolb." Or you might want to give landmarks: "We're two blocks south of Midtown Elementary School."

If a child or teen calls—parents often put them up to it—follow the same steps you would for an adult. Listen to his needs. Match benefits to those needs. Get the information you need. And give the child the information he needs. You will probably be a little more casual with a child than you would with an adult. But be sure to treat the child with respect. You want the child as a student, so you should treat him with the same respect you treat all your students.

When anyone under eighteen calls, your mission shifts a little bit, however. Of course, you still want to convince the caller to study with you. But you must also convince the child that he must bring a parent in to sign up. You should have a policy that a minor cannot sign up without a parent's signature. Not only does this help you deal with liability issues, it also gives you an opportunity to explain the value of your program to the parent. Having a parent who believes in the value of martial arts training is crucial for any child's success in the arts. So if a child calls, you win over the child but also give the child what he needs to win over the parent. You make sure the child understands that if he wants to study the martial arts, it is necessary to bring his parent to see you. Then get an address or phone number. Try to send information to the parent, talk with the parent, and make an appointment with the parent.

Child or adult, your ultimate mission during a call from a prospective student is to bring the person through the door.

Win Over Your Walk-In Customers

Once a potential student walks through your door, your mission shifts. Now everything you do and say works toward signing that person up. Many customers make up their mind within the first thirty seconds after entering your school. You have that long to create a positive impression and capture their interest.

We're not talking "hard-sell" tactics. Most people, martial arts school owners included, are not born to be high-pressure salespeople. What we're talking about is problem solving. The prospective student who just walked through your door did so for a reason. If you can find out what that reason is, maybe you can provide what that person wants. It's OK to make prospective students feel comfortable buying your services. It's OK to help them resolve any ambivalence they might have about signing on with you. It's OK to say, "I'd like to have you as a student. Let's sign the agreement now." In fact, it's more than OK; it's your main goal from the first second they walk through your door.

The basic principles for handling visits are much the same as the principles for handling calls. You practice active listening to find out what they are looking for. You build their interest with benefits that will meet their needs. You get the information you need and give them the information they need.

The main difference is that now your mission has changed. Your mission when fielding a phone call was to get the person to come in. Your mission now is to close the sale and start a new student training.

Create a Strong First Impression

What do people see when they first walk through the door? Chances are they see things you don't even notice anymore. You've learned to ignore the water stain on the ceiling, the heap of equipment and uniforms in the corner, the junk piled on the chair next to the desk. You see them so often, you hardly know they're there. Yet for first-time visitors, they're part of a first impression. That first impression can make prospective students want to turn on their heel and walk back out the door. Or it can be your first sales tool. Create a positive environment. Train yourself to notice details.

Put up an "Open" sign. Put some chairs in a place where prospective students or parents can sit and watch a class. Straighten up the day's clutter and clean the training floor. Get ready for the next day before you leave for the night. Be inviting. Look welcoming. Appear ready for business, and you'll draw business.

Martial arts schools must also consider another important first impression: the one that is made on a visitor's nose. Walk outdoors occasionally. Fill your lungs with fresh air (or what passes for fresh air in your part of town). Then walk back in. If you didn't own the place, is

---

IS YOUR MARTIAL ARTS SCHOOL INVITING TO PROSPECTIVE STUDENTS?

Don't rely on your memory to help you answer these questions. Walk around your school. Try to see it as a prospective student would see it.

___Are the sidewalk, parking lot, and entryway clean?

___Are the windows clean?

___When you look through the window from outside, does the school look ready for business?

___Is the doorway clear, not crowded with people, shoes, gear, etc.?

___Is the waiting area free of gear, shoes, stray magazines, and toys?

___Are brochures, schedules, and business cards readily available?

___Is everything in your office businesslike?

___Are dressing areas clean and well lighted?

___Is training equipment that is not being used neatly stowed?

___Is the air fresh and moving?

___Is the temperature suitable for the activity on the floor?

___Is the floor clean (especially important if you train barefooted)?

___Are the walls and ceiling clean and in good repair?

·this a room you would voluntarily spend time in? Is there anything more than "prebreathed" air for the students to inhale? Is it time you got rid of the pile of dirty uniforms in the corner? Enough said.

While you're looking around the school, also look in the mirror. See the reflection in the mirror as someone who just came in from outside would. Check your hair, your breath, your smell. Make sure you aren't wearing heavy perfume or aftershave. Be aware of these things, especially if you go directly from training to meeting prospective students.

Look also at the way you dress. Dress neatly and professionally. Of course, that doesn't mean you have to put on a suit every morning. But neither should you go to the opposite extreme. Save the five-year-old pair of "lucky" sweat pants for when you work out in your backyard. Get rid of the muscle shirts, tank tops, and the "Kiss me I'm a martial artist!" T-shirt, too. If your school has a standard uniform, a clean, pressed, well-cared-for version of that uniform is fine. If not, you might want to devise your own uniform—a polo shirt with your school logo on it, worn with clean jeans or chinos, for example. Whatever you decide to wear, it should say, "This is my school, and I'm ready for business." If it looks as if you dressed out of a soggy pile on the bottom of your gym locker, you will be chasing away prospective students.

Next, look at your current students. In many schools, students hang around the front door or in the office joking with each other and swapping stories. It's part of the life of a martial arts school. Yet think of what that might look like to a visitor. To them, it looks like a bunch of strangers—strong, confident strangers, maybe in intimidating martial arts uniforms. And these strangers are standing between them and something they may be unsure about in the first place. Don't make prospective students run a gauntlet to get to you. Current students need a place to talk with friends and fellow students. But that place isn't the main entryway.

Welcome the Person

No one should come through the door without being noticed and welcomed. This is true of students, but it is particularly true of first-

> **WHEN PEOPLE WALK THROUGH YOUR DOOR FOR THE FIRST TIME, THEY AREN'T STRANGERS. THEY ARE PEOPLE WHO MAY BECOME SENIOR STUDENTS, OR EVEN GOOD FRIENDS. THEY AREN'T AN INTERRUPTION. THEY'RE THE REASON YOU'RE IN BUSINESS.**

time visitors. Someone—you, your assistant instructor, your office manager—should have one eye on the door any time you're open. Greet people enthusiastically and with a smile. If someone can drift in unnoticed, they—and their business—can drift out unnoticed.

What this means, if you're a one-person operation, is that you need to be able to see the door from the teaching floor. You don't have to drop everything when someone new comes in. In fact, leaving students alone in the training area while you talk with a prospective student sends a bad message. It says you don't take very good care of your current students. If you're the only instructor, and a prospective student walks in, take a few seconds to greet that person warmly. Tell the person when you'll be free, invite him to watch, and then get back to your teaching.

When possible, focus your attention solely on this potential student. For those first few moments, he is the only person in the room. Take your mind off your students, the class you just walked out of, and greet the person with a smile. Get his name. No, don't just ask for the prospective student's name; get his name. Learn it. Memorize it. Call the person by name regularly. Break the ice by treating the prospective student as you would a guest in your home.

Treat the person with the same respect you treat your students. In a sense, when that person came to you to learn about your program, you became his teacher. Walking through the door was the prospective student's first martial arts lesson. That person worked up the courage to approach a strange, new place and to ask for what he wanted. For many people, doing that is a major accomplishment. Reward that accomplishment as you reward all your students' accomplishments.

If your guest is someone you've met on the phone, you already have some basic information about that person. Review your information sheet before the prospective student comes for his appointment. A word of caution, though: people can be very different in person than they are on the phone. They may express a completely different set of needs once they begin talking to you in person. Don't assume that you know why a person has come to see you. Keep listening.

If your guest hasn't called first, you need to get the same kind of information you would get from a first-time caller. Ask the prospective student a few questions and fill out the information sheet. Or have the prospective student fill it out.

Show the Person Around

After you've greeted your guest, take about five minutes to show the person around. Show the prospective student where she will be training. Physically take the person around your school, let her touch the training equipment, while you briefly explain the benefits of using each main piece of equipment. If children are along, don't let them go wild, but let them try something safe they will think is fun. Don't talk down to them. Treat them with the respect you show all your students. Give both children and adults a thorough tour. Even show them the dressing rooms and rest rooms. They should be clean and sparkling, another selling point for your school.

Consider, too, that you aren't just showing a prospective student your school; you're showing her yourself as well. You'll be spending a lot of time with this person if she becomes your student. Your personality, your style, and your methods of teaching are an important part of what you're "selling." If your student is going to learn from you, she must first respect you. If the two of you don't connect, you won't be able to work together.

Match Needs to Benefits

While you're showing prospective students around, ask questions about what they want to accomplish for themselves (or their children) by becoming a part of your school. Find out what they want, what they need. Then show them how you can meet that need. Again, in your own mind you are going back to your marketing identity, to the most persuasive features and benefits you have to offer. Let's say a person is looking for a way to relieve stress. Take her over to your heavy bag rack (if that's one of your most impressive features) and explain about some drills you do using it. Show the prospect what you have to help relieve her stress. Encourage the person to join a class, so she can feel what you have to offer.

Don't be shy about the features and benefits you have to offer. But don't monopolize the conversation either. Rule number one is to listen more than you talk. Ask questions, and listen to answers.

A brief word to experienced teachers: most teachers have the tendency to talk too much at this stage of the sign-up process. Teachers are used to giving information, used to explaining things. However, when you're meeting a potential student, you have to talk only enough to draw that person out. Then you must be quiet enough to hear what she is saying. Don't assume that what you like most about your school will be the benefit the student values most highly. First, figure out what things are important to that person, what she needs from you, and then let the person know how you can provide those services.

Whatever you do, don't lie to a prospective student. People can smell a phony. If you can't meet a person's needs, let her know. Be positive about what you can do for the person, but don't make things up. When you're forging connections with a potential student, forge honest ones, not ones based on hollow flattery. Approach sales with the same integrity you approach your art. You won't succeed in either the martial arts or business world if you think fast talking can be a substitute for honesty and hard work.

When signing up a new student, enthusiasm and positive energy go a long way. You'll have bad days. We all have bad days. On those days, you just have to pull it together and do what needs to be done.

Just as you have to get yourself mentally ready to start a class, you have to focus your energy and enthusiasm when you talk with a prospective student.

Again, don't answer every question. Don't explain everything you do. Be especially careful of questions that compare different styles of martial arts. Leave some mystery, especially about technical issues. It's appropriate that a prospective student not find some things out until they've become a student. If you say something like, "That's a good question. We teach you that in your first class," it gives the person something to look forward to. Don't answer every question, but do give reassurance that you can provide what the prospective student needs, that becoming a student at your school is a good decision.

Master the Art of Closing

Closing is simply taking a prospective student from being interested to enrolling as a student. Does the prospective student want to take classes? Then bring that person to the point where he is ready to sign up and can get on with taking classes.

Closing does not have to be traumatic for you or your prospective student. A little forethought and a few simple techniques can smooth the way through the decision-making process so both of you can get out onto the floor and begin training.

Closing techniques are a little like self-defense techniques in the sense that some will feel more comfortable than others. You may rely mostly on your favorites. Yet you need more than one or two.

When do you use closing techniques? As soon as the prospective student starts looking interested. If a prospective student looks enthusiastic about something you've shown her, go ahead and close. If a prospective student looks as if he is beginning to picture himself as part of your group, close. Before they have a chance to talk themselves out of it, close.

"Closing" means asking for the sale. That bears repeating: Ask for the sale. Tell your guest you would like to have her as a student, and ask if she would like to become part of the school. It seems simple enough, but you'd be amazed how many people don't do it. Ask.

Closing #1: Straightforward

You: "Do you like what you see?"

Other person: "Yes, I do."

You: "Then let's do the paperwork and get you started."

The straightforward closing is just that. Some people are ready to buy when they walk through the door. Some people know they want to study martial arts, and they want to do it with you. Let them. Stop talking and start writing. It's as simple as that.

Closing #2: Checklist

Let's say you've listened to your prospective student, determined his needs. You've introduced the person to the benefits you have to offer, and the person seems enthusiastic. You think that the prospective student's needs and your school are a good match. Tell the person so.

You: "OK, you're interested in fitness. For that we have the sweat and stretch class you said you were interested in. We have the morning class for those days when you have to work graveyard shift. Also, there's the self-defense techniques we teach in every class to help you feel safer taking the bus to work. I think we have a good match between what you want and what we have. Let's get you started!"

Closing #3: Assumptive

You've been showing the prospective student around. You can tell the person wants to be out there doing, not just talking. You make the assumption that the person wants to start.

You: "So, do you want to start in the six o'clock class or the seven o'clock?"

Other person: "Well, I guess the six o'clock would be fine."

You: "Great! Welcome aboard! Let's finish the paperwork and get you a uniform so you'll be ready to start at six."

Closing #4: Answering Objections

Occasionally you get a potential student who looks interested, but you can tell something is holding the person back. Ask what the problem is.

Other person: "It looks like a lot of fun, but I don't know if I'm really ready."

You: "What's standing between you and your being ready?"

Maybe the objection is something straightforward. The person doesn't want to start until after final exam week. She has to arrange for babysitting. She wants to check with a spouse before signing the check. You might suggest the person sign now, take care of all the business details now. Then when she gets the problem straightened out, she can come in and begin classes without any hassle. You can encourage prospective students by making sure they have nothing to lose. Tell them if they can't get the problems straightened out, you'll refund their money anytime within a week (or two weeks, or a month).

Often the objection is a money problem. For example, a person can afford the monthly dues but doesn't have the money for the registration fee or the uniform or something else. That's easy. Arrange a down payment that day, followed by a specific plan to pay off the rest of the money. Ask the prospective student to suggest the payment schedule—the person knows his budget better than you do—then get a firm commitment to follow that plan.

Sometimes the objection isn't that specific. The prospective student is telling you, "Well, it's a lot of money." Or, "I just don't know if I have the time." But what she means is that she's a little frightened or shy or afraid of trying something she may be unable to do. In that case, think back to when you were showing her around. What benefits did she "connect" with? Remind her of what excited her about your program. Maybe she just needs some reassurance that she's doing the right thing.

Answer prospective students' objections one at a time. Take each one seriously. But always steer the conversation toward a close. If at the end of the conversation, the student still isn't ready to sign up, make sure you have her name, address, and phone number. Part on friendly terms. Then follow up. If the person is really interested, and if you do your job right, you will see that person again.

Closing #5: The Special Offer

You've probably heard the line: "Buy now, and we'll throw in this beautiful _____ at no additional cost! Act now! Supplies are limited!"

Did it work on you? Or did you just tune it out because you've heard the line a hundred times and don't pay any attention to it any more?

Making a "special offer" is one way to close. If the student signs up now, you'll throw in a free piece of equipment. Or you'll split the registration fee with the person. Or you'll give him two free private lessons.

Sometimes the "special offer" works. Sometimes your prospect will just tune it out. Sometimes the person will leave to find another teacher who doesn't sound so much like a late-night infomercial announcer.

If you can make the "special offer" fit with your image, it can be very effective. However, it needs to be used with integrity and with the same honesty you bring to your teaching and your art.

Get down to the Nitty Gritty

The prospective student has said, "OK." He wants to see the agreement, is ready to do business. What next?

Invite the student into your office. If possible, sit on the same side of the desk with the person. Better yet, have a round table set up just for this purpose. Seat the prospect where he can see your P.O.P. materials. (See chapter 9 for more information on P.O.P. materials.)

Then get down to business quickly. If you haven't already done so, explain your schedule, your prices, and when the person's first class will be. Every time you show the student something—your schedule, your prices, and when the first class will be—ask the person if it fits in with his schedule or budget. If it doesn't, you may need to do some troubleshooting. Suggest an alternate schedule, if you have one. Offer information about how other students have solved that particular problem. At the very least, if the prospect balks, don't continue until you have reminded him of the pertinent benefits of your school. Don't let him talk himself out of what you have already agreed is right.

How much pressure you put on the prospective student depends on your personality (and the other person's). But remember, he is agreeing to a long-term training schedule. The decision is not just about parting with money. It's also about committing time and energy. Sometimes people really do need to "think about it" or rearrange their schedule.

What if a prospective student is interested but wants to negotiate the monthly dues? What's negotiable? Most people will say "anything's negotiable," but is it? You've carefully determined what you need to be paid to stay in business. First, ask yourself, "If this is what my services are worth, why should I take less?" You have come up with your prices after careful calculation. Believe in them. Don't apologize for them. Second, understand that if you start bargaining, even with one student, word will get around. Soon you'll find yourself with a school of good negotiators who are not paying you enough for you to meet the rent. Besides, how much respect do you think you will get as a teacher if you have the reputation for being a pushover at the bargaining table? Set your prices and stay firm. The only time possibly to bend is for a college student, for someone on a fixed income, or for a large family. For these people, have a special student or family rate, with strict criteria as to when it can be used.

Regarding barter, some students may wish to barter goods or services in exchange for tuition. If you are considering such a deal, be sure you trade retail value to retail value. For services, barter at the highest price. For instance, if you usually give private lessons at $50 per hour, but offer a discount to students who purchase five lessons or more, you would barter at the $50 rate, even if the student was bartering for more than five lessons. In other words, if your tuition is $60 per month, and the object your prospective student wishes to use as barter is worth $60 at retail price, you have an even trade. When students come to you wishing to barter, your primary consideration is whether you can use the particular goods or services they are offering. Would you spend money on it if it were not a student offering it to you? Remember, too, that the IRS treats barter the same as money. Ask your accountant how to account for it in your income statements.

A word about contracts: "Contract" is a scary word. It brings up visions of complicated legal language, of getting trapped in a legal net you can't get out of. "Agreement" is probably a better term, at least a less frightening term. At its essence, a contract is merely a mutual agreement to do business—you agree to teach someone and that person agrees to pay you.

The reason that a time period is stipulated in the agreement is so you can plan for the student's future. You would probably teach an introduction to a long-term course of study differently from a one-month, stand-alone program. The contract lets you know which you are dealing with. Furthermore, when a student agrees to a longer term of study, that commitment is likely to spill over into their attitude toward training. It's easy for a student who is paying weekly to skip a week—both of payment and of training. However, a student who has committed to regular monthly payment for a year is less likely to skip time he has already paid for or committed to.

The agreement also allows you to get basic information you will need during the time that the student studies with you—name, address, phone number, and any physical/medical challenges. You should also get emergency contact information and permission to act on the student's behalf in an emergency. (For more information about drawing up your agreement, see chapter 6.)

The agreement needs to be a legal document, something you can enforce if you must. Have it reviewed by your attorney before you start using it. Present it as a serious agreement. But don't make it frightening.

Still some people will balk at a long-term agreement, especially with someone they have just met. For these people, a very effective sales tool is the first-month introductory course. This offer lets the person make a short-term commitment to see if he likes it. Here's how it works: Let the person experience one full month of your regular classes at the regular price or, if you can afford it, at a special reduced price. Then, at week three—or when the student has developed an enthusiasm for the art—discuss his continuing on a more permanent basis. Another possibility is to have the student sign up for a six- or twelve-month agreement and give the person thirty days before he has to pay enrollment or startup fees. Or offer the student a thirty-day, money-back guarantee. Or include a uniform or piece of equipment or a cash discount as an incentive to commit to a longer-term agreement.

So let's say your meeting with your prospect is ending. He knows the terms of the agreement you're offering. You've presented the schedule of classes. He has no further questions. What remains?

Follow Up, Follow Up, Follow Up

What exactly do you want to carry away from your meeting? A one-year agreement paid in advance would be nice. But meetings with prospective students don't always turn out like that. Much more realistic would be an initial commitment to an introductory offer. Try to get a financial down payment—even if it's only ten dollars. People's minds and hearts tend to be where their wallets are. Getting an initial down payment helps ensure that you won't be just a passing fancy.

Barring that, at least get an address and phone number. After prospective students leave, make a few notes about interests or special needs on their information card. Not everyone will enroll in your school the moment they come through the door. Realistically, very few will on the first visit. It's understandable: they're not only committing money, but time and effort. They may even be committing to a new diet, a new lifestyle, or a completely new schedule. That doesn't even take into account coordinating with spouses, arranging car-pooling for children, and logistical details they don't even hint at. It takes time to work out the details for all of this.

Put your walk-away package into their hands, and then give them time to arrange logistics. But don't just twiddle your thumbs while you're waiting. While they're rearranging their life, you're following up.

The first thing you do when a prospective student leaves without signing up is send a thank-you postcard. Do it that day. The postcard should have your logo and your address, and it should say simply, "Thanks for coming by to see the school." Don't say anything personal. Don't try to force the sale. Don't even say "hope to see you again." Just thank the person for stopping by. All you're doing is keeping the lines of communication open.

Two or three days later, call the prospective student. Ask what she thought of the tour and your offer. Remind the person of the things that excited her. Ask when she will be ready to start.

Keep the prospective student's information card on file along with information cards for prospective students who called and leads you've received from other sources. Contact each of these people at least five more times over the first three months. This contact can be done by phone, answering machine message, note, e-mail, or postcard. During those five months, send them your newsletter and any tournament or special event flyers you may be sending out. If you were able to get their birth date, send them a birthday card each year. Stay in front of them, but not under their feet.

Don't fool yourself, however. When someone leaves your office without scheduling his first class, ask yourself why. If the person wasn't impressed, have someone else call him to reemphasize the benefits of your program. Don't take it personally—sometimes two personalities just don't mesh. Even so, if most prospective students are walking back out the door, perhaps you need to examine your approach.

What if they do sign up? You're finished selling then, right? Not quite. It's part of the psyche of the American consumer to second-guess everything we buy. We're prone to "buyer's remorse," the need to justify our purchases. Think about the last time you bought a car or a piece of furniture. After you got it home, didn't you tell someone about it? Didn't you tell them about the sale price or all the great features it has? Didn't you want reassurance that all those zeroes you wrote on the check were worth it?

Now think about your students. By committing to a martial arts program, they've gone out on a limb. They've just made a big financial commitment, not to mention the commitment of time and effort. You need to reassure them as soon as possible that they have made the right choice—and that they don't want to back out now.

Send them a postcard. It doesn't have to be elaborate, something like "Welcome to the family! We're looking forward to working with you." Put it on a card with your logo, sign it, and send it off immediately. Then be sure to welcome them in their first class. Introduce them to some other students. Ask a student to show them around. Make them feel at home and comfortable as soon as possible. A little enthusiasm goes a long way toward making new students feel welcome.

Work with Your Employee

A word about what to do when you have an employee whose job it is to approach prospective students instead of you: Your employee needs to be totally comfortable with your marketing identity before beginning to work with her prospects. Just as you must believe in what you have to offer, your employee must believe in it as well. She must also be comfortable with the techniques you use to sign up students. Work with your employee. Train and practice often. Make sure she is prepared to represent you properly.

Sometimes the employee is so enthusiastic she can't slow down enough to listen to the prospective student. Every person has her own agenda, including your employee. Be clear about how important it is to

---

FOUR RULES FOR
TRAINING EMPLOYEES

1. Communicate your expectations.
2. Correct the employee in private.
3. Praise the employee in public.
4. Give the employee daily encouragement.

---

focus on the prospect's agenda—not her own. Encourage your employee to listen, to discover as much as possible about the prospective student's needs.

After the prospective student leaves, spend a moment with your employee for debriefing. Ask what went well, what could have gone better. Ask what she could do to improve. Practice your active listening skills when working with your employee. Emphasize what they did well. Praise them when they deserve it, even for something small.

Teaching an employee sign-up skills requires the same methods as teaching a very complicated martial arts technique to a student. You constructively, foster practice, praise, and give the employee credit for a job well done.

Trust your training. Let the employee do her job. Don't jump into the middle of the employee's presentations. At first, your employee may be less effective than you. She may do things a little differently. But with time, practice, and guidance, your employee can develop into an excellent representative for you and your school.

Selling your program doesn't have to be traumatic for either you or your prospects. Signing up new students is just an extension of believing in yourself and what you have to offer.

Know your school, your program, the benefits you have to offer. Then match what you have to offer to what your prospects need. Smile. Invite them to join you, and make it easy for them to do so. Developing strong sign-up skills is the first step toward maintaining a healthy school enrollment.

Chapter Eleven:
Keep Track of Your Students

If you have never run a business of your own before, you will be amazed at the amount of record keeping involved. You will probably be tempted to keep things in your head rather than on paper. You may be tempted to "manage your finances" by balancing your checkbook occasionally. Yet without accurate records, you are flying, and often crashing, by the seat of your pants. With good records, you can troubleshoot problems before they become too big to correct. You can make informed changes to your program and decide whether changes are financially worthwhile. In short, good records can help you keep the money coming in.

Your records serve two purposes: to keep track of your students and to keep track of your money. You use the first kind of records to make decisions about scheduling and student retention. You use the second to make decisions about taxes and profitability. In this chapter, we'll look at student records. In the next chapter, we'll discuss how to keep track of your money.

Set Up Student Files

If you decide to use a manual system, it will probably be made up of a set of file folders and index cards. For each student, keep a permanent, individual file folder. The folder should contain the student's agreement (contract). On the agreement should be the student's name, address, phone number, parents' or spouse's name, and emergency phone numbers. It might also include a work address, mobile phone numbers, and e-mail addresses for your student or his parents. The agreement also contains financial information: how much the student pays, when he pays, when payment is overdue, and what late fees will be charged for overdue payments. Each student's folder must also contain a liability release form. If you require a medical release form, it too should go in their folder. If you have a rank or promotion system at your school, also keep information about current rank, past promotions, and when promotion is due. You may also want to keep a permanent record of attendance and any equipment purchases the student makes.

These file folders are your permanent records of your students. Keep them arranged alphabetically in a file drawer, not on top of your desk where they can be lost.

When putting together these student files, be aware that they may be subject to your state's freedom of information laws. If this is the case, the student, or the parent of a minor, may be entitled to read the entire file anytime. Student files are not the place to record disciplinary infractions, or observations about a student's basic capacities. In short, if you would not want the students themselves seeing particular information, don't put it in their permanent files. On the other hand, these permanent files are confidential records. Things like phone numbers and addresses should be kept private. Ask permission from the person involved before handing out phone numbers or other information. Better yet, make it a policy never to hand out personal information on a student.

Track Student Attendance

Attendance records help you accomplish two goals. First, you can track specific students' class time. If attendance is a factor for promoting students at your school, you need precise attendance records. But even if you don't use attendance records for promotion, you need to know when a student's attendance is falling off. If you know immediately when a student's attendance pattern changes, you can follow up before they become a drop-out statistic.

Second, you can track fluctuations in overall student attendance. You will have specific times of the year when your attendance drops off. Every business does. If you know, for example, that your attendance always drops off during summer vacation season, you can plan. You can save money to cover expenses. You can boost your advertising and bring in new students. You can run a short-term program, a self-defense seminar, or children's camp to bring in extra cash. You could even plan a vacation for yourself during a slow week. But before you can plan, you need to see the trends. The way you see the trends is by keeping and analyzing attendance records.

A Manual Tracking System

One way to track individual student attendance is to create individual student cards. An 8-1/2" x 5-1/2" card has room on the front for a student's name, ID number, and picture. You can also record the student's birthday, a list of promotions, seminars attended, any other information you might want to record about the student on a day-to-day basis. On the back you can put a grid to record up to a full year of attendance. Twelve rows down will accommodate the twelve months. Thirty-one squares across will accommodate the days of the month. When a student attends a class, check or color in the appropriate box on the grid. You can also line up the grid by days of the week. That way you can look down the card quickly to see which days of the week the student generally attends classes.

The only way to see patterns in overall student attendance is to record attendance in each class faithfully. From the individual attendance cards, create an overall summary sheet on which you can list how many students attend each class each week. Record enough detail to know if, for example, your children's class attendance is falling off, or if a specific day of adult classes has attendance problems in the summer.

A Computerized Tracking System

Although you need to have files for contracts and release forms with original signatures, you can keep most of your student information in computer files. One advantage of keeping a computerized database is the reports it can generate. Computers excel at shifting and sorting great piles of mind-numbing detail. Do you need to know if your average attendance for your children's Tuesdays and Thursdays classes has grown over the last two years? A computer with the proper program can save you the trouble of a manual count. Need a list of students who haven't been training during the last month? The computer can do it in a fraction of the time it would take you to do it manually. It can even give you a list of contact phone numbers.

Several companies offer business software programs set up for martial arts schools. These programs' features and price vary widely. You'll need to decide what you plan to use the software for to select a package to meet your needs. At the very least, make sure the software you select handles these things:

STUDENT MANAGEMENT SOFTWARE
ATTENDANCE TRACKING INFORMATION

Minimum requirements:

A database containing all your students, including
names, addresses, and phone numbers

A list of students by rank or class

A count of students, active and inactive

Attendance for a particular student

Attendance for a particular day or class

Seasonal fluctuations in attendance

Drop-out ratios

Reports of who is eligible for promotion
(according to specific criteria you have put in)

A record of what equipment a student has purchased

Personal health statistics

Reports of birthdays and anniversaries

Labels for mass mailings

Your management software should produce reports to help you with student retention. It should let you know which students have stopped attending. It should chart seasonal attendance fluctuations. It should be able to give you information about whether a particular class has grown. It should be able to produce labels for mass mailings, reports of birthdays, anniversaries and student promotions as well as general counts and drop-out ratios.

For example, let's say that you have eighty students. If five of those eighty suddenly stopped attending, how long would it take you to notice? You have less than three weeks to catch drop-out problems. In three weeks, not attending has become a habit. If a student hasn't shown up for a week, your management software should notice that, even if you haven't.

Selecting software is a personal thing. You need to find a package that meets your needs, can run on your computer, and suits your personality. Read industry magazines for advertisements for martial arts computer programs. Search the Internet. Most companies offer demo discs. Order one and take the time to try it out. Add and subtract real information to see if it will help you or be more trouble than it is worth. It always takes a lot of time to set up and learn a new computer program. But once set up, it should save you time and give you the reports you need. If it doesn't, it's not worth the price, even if it is free.

When choosing a management program, you might be tempted to consider a custom-made database. Having a program tailored to your needs has its advantages. But buying a software program off the shelf is generally much less expensive and more time-efficient. Even if you have a student create a custom database program for you in exchange for lessons, think about how long it's going to take to set up the system. Think about how long it's going to take to work out the bugs. Think about what you're going to do should the student move away and you have problems with the program. A management program purchased from a reputable software company will be ready to use right out of the box. It should also have technical support and upgrade capabilities.

Though the advantages of keeping your records on computer are many, the disadvantage is the temptation to waste time and energy creating fascinating reports containing information you don't need. No matter whether you gather information manually or electronically, compile only what you will need and use. Your main job is to teach martial arts, not generate computer reports.

Several school management programs will handle not just student records but also accounts receivable and basic accounting. (You can find more on those two topics in chapter 12.) Know what you need your software to do, then shop around. The time you spend doing so will save you time in the long run.

Take In Student Payments

In addition to tracking student attendance, you must also be able to track student payments. You must be able to collect money quickly and efficiently. You must be able to account for every cent that comes into or leaves your school. And you must be able to ascertain quickly and easily who owes you money and who doesn't.

Set Up Payment Policies

Generally, your students will pay their bills using one of five methods: cash, checks, traveler's checks, cashier's checks, or credit cards. Which of these methods you accept is your decision. Discuss it with your banker. Then write down your payment policy so that any employee accepting money in your office knows exactly how you want it handled.

If you decide to accept checks for payment, decide whether you want to require check guarantee cards or picture identification. Remember that most checks will be from continuing students. You may wish to have two ID policies: one for registered students (or members of your school), another for nonmembers buying merchandise, trying out a class, or paying a mat fee to train for a limited time. Also establish a fee for checks that fail to clear the bank (bounced checks). Make a sign and hang it in the office where people can see it as they write checks.

Will you take credit cards? Think carefully before answering this question. Accepting credit cards costs money. But it also offers an important benefit for your students. Whether credit cards make sense for your school depends on your students and their buying habits. (See chapter 6 for more information.)

Collect Payments Efficiently

Once you've set up your basic payment policies, make sure you can take payments quickly and efficiently. You'll need to be sure you always have enough cash to make change. You'll need to keep track of petty cash. You'll need to make sure that students who have paid their bills get credited and students who haven't paid their bills get reminded. Day-to-day money management means setting up and following a few common-sense procedures so you can manage your money well and still have time to teach.

Consider when you take in most of your money. If you are like most schools, it will be just before class or just after class. In other words, students will be paying while you are gearing up to teach or while you are trying to touch base with students and parents before they leave. You need to have a quick and efficient system for taking in and recording payments. If you don't have such a system, you might be tempted to forgo record keeping. Doing so is asking for trouble. You must know where your money comes from to ensure that it keeps coming in.

WHAT TO KEEP AT THE DESK WHERE YOU TAKE IN MONEY

1. Change—enough to break a $100
2. Blank receipts—either generic or custom made
3. Your accounts receivable records
4. Credit card receipt forms and capture machine
5. Blank copies of your daily balance sheet
6. A petty cash receipt envelope
7. Several inexpensive but reliable pens

First, set up a cash drawer or box where you always keep your school's money. Keep a specific amount of cash (ones, fives, tens, and coins) for change. How much cash you keep depends on how your money comes in. Generally, you want to keep as little as possible and still be able to break a $100 bill when it comes in for tuition payment.

Keep your accounts receivable records and your receipt forms near that cash drawer. Always take in tuition and other payments in that specific place. That way you can keep all your money together, make change, and quickly record the information you will need later for your books and inventory records.

Have a specific receipt form you always use every time you take in money. You can buy NCR (no carbon required) cash receipts at any office supply store. The advantage of these generic receipts is that they have two copies, one for you and one for your customer. The disadvantage is that they aren't tailored to the kind of business you will be doing and will often take more time to fill out than a custom receipt.

Making your own custom receipts is easy and will suit your needs better than a generic form. Your receipt can be a photocopied half sheet of paper—8-1/2" x 5-1/2". Create a space for the student's name, the date, the amount paid, what was paid for, and whether payment was made by cash, check, or charge. If you normally take in money in only a few categories—tuition, private lessons, and testing, for example, you can create a box to be checked for each kind of payment. Similar boxes for method of payment (cash, check, or credit card) can save you the time spent writing those things onto the receipt. If you want use the same receipt for your pro shop, create spaces for a description of the item being purchased and for sales tax. When you take in money, fill in the blanks in your receipt, fold the sheet in half, tuck the check or credit card receipt into the folded sheet of paper, and put the package in your cash drawer or bank bag to record later.

You can also record all the payments for the day on a single sheet of paper. Each transaction goes on a separate line. Each column gives you a piece of information about that transaction: who made the payment, what the payment was for, how payment was made, and how much was paid.

The advantage of keeping receipts is that they are quick and accurate. You don't have to try to enter information into your financial journal, your tuition payment records, or your inventory records while you're trying to take care of your customers. You just fill out a receipt every time money comes in. Then at the end of the day, or during a slow period in the day, you can sort the information into its proper place.

If you are running your school by yourself and you find you don't have time to fill out receipts each time you take in payment, you may want to create a lock box for collecting tuition. A lock box is a strong, padlocked box with a slit in the lid big enough for an envelope but too small for fingers. Next to the lock box, provide envelopes with a form printed on each. Provide a space for the student's name, another for the date, and another to note what the payment is for. In other words, print on the envelope the same information you put on your receipts. Students put their payment in one of these envelopes, fill in the blanks, and put the envelope in the box via the slot in the top. You empty the box at the end of the day and record the payments appropriately. This system is easy, and it doesn't tie you up during or between classes. However, it doesn't allow you to straighten out any financial mix-ups on the spot, and it doesn't allow you the personal time with each student that you get when you collect payments individually. A lock box works best if your students pay the same amount each month. If payments get complicated, you may need to take them in personally or hire someone to do so.

Whatever payment collection system you choose, you must be sure of one thing: at the end of the day, you must have written records accounting for every cent that has come into your business. These written records allow you to balance your daily receipts and keep accurate financial records. (See chapter 12 for more information.)

Track Student Payments

"Accounts receivable" is accounting jargon for the money you are supposed to be paid for services you've performed and the goods you've sold. In a martial arts school, where most of your income comes from student payments, your accounts receivable is the record of what your students owe for either goods or services.

Some of your students will pay you every month like clockwork. Some will forget to pay you until you bill them. And a few others may not pay you until you have reminded them two or three times. For the health of your business, you need to be able to know for any given month which students are which. You need to have a clear, simple way to record when students pay you and what they pay you for. And you need to have a plan you put into action when they don't pay you or when they pay you late.

A Simple Manual Tracking System

A manual system for keeping track of student payments can be as simple as a grid with student names down one side and the month(s) across the top. You check off the box or fill in the date or amount when they've paid.

The names in the first column are arranged alphabetically, not by rank or student number. This arrangement allows you to find the student's name and record the payment quickly and efficiently. If it takes you twenty seconds to find a student's name each time he pays, and if you have 200 students, that's an hour of your and your students' time you waste every time you collect tuition. Taking a few minutes to set up an efficient system saves time in the long run.

If students' tuition comes due at different times of the month— some on the first and some on the fifteenth, for example—you can

Tuition Payments 1/02-3/02	January			February			March		
	paid	amount	notes	paid	amount	notes	paid	amount	notes
Anderson, Joe $65 due on 1st	1/1	$65				billed 2/6, 3/6			billed 3/6
Carrera, Maria $60 due on 1st	1/1	$60		2/2	$60		3/1	$60	
Jones, Mike $65 due on 1st	1/20	$65	billed 1/6	2/1	$65		3/1	$65	
Lee, Vanessa $65 due on 1st	1/3	$65		2/10	$65	will pay 2/10	3/2	$65	
Walters, David $65 due on 15th	1/15	$65		2/15	$65		3/14	$65	
Total		$320			$255			$255	

arrange the first column by date and then by name beneath those dates. If different students pay different amounts for tuition, you might want to note their tuition amount by their name. Or you might want to fill in their box each month with the amount they paid. If some students prefer to be billed for their tuition (rather than paying it in the office), have a space to note that as well.

If you also collect promotion or tournament fees, you can use a similar sheet for those payments. Keep all your accounts receivable records in a single binder. That way you need to look in only one place to see if someone owes you money.

Another system for tracking student payments is to have a cover sheet stapled inside each student's permanent file. This cover sheet records what the student's payments are, when each was made, and whether the student owes you money. The advantage of this system is that all the things you need to know about a given student—his signed contract, release form, record of promotions, and financial records—are in a single place. The disadvantage is that you must pull all the folders every time you want to figure out who is past due on their payments.

You may wish to use a combination of both methods. Use a master list each month to record tuition for the whole school. Then record each student's payments at the end of the month in their individual folders. This system gives you the opportunity to make sure you have sent out reminder notes and bills on time. It also allows you to establish a backup system in case the master list gets lost. It is, however, somewhat time-consuming.

Although regular tuition and fees will probably be the bulk of your accounts receivable, they will not be all of it. Beyond accounting for regular fees, you also need to account for miscellaneous payments and purchases. For example, if a student has a uniform on layaway and forgets a payment, how will you know? If you've agreed to allow another student to pay off a testing fee over two or three months, how will you keep track of that? One easy way is a twelve-month accordion file. Allocate one slot for each month (or week or every two weeks, depending on how often you send out bills). Every time you agree with a student that he owes you money, make a note of it and drop the note into the slot for the month when the money is due. If you need to send out invoices, note money owed for off-site seminars or other special projects in the file as well. You might also want to put reminder notes in this file when a student's contract is due for renewal.

A Computerized Tracking System

A simple system may work fine if you have a small number of students and if student payments are simple and straightforward. If you have a large number of students, these systems become cumbersome. If you find you are wasting time hunting for student names, or if you find yourself unsure of who owes you what, it may be time to go to a computerized system. Similarly, if you add testing and seminar fees, payment for retail purchases on layaway, family discounts, scholarships, or any other complication, you may find you need a more elaborate tracking system.

STUDENT MANAGEMENT SOFTWARE
ACCOUNTS RECEIVABLE INFORMATION

You'll need to know:
How much a student's tuition is and when it's due.
What payments the student has made.
What payments the student owes.
The total amount of money owed by contract (to be
    transferred to the assets section of your balance sheet).
Past-due notices.

Most school management software will enable you to track student payments. You especially need to know who owes money, how much is owed, and when it's due. You also need to know who paid how much and for what.

Should you have financial problems some month, your student management records should be able to tell you what happened. For example, let's say again that you have eighty students. Two months ago you had an income of $8,000 from those eighty students. Last month your attendance was still eighty, but your income was $6,500. Your records should tell you if the difference occurred because students weren't paying their tuition or if they weren't buying extras. Maybe no one bought equipment last month. Maybe the problem was that seminar and tournament attendance was off. Maybe you were giving too many scholarships.

Your management software should help you chart all the money that comes in. It should give you reports on where it came from and when. It should tell you who has paid their bills and who is overdue. If you have a sudden drop in income, your management software should help you pinpoint the problem.

Chapter Twelve:
Keep Track of Your Money

Your financial records allow you to do two things: First, they allow you to track your income and expenses. In these records you record every cent entering or leaving your business. Second, they give you the information you need to generate financial reports. These reports are the tools you use to assess the financial health of your business.

Your financial records help you keep the government, your creditors, your landlord, and your accountant happy. And they help you know what money is yours to keep as profit.

What are the minimum financial records you will need? At the very least, you need to satisfy the basic Internal Revenue Service (IRS) requirements. The IRS provides free publications to help you set up a recordkeeping system. Publication 538, "Accounting Periods and Methods," explains the kind of accounting you need to satisfy tax audit requirements. The IRS Small Business Tax Kit illustrates how you might comply with the basic filing requirements.

The government sets the minimum standard for your record keeping. But you must go beyond the minimum standard if you want your business to thrive. Your financial records are a crucial tool for tracking your business's progress and diagnosing problems before they become too large. Beyond keeping the obvious record of inflow and outflow of money, you should learn to keep track of monthly and yearly profits or losses, trends in student payment, cash flow, equity in the business, and other statistics necessary to grow a successful business.

What if you hate accounting and bookkeeping? Then you'll want a simple, common-sense way to keep track of financial transactions. A good computer accounting program can make entering information no more painful than keeping a checking account register. It will produce on command all the reports you need. It will even do the math for you. If you don't want a computerized system, discuss with your accountant how to keep a simple manual bookkeeping system. You can record transactions, and then at the end of the year give "the books" to your accountant to do her accounting magic on them. But to keep even these simple books, and to use them for effective business planning, you will still need to know the basics of bookkeeping and accounting.

Balance Your Daily Receipts

Balancing daily receipts is a matter of making sure that every transaction has a receipt, and every receipt placed in the cash drawer is accompanied by cash, a check, or a credit card payment. In other words, balancing your receipts is making sure your records match your money.

Petty Cash

You will need to set up a way of tracking petty cash. Petty cash is the money you use to make small purchases. Of course, you will want to pay for as many purchases as possible by check. Doing so allows you to keep track of your business expenditures by simply looking at your check register. However, for small purchases—a couple of stamps, a two-dollar furnace filter, a handful of photocopies—you may want to pay in cash. A simple way to keep track of these cash payments is to have an envelope for receipts. Every time you make a purchase using petty cash, draw the cash from your change drawer. Then, note on the receipt or cash register tape the amount, the date, what it was for, and who made the purchase. Put the receipt in the envelope in your cash drawer. At the end of the day, pull the petty cash receipts from the envelope and put them with the rest of the daily receipts to be accounted for in your daily balance sheet.

Daily Balance Sheet

Your daily balance sheet cross-checks your receipts with the money that has gone into and out of your cash drawer. At the end of the day, count your money—all the cash, checks, and credit card receipts in your cash drawer. Write down in the first column on your balance sheet the total amount of money in the drawer. Subtract from that total the fixed amount of cash you always keep in your drawer for petty cash purchases and to make change. In the second column, add together your paper receipts for the day—all those NCR or custom-made receipts recording cash, check, or credit card income for the day. (See chapter 11 for more information on receipts.) Subtract from the total any petty cash receipts you may have. The totals for the two columns should match. If they don't, you may have missed filling out a receipt. Or you may have taken in money that didn't find its way into the drawer.

DAILY TRANSMITTAL SHEET

DAY————————— DATE ————————BY ——————

Beginning Balance=Cash **Ending Money in Drawer** --Including Cash, Checks & Credit cards	$ $	Number of Receipts Cash	$
		Checks	$
		Credit Cards Number____	$
Less Change for Drawer	($)	Credit Cards Balanced?	Yes
Total Money Received	$ A	**Total Receipts**	$ B

A=B to Balance

A daily balance sheet gives you the chance to double-check that nothing was misplaced. It also reminds you to settle your credit cards daily. When you're finished balancing the daily transactions, the money from the day goes into your bank deposit. The information on the receipts is transferred into your financial journal, your inventory records, and your accounts receivable records. (More information on those financial records and reports later.)

Write down these day-to-day money-handling and balancing procedures. That way, no matter if you or your employee do them, they will always be done the same way. Consistency is essential in accounting procedures.

Collect Your Debts

On a specific day each month, perhaps on the sixth if tuition is typically due on the first, sit down and determine which students owe you money. Go through all your accounts receivable—your tuition for equipment purchases, everything on your accounts receivable lists or in your accounts receivable accordion file. Make up bills and mail them.

Office supply stores have a selection of professional-looking forms. All you need to do is add your name at the top, fill in the particulars, and send them off. Or you can make your own. Bills should contain the student's name, the amount due, what it is due for, when it is due, and where to send the money. Each time you send a bill, put a copy in the student's file and make a note on your accounts receivable record. Follow up if the students fail to pay the bill or make arrangements with you within one week. Find out what is wrong. If your student has a good reason for not paying, you need to make arrangements or risk losing that student. Remember, however, that you are providing students with a service. You deserve to be paid according to your original agreement with them.

Track Accounts Payable

Beyond keeping track of the money coming in, you will need to keep track of when your accounts payable are due. Accounts payable are bills, money you owe and need to pay out. For example, rent, utility bills, sales tax, and payroll taxes are all accounts payable.

A simple way to organize your accounts payable is to use another large monthly accordion file. When you pick up the mail, immediately sort the bills into the file by the month they are due. This file makes sure you can find the actual forms and bills when you need them.

To make sure you don't miss a payment, create a monthly checklist of which bills are due and when. For example, you know your monthly bills always include rent, phone, electric, gas, water, payroll, payroll taxes, and sales taxes. Create a list for each month that includes these normal bills. Then leave room to list any additional bills for that month.

When you pay bills, pull the invoices, bills, and statements for the month from the accordion folder. Sort the ones you want to pay immediately from the ones you want to pay later in the month. As you pay each bill, mark on the checklist the date you paid it, the amount, and the check number. When you are through, place the checklist and any unpaid bills back in the appropriate month's slot. Next time you pay bills, you will have a record of what has and hasn't been paid. At the end of the month, when all the bills have been paid, move your checklist to your receipts file. If you keep an accounts payable checklist, you won't miss paying a bill because you didn't get it in the mail, thought you paid it but didn't, or misplaced it when it came in.

Receipts Files

You will also need a way of keeping receipts. A simple way is to use either files in a file drawer or yet another accordion file. When you pay a bill, file the receipt under the appropriate month. When you make your weekly bank deposit, record the deposit in your checkbook, and then file the receipt. If a piece of paper contains information you may need to support your tax forms, file it, too. Always make a file copy of every report you fill out for the government, landlord, or insurance agency. In short, if it records a financial or legal transaction, file it in your receipts file.

Why should you save your receipts? Sometimes you will need them to double-check an entry in your financial journal. Sometimes other people will need to see them. If you are ever required to provide a certified financial record of your business, you will need to produce a paper trail of your financial transactions. A CPA will come into your business and will use that paper trail, your receipts, to produce a new financial record. You may also need receipts for an IRS audit. Most of the time, the IRS works from the information you give them on your tax forms. But if they ever audit you, they may ask you to produce receipts to prove your tax forms are accurate. Check with your accountant, the IRS, and your state tax agency to learn which receipts to keep and for how long.

Checking Account Register

One simple technique that will help you keep track of your money is to always put money into and take it out of the same place. For example, have one checking account that all money gets deposited to and all bills are paid from. Minimize cash outlays. If you have a savings account, put the money in your checking account first and then transfer it to savings. Make detailed notes in your check register about where the money came from, where it went, and why.

If you funnel all your money through your checking account, your check register becomes a permanent record of your receipts and payments, much like a bookkeeper's journal. If you need to know when you got paid for a private lesson, look at your check register. If you need to double-check whether you paid a particular bill, look at your check register.

Your check register does not, however, take the place of a financial statement. Other more detailed, more sophisticated record systems can help you spot trends and diagnose problems in your business. But the simple check register is the quickest, easiest way to answer day-to-day questions about your money.

Try to set up a record keeping system that's easy to use, and requires a minimum of shuffling papers and copying information. When setting up your system, it's your goal to make being organized easier than being disorganized. If you have a specific place for each piece of paper, a place that is close to where you take in that paper, chances are you will use that place and be organized. But if your system is too complicated or time-consuming, not only will you waste time using it, but you will also probably eventually start ignoring it. Doing so will leave you operating your business blindly, without proper feedback for success.

Manage Your Finances

Keeping track of the money coming in and going out of your business is not an end in itself. Financial record keeping gives you the data you need to determine your tax liability. It also gives you information you can analyze to assess the financial health of your business.

Overall, financial records are built from smaller parts into larger. Information from receipts and checking account register are entered into a financial journal (or the computerized version of a financial journal). Information from the journal is used to build profit and loss statements and to track cash flow. At the end of the year, all your financial information is brought together and summarized in annual financial statements.

Financial Journal

Your financial journal, also called the general journal, is the place you record every individual financial transaction. If you take in tuition money, it goes in the journal. If you sell a piece of equipment, it goes in the journal. If you write a check, it goes in the journal. If you make purchases out of petty cash, it goes in the journal. Any money coming in or going out goes in the journal. If you need to know what happened financially on any given day, you look at your journal. If you need to look up a specific financial transaction, you look in the journal.

If you run all your financial transactions through your checking account, and if you keep a detailed check register, your check register can function as your disbursements and receipts journal. Technically speaking, a true general financial journal includes double entry. For every debit, you also find a credit to record. The financial journal also contains disbursements and receipts, accounts receivable and accounts payable records. It contains information about how much you paid, to whom, and why, and it helps you sort all expense and income information in proper categories. At the most basic level of record keeping, however, the most important thing is not form but clarity and accuracy.

If the financial records on your checking account register are accurate and clear, you, your accountant, or your computer program can put them in proper accounting format later.

Get either a business checkbook or the kind that has three checks per page. What you are looking for is a large enough checking account register that you can record extra detail on it. Each time you make a deposit, note on a register how much you deposited and where the money came from: tuition, testing, retail sales, sales tax, or other source. Each time you write a check, record to whom it was written, for how much, and for what. In short, your check register can function as your disbursements and receipts journal only if you include enough information in it to account for where every cent came from and where every cent went. On the following page is a sample checking account register.

On your checking account register, it's unnecessary to mark who paid you. That information is on your receipts and your accounts receivable lists. What is necessary is to differentiate between kinds of income such as tuition payments and other types of payments. Tuition payment is recorded separately from payment for merchandise. Sales tax is differentiated from payment for services. If two sources of income go on different lines on your profit and loss statement (P&L), they need to be differentiated in your journal. (More information on P&Ls later in the chapter.)

When you pay expenses, differentiate them by category as well. For example, if part of your phone bill is for phone service and part for your Yellow Pages ad, make sure you record two expenses, not just one. Distinguish rent from taxes, office supplies from advertising. When keeping records in your journal, think about your P&L. If two expenses go on different lines on your P&L, they need to be differentiated in your journal.

Another method of keeping a simplified financial journal is a posting system, also called a pegboard system. Each time you take in money and write a receipt, you also make carbon copies on a permanent journal page and account card under the receipt. The system is called a pegboard or posting system, because you attach the receipt to

SAMPLE CHECKING ACCOUNT REGISTER			
9/18/02			Balance
			$1,000.00
Deposits		+$3,161.34	$4,161.34
tuition	$3,130.00		
sales (mouth guard)	$ 1.25		
sales tax	$ .09		
private lesson	$ 30.00		
Checks:			
#1546 XYZ Company (landlord)			
rent		-$2,250.00	$1,911.34
#1547	US Phone	-$ 85.00	$1,826.34
Yellow Pages ad	$ 65.00		
phone service	$ 20.00		
Petty cash:			
cleaning supplies		-$ 32.00	$1,794.34

pegs before writing it. These pegs line up the carbon copies to form lines in your journal. If you also use a pegboard for your checking account, it creates a separate disbursement journal on its receipt page.

The advantage of a pegboard system is that you don't have to recopy your information from your receipts to your journal. The disadvantage is that it may be more time-consuming at the time you record the information, and the pegboard itself is physically cumbersome.

Several other methods of keeping a financial journal are available for small businesses. By far, the most labor-saving one is a computerized system. Sure, you have to invest a certain amount of time to learn to use a new program. But once you do, you will never have to recopy information. The computer will add and subtract for you. It will even generate the reports you need automatically.

To find a way of keeping a financial journal that suits you and your business, talk to your accountant. Look at what is for sale in a local office supply store. Talk with your dentist, veterinarian, or any other local small business owner to see what works for them. You might learn about something you can easily adapt for your own purposes.

PROFIT AND LOSS STATEMENT FOR ARIZONA KOBUDO ACADEMY JANUARY 1 TO JANUARY 31, 2002

INCOME

Classes outside the school	$200.00	
Other service income	$100.00	
Private lessons	$500.00	
Seminars	$400.00	
Testing and promotion	$1,000.00	
Tournaments	$0.00	
Tuition	$5,200.00	
Gross Service Income:		$7,400.00
Retail sales	$1,200.00	
Less cost of goods sold	($720.00)	
Gross Profit from Retail Sales:		$ 480.00
TOTAL GROSS INCOME:		$7,880.00

EXPENSES

Advertising	$350.00	
Bank charges	$20.00	
Insurance ($3,000 per year/12)	$167.00	
Interest expense	$20.00	
Maintenance	$35.00	
Office supplies	$25.00	
Printing & postage	$200.00	
Rent	$2,000.00	
Salaries	$3,000.00	
Taxes—payroll	$387.00	
Taxes—sales tax on retail sales	$154.00	
Telephone	$125.00	
Utilities	$350.00	
TOTAL EXPENSES		$6,833.00

NET PROFIT		$1,047.00
Profit percentage	13.29%	

Profit and Loss Statement

Information from your financial journal is collected and summarized each month to produce a profit and loss statement. The purpose of a profit and loss statement is to give you an overall picture of your business finances: your income, expenses, and bottom line. The P&L is one of the two most important reports you will produce, the other being the balance sheet. On the preceeding page is a sample profit and loss statement.

Notice that the P&L makes the distinction between service and retail income. Service income is money you take in exchange for your time and effort: for tuition or in payment for private lessons, for example. In many states, service income is not subject to sales tax. By contrast, retail income is money taken in payment for tangible goods, the things you sell in your pro shop. Retail income is taxable in most states and in some cities. If your P&L contains a line for retail income and that retail income is taxed, the expense section of the P&L must have a line for sales tax.

What categories of income and expenses should appear on your P&L? That depends on what you want to track. Profit and loss statements often contain certain standard categories—service and retail income, advertising, utilities, rent, and payroll expenses. But the categories you choose depend on what you want to know about your business.

You must produce a P&L at the end of each year. You should produce one every month, or at the very least quarterly. If you have a computer accounting program, all you have to do is regularly enter income and expenditures, and the program will generate a P&L on command. If you don't use a computer to keep your financial records, you will need to sort the entries in your journal by category. Add up each category and transfer the totals into your P&L.

From the profit and loss statement, you can easily figure income percentages. To do so, divide any given kind of income by your total income; then multiply by 100. In the example, the Arizona Kobudo Academy took in $5,200 from tuition, $500 from private lessons, and $480 gross profit from retail sales. Their total income was $7,880. That means that the percentage of their income coming from tuition was (5,200 / 7,880) = .66, or 66 percent. Roughly another 6 percent came from private lessons and 6 percent from retail sales.

To Calculate What Percentage of Your Income Comes from Any One Source:

One source of income / total income

Divided By 100

Equals The percentage of your income from that source

Calculating income percentages enables you to see at a glance where your income is coming from. It also helps you compare income sources from month to month, even though dollar amounts differ from month to month. For example, are you getting more of your income from retail this month than you did six months ago? Are private lessons playing a larger or smaller role in your income now than they were a year ago?

To Calculate What Percentage of Your Income Goes Toward Any One Expense:

A specific expense / total income

Divided By 100

Equals The percentage of income going toward that expense

Calculating expense percentages allows you to keep an eye on your expenses. How much of your total income goes toward fixed expenses, the monthly costs of doing business that do not fluctuate with an increase or decrease in business? What percentage of your income goes to optional purchases such as nonessential equipment? Has your advertising budget been growing or shrinking in relation to your income? When you compare them with your overall budget, are any of your expense categories getting out of line?

In short, a profit and loss statement allows you to see if you are making or losing money. It gives you an overview of where your money is coming from. And it tells you how much of your income is going to which expenses. A profit and loss statement is often your first clue if something is out of balance in your business—if you are spending too much money on nonessentials, or if your income from private lessons has fallen. Without one, you don't know if changes you've made to your business are paying off. Without one, you could be on a self-destructive course and not know until it is too late to correct. If you're serious about keeping your school successful, you need to produce and analyze a P&L every month.

Balance Sheet

At the end of each year, you should generate a balance sheet. A balance sheet shows your current, fixed, and other assets (things you own), shows your current and long-term liabilities (things you owe), and calculates your net equity in the business. A balance sheet takes the information from your profit and loss statement, combines it with other figures, and looks at it in the context of your business as a whole. On the following page is a sample balance sheet.

A balance sheet is very helpful when you are expressing your business value to a lender. But it can also help you make sure your business is moving in a positive direction.

For example, what is your asset-to-liability ratio? A healthy company has an asset-to-liability ratio of 1.5 or 2 to 1. In other words, it owns one to two times more than it owes. Let's say that you look at your balance sheet and see that you owe more than you own (a common situation for a business that is just starting out). If you compare this year's balance sheet to last year's balance sheet, has your asset-to-liability ratio improved? If so, your business is growing in a healthy direction. If not, you may be headed toward trouble.

What is your return on investment (ROI)? In the example company, the ROI is 2.5 percent. The net profit (bottom line of the P&L) is $1,047. The total assets (on the balance sheet) are $41,875. Net profit divided by total assets, 1,047/41,875, equals .025, or 2.5 percent.

BALANCE SHEET
ARIZONA KOBUDO ACADEMY
YEAR ENDING 12/31/02

ASSETS

Current Assets

Cash in Checking Account	$3,883.00	
Cash in Savings Account	$1,000.00	
Petty Cash in Drawer	$42.00	
TOTAL Cash (Liquid Assets)		$4,925.00
Inventory for Resale (at Landed Cost)	$15,000.00	
Accounts Receivable (Immediately Owed to You)	$4,500.00	
TOTAL Current Assets		$24,425.00

Fixed Assets

Accumulated Depreciation		($ 5,050.00)
Computer and Software	$2,000.00	
Furniture and Fixtures	$2,500.00	
Leasehold Improvements		$6,000.00
Signs	$4,000.00	
Training Equipment	$5,000.00	
TOTAL Fixed Assets		$14,450.00
Other Assets		
Security Deposits (Rent,Utilities)	$3,000.00	
TOTAL Other Assets		$3,000.00

TOTAL ASSETS $41,875.00

LIABILITIES:

Current Liabilities

Accounts Payable (Current)	$100.00	
Rent—One Year	$24,000.00	
Current Portion of Loans (due in one year)	$1,200.00	
Payroll Taxes Due	50.00	
Sales Taxes Due	25.00	
TOTAL Current Liabilities		$25,375.00

Long Term Liabilities

Long Term Loans (over one year)	$3,800.00	
TOTAL Long Term Liabilities		$3,800.00

TOTAL LIABILITIES $29,175.00

OWNER'S EQUITY:

Common stock	$ 5,000.00	
Accumulated Earnings	$ 7,700.00	
TOTAL OWNER'S EQUITY		$12,700.00

TOTAL LIABILITIES AND EQUITY $41,875.00

Asset to liability ratio: 1.44:1
Current ratio: .96:1
Return on Investment: 25%

Ratios You Can Get from a Balance Sheet

Acid test ratio: Liquid assets (assets that can be readily turned into cash) divided by current liabilities equals the acid test ratio. It measures how much money your business has immediately available. A ratio of 2:1 is considered good.

Asset-to-liability ratio: Total assets divided by total liabilities equals the asset-to-liability ratio. A healthy company has an asset-to-liability ratio of 1.5:1 or 2:1.

Current ratio: Current assets divided by current liabilities equals the current ratio. It tells you what proportion of your total assets you could convert to cash within a short period of time. In other words, it is a measure of how liquid you are. A ratio of 2:1 is considered good.

Return on investment (ROI): Net profit divided by total assets equals ROI. It measures profitability. ROI is typically expressed as a percentage. The lowest acceptable ROI is around 1 percent to 3 percent; 5 percent to 10 percent are good ROIs.

In a small business you don't want a return on investment that's too high because you pay taxes based on that number. Any profit is acceptable, but you should be getting 1 to 3 percent at a minimum, depending on the salary you take out of the business. A lender or investor will ask about your return on investment. Since you are probably your own biggest investor, shouldn't you know your ROI, too?

Learn to read a balance sheet. Learn to calculate and interpret ratios by applying them to your own numbers. Spend time with your accountant and banker and ask them about what things they look for in P&L statements and balance sheets. Find out what ratios are important to them. Profit and loss, cash flow, balance sheets, ratios: these are the language of the financial world. Don't be afraid to let the experts teach you how to speak it.

Learn to Keep Your Own Books

You don't have to be an accountant to keep the books for your business. But if you haven't kept financial records for a business before, it is a skill you will need to learn. For a quick and dirty introduction to the records the IRS requires, order a copy of IRS Publication 334, "Tax Guide for a Small Business." But these minimal records will not allow you to do all the analysis you need. Seriously consider spending the time to learn some basic bookkeeping and financial management skills. Get a good basic bookkeeping book and a small business financial management book. Or take a few vocational school or community college courses.

Seriously consider learning to use a computerized accounting program. Doing so will save you both time and money. Many small business accounting programs today are very user-friendly. Talk to your accountant for recommendations. If you have some computer experience, you can probably learn to use your accounting program by playing with trial data. If you need more help, your local community college will probably have classes available. The SBA's Information Centers also help small business owners learn to use computers. If you have the money, you can hire a private company to set up your business computer system and teach you to use it. Or you may have a student who can help you learn. (Be careful, however, not to entangle your student in your personal financial matters. Students come to study with you to get away from their own day-to-day computer and financial traumas.)

Part of keeping good records is simple common sense. Know what information you will need and make sure you can lay your hands on it when you need it. Part of keeping good records is learning some basic skills and applying them consistently. Keeping good records helps you keep out of trouble with the IRS. It helps you troubleshoot financial problems that could sink your business. And it helps you increase your profits and meet your financial goals. If you don't know how to do basic bookkeeping, learn. If you don't know how to use a computer, learn. If you don't know how to produce and analyze small business financial reports, learn. The success, in fact the very life, of your business depends on your ability to manage its finances well.

CHAPTER THIRTEEN:

KEEP THEM COMING BACK FOR MORE

Nothing hits you in the gut quite like a student's leaving. You've invested your time, your energy, your sweat in this person. You trusted them. Now they're packing their gear, walking out the door, not showing up, making excuses when you call to check on them. Not many teachers can watch a student leave without some sadness, anger, hurt, or confusion. Yet few situations demand of you more hardheaded realism as a business person. Quite apart from the relationships—the personal qualities that go out the door with each student who leaves—there is the issue of paying the rent. If you're going to stay in business, you must hang on to your students.

Keep Your Regular Students

To keep your regular students active over the long term, make sure they don't leave for very long in the short term. Do you remember the last time you were off work for a week or two for vacation or illness? Do you remember how difficult it was to get back into the regular routine? Think about that next time a student comes to you wanting to "take a little time off." In three weeks, staying home will have become a habit. In a month or two, their skills will have gotten rusty. In six months, they will have slid way behind their peers who have continued to train. Dropping out permanently will become much easier than working to catch up.

It's Newton's first law of motion: A body in motion tends to remain in motion. A body at rest tends to remain at rest. OK, so he wasn't exactly talking about your school. But the truth remains: Once a student's southern hemisphere has been planted at home in couch-potato position for a week or two, it is tough to get it up and back in the studio training. Time taken away from training is time spent inventing excuses not to train.

So how do you keep your students from drifting away?

Keep your eyes and ears open. Know the people who study with you. If yours is like most schools, you have four kinds of students. A few of your students are there when you open for business and there when you close for the night. They're at all the special events. If they could figure out a way to pitch a tent in your parking lot, they would spend twenty-four hours a day at your school. Other students have a regular training schedule and are in often enough to excel. Studying with you and helping out with classes are high priorities for them, and they make time for it. These first two kinds of students are the backbone of your school. The third kind have many things in their life that take priority over training with you. They're good students when they're with you, but they're with you infrequently. The fourth kind of student drifts in and out. They don't stay motivated for long. They're only one step away from disappearing completely.

If you want to keep students from drifting away, you not only have to recognize when the fourth kind of student is on their way out; you also have to recognize when the first kind is beginning to burn out. You have to recognize when the second kind of student is slipping into the third category or the third into the fourth. It's tempting to think of drop-out prevention as trying to persuade students who haven't been attending to come back. But that perspective can cause you to take the first and second type of student and their regular attendance for granted. Doing so is a dangerous habit that can spell disaster for the school owner. If you're paying attention, you can usually see early warning signs before a student walks out the door. Keep your eyes open for signs of dissatisfaction or restlessness.

Keep Them Interested

One of the biggest reasons that students drop out is that they get bored and lose interest. Or other things start to interest them more. As a teacher, you can't do much if a student leaves because she just got a driver's license, wants to spend more time with a girl/boy friend, or needs a second job. You can't control outside influences in your students' lives. But if the problem is inside your school, you must do something about it. You must learn, practice, and refine the skills you need to keep each one of your students interested and motivated.

Motivation

What do you know about human motivation? Are you able to see the differences in the way different people are motivated? Are you able to capitalize on what motivates each individual? Have you ever talked to your students about what makes them want to excel?

Different people begin studying a martial art for different reasons. Some come to class to meet people or to feel as though they belong somewhere. Some are looking for authority and the prestige that goes with it. Others are motivated by their mind—they enjoy learning new things, continually challenging themselves. Some just want a good workout. Still others are in it for the fun. To keep these different kinds of students motivated, you must focus on different aspects of your classes. A student who is motivated by learning may be bored by a "good workout" class. But a student who is motivated by fun may balk at too many intellectual requirements. A student who is looking for prestige or recognition may consider special

> **KEEPING STUDENTS MOTIVATED**
>
> 1. Believe your students will be successful. Create a "can do" atmosphere.
> 2. Be aware of the unique needs and motivations of individual students.
> 3. Acknowledge good attitude and good effort.
> 4. Help students put failure behind them. Let students start each new attempt at a task with a clean slate.
> 5. Praise specific behaviors. Correct specific techniques. Be honest in your praise and correction. Show your students that you are paying attention.

private lessons with you to be a privilege. One who is looking for social connection might dislike private lessons because they lack the noise and interaction of a large class.

Listen to students. Watch when they train, not just for technique but also for what fires them up. Look at their faces. Read their eyes. Notice when they drift off. Then, when you design classes, design them with your students' motivations in mind. Rotate through different kinds of activities to appeal to different people either on a daily or weekly basis.

As a teacher, you must be a student of human beings and what makes them do what they do. As a school owner, you must be a keen observer of your students (and your students' parents). You must be an expert on what motivates them to excel.

Children

If you find you lose children more regularly than adults, ask yourself what you know about the cognitive development of the age groups you teach. Are you expecting things from your six-year-olds that typically don't develop until children are in their teens?

Children can learn amazingly detailed and complex skills, but they tend to learn more holistically than adults. A detailed verbal analysis of each technique typically won't work for a six-year-old. But simply moving well yourself and asking the children to move with you often will.

Children have shorter attention spans than adults. Although attention spans vary widely from individual to individual, a simple formula can help you not overextend your children. Consider the ages of the children in the class. For a class of three- to five-year-olds, figure a three- to five-minute attention span. For a class of six- to nine-year-olds, six to nine minutes. For adults, figure twenty to twenty-five minutes. Before you hit maximum attention span, you need to change the exercise—change the drill, change the pace, face the class a different direction, line them up in a circle rather than a line. Of course, with practice, students can stretch the length of their attention. In fact, part of martial arts training is learning to focus even when the natural impulse is to let the mind wander. If, however, you continually push the upper limits of your students' attention, they will not only lose focus, they will lose interest.

Never underestimate your children. But if you treat your children like adults, don't be surprised if they fail to live up to their potential as children.

Parents

Behind every child in your martial arts class is a parent, guardian, grandparent, aunt, or uncle. They pay for lessons, drive their child to class, celebrate their child's successes, encourage their child when he gets frustrated. If a parent believes in what you are doing, you have the most valuable ally you could hope for. If a parent doesn't approve of what you are doing, keeping their child motivated is the least of your worries.

Listen to your students' parents or grandparents. Make sure you know them by name. Encourage them to give you honest feedback. Know why they have brought their child to study with you. Beyond that, let them know that you appreciate the time and money they sacrifice to keep their child in the martial arts. Work with them for the good of their child.

Innovation

Understanding motivation and attention span is one thing. Building that knowledge into an interesting class session is yet another. Consider how much time any given student spends with you. If she attends class three times a week for a year, that's more than 150 hours of class. If you want to hold a person's interest for 150 hours, you will need to incorporate some variety.

Granted, a certain amount of repetition creates both good technique and a certain amount of security. Students, particularly children, often like to use the same warm-up or cool-down each class. It allows them to settle into the routine of a martial arts class and leave the outside world far away. Repetition can be purposeful. Purposeless repetition, however, leads to boredom. Most students have a pretty good instinct for activities that merely fill class time.

Invent new drills. Trade drills and teaching techniques with other teachers. Read books and trade magazines to learn new teaching ideas. Take a teaching seminar.

Keep written records. One of the most common reasons for lack of variety is that teachers don't write, follow, and keep lesson plans. If you walk into a class without a lesson plan, chances are you will fall back on the same old drills.

Even if you can't imagine yourself following a lesson plan, you should have a library of drills that you keep in written form and look at regularly. Try a new drill at least once a week, and note the ones that work and those that don't. If you've been teaching for a while, you've probably forgotten more drills than your students have seen. Written records keep those drills alive.

At the beginning of the week, choose a theme. List the skills your students need, and rotate through the list. One week work on footwork. The next focus on correct blocking technique. The week after that look at takedowns. Go ahead and work your usual combinations, forms, prescribed drills. But when you break them down to drill them and when you select which supplementary drills to use in each class, keep your theme in mind. Keep a record of your themes for each week. Doing so will help you train more well-rounded martial artists. And it will keep your classes from falling into ruts.

Consistency

When students drop out, do they say things like, "It wasn't what I expected"? Your students were interested when they signed up. If they're losing interest now, is it possible that you've changed?

Make sure that your classes reflect your marketing plan. Let's say you have always billed your school as a training ground for serious competitors. If lately you haven't been seeking out tournaments and haven't been holding competition classes, you've taken away the thing that's most likely to keep your competitive students interested. Conversely, if you have signed up students who are mostly interested in fitness and stress reduction, and now you're pushing competition, you may be losing students who just aren't interested in your new emphasis.

It's OK to change your marketing identity and your classes to match, just make sure you do it consciously and consistently. And make sure you are willing to accept the consequences of that change.

Make sure, too, that you are consistent in your attitude and habits. Start and stop classes on time. When you step onto the training floor for a class, make sure you're ready to teach.

Keeping a class interested month after month is not easy. It requires that you not only become a student of human motivation but also conscientiously train your teaching skills. Always remember: Your students are not just paying for information. They are paying you to meet their needs—real and imagined. Learn what those needs are. And learn how to meet them as skillfully as possible.

Keep Them Playing

Another common complaint of students who drop out is "it was all work and no fun." Children need stimulation, excitement, regular changes of pace. Adults, whether they know it or not, need the same thing.

When we get serious about our martial art, we tend to "train," to "work out." We all too often lose the ability to play. Serious training and fun don't have to be mutually exclusive.

Many of your students will be coming to your classes for recreation, to have fun and get some exercise. Go ahead and work your students hard. Challenge them. Make them sweat. But smile now and then while you do so. Show your students that you are having a good time. Enjoy their company. Find a way to present class material in a fresh, fun way. Make sure each class ends with something the students like to do. Send them home with smiles on their faces.

Fun is a powerful motivator. Help your students—both adults and children—play while they make progress, and they will keep coming back.

Keep Them Working

Many students have trouble practicing at home. They have trouble making the time, or they don't have the willpower. So they enroll in an organized school, make attendance a habit, and rely on you to help them get the exercise they need.

It's up to you to keep them working. Let them build up a sweat. Don't let them cool down too much between drills. Go ahead and explain what they need to do and why. But if you feel the temptation to begin a lecture, ask yourself if the lecture is more important than your students' exercise and practice time. In other words, don't talk about martial arts. Do martial arts.

Keep Them Loyal

A common reason students drop out, and one of the toughest ones for a teacher to take, is simply, "I didn't like the teacher." Personality differences are, of course, unavoidable. But a good teacher will minimize those differences, focusing instead on the students and their needs.

Listen Well

How do you reduce the chances of students dropping out because they didn't like you? Listen. Draw your students out. Let them tell you what they need. Of course you have a commitment as a teacher to give students what they need to learn the art. But within those bounds, you also have to give them what they themselves believe they need.

What happens if you don't listen? What happens if you believe you always know better than they what they need? What happens if you merely pass along technique, just as your teachers, and their teachers before them, did? What happens is that you appear to care more about the art than you do about the people you are training. If that image is a conscious choice, and if you are willing to accept the repercussions, it is your decision to make. But understand that not many people can relate to a teacher like that. People in our consumer culture are used to comparison shopping. They select products and services that suit them. If their doctor, dentist, hairdresser, or church isn't listening to them, isn't meeting their needs, they will find another. In the eyes of the average American consumer, you can be replaced. But if you continue to listen and meet your students' needs, you will remain an important part of their lives.

Praise Well

How much do you praise your students? People don't move forward in their training fueled solely by criticism. Take a hint from Dale Carnegie—praise, correct, praise. For example, "Your hand position is great. Now let me show you how to get more power into the technique . . ." Then, as soon as your students begin to make progress, let them know. Praise them for improvement, not just perfect technique. But what if a student isn't doing much of anything right? Find something. Praise does not have to be "you did that perfectly." It can be "you did that better than last time." It doesn't have to be "that was Olympic caliber." It can be "your left foot position was very good." Praise regularly. Don't lie. Don't exaggerate. But learn to recognize and celebrate your students' small victories.

When praising, remember that children and adults both can sense insincerity. If you walk by when they're floundering, goofing off, or just having an off day, and you say "Good job!" they may assume that you are lying or not paying attention. But if you try, you can find a compliment for every student every day. It may simply be that a student finally made a fist correctly, or was concentrating on his technique. It may be that a student's technique was ever so slightly better than it was yesterday. It may be something small, but it has to be something real. Teach yourself to look for improvement, to notice achievement as much or more than you do problematic technique. Praise growth, and you will encourage growth.

Don't forget to praise your exemplary students, the ones who seem to need very little outside motivation to excel. They still need praise, sometimes more than the others. Be careful not to fall into the habit of being harder on your good students "because they can take it." Encourage them. Push them to excel if you think they need it. But watch for signs of burnout.

Correct Well

Sometimes, though, you will need to criticize. When that time comes, criticize behavior, not people. All of us can probably remember a coach or teacher who used to attack us personally, a coach who used to tell us we were clumsy rather than teaching us better footwork, a coach who used to call us lazy rather than encouraging us to work to our full potential. Do you have fond memories of those insults? Probably not. When a student makes a performance error, correct the error. Make your correction specific. Tell students what they are doing right as well as what they're doing wrong. Avoid statements like, "There you go again. You always mess up that technique." In other words, don't attack your students; teach them the specific things they need to do better.

Your students with a strong self-image should receive at least 60 percent positive feedback and no more than 40 percent corrective feedback. If you have shy or insecure students, they should receive more like 80 percent positive feedback and no more than 20 percent corrective, constructive feedback.

SIX STEPS TO BETTER CORRECTION

1. Recognize accomplishment first.
2. Correct specific techniques and give specific advice.
3. Avoid generalizations and personal attacks.
4. Correct only one or two things at a time.
5. Be empathetic when wording your correction.
6. Recognize and praise improvement.

When you correct students, don't give them more than two things to work on at any given moment. Granted, at the beginning a student is probably doing a lot more wrong than right. Picking just one thing for the student to work on may be hard. But if you overload students with all the things that need work, they will short-circuit. Give them one thing at a time, one thing they can succeed at. Watch them succeed. Praise them when they do. Make each session a series of small successes rather than a steady stream of criticism. Structure your classes for the success of every student. Help them be winners in several small "contests" every day.

Finally, don't punish a student for mistakes in technique. Punishment occupies the teacher's time, time that could be spent teaching, and it drains the students' energy, energy that could be put into a focused second attempt. Punishment brings up feelings of anger, resentment, self-pity, and self-justification in the person being punished. It floods that person with a wash of thoughts, memories, and emotions that make it even more difficult for her to train well. Sometimes punishment for behavior problems is necessary. But punishment for mistakes in technique is almost always counterproductive.

Communicate Well

What causes a breakdown of loyalty? One of the biggest causes is students' believing you are not loyal to them. Do you hold yourself to the same standards you expect of them? Do you treat them honestly and fairly? Most of us do. But sometimes loyalty breaks down anyway. In those cases, check to see if you are expressing yourself well. If your expectations are reasonable, are they clear? Do you and your students know what you expect of them?

It's an old story: Years after training is over, a student and his mentor, coach, or teacher, get together. The coach tells the student, "I was always proud of you." The student is surprised, shocked. The student has believed for years that he was never good enough to please the coach. What happened? Probably a break down of communication. The coach remembers pushing the student to get better, to work up to potential. The student remembers the criticism, the way his technique was never quite up to the coach's standards.

As a teacher, you must find a way to tell your students that you're proud of them. Find a way to celebrate not only their large victories but their small ones as well. Find a way to let them know that they as people are valuable to you.

One way to express to your students that they are valuable to you is to write personal notes. One karate sensei has 500 students. He has made the commitment to write and mail personal notes to five students each day. That way each of his students get a personal note from him roughly once every four months. Could you do something similar? The notes can be about anything: congratulations on an achievement, a thank-you for help, a comment on progress. The only restrictions are that they should be personal, specific, and positive. But what if you can't find something personal and positive to say about each of your students? Then either you're not paying attention or you're not teaching very well.

An occasion you might want to mark is the anniversary of a student's first day of training. A simple note will do: "The last year has been great. You've made very good progress. I'm looking forward to the next one." Pay attention to milestones in your students' lives: testing, promotions, first tournament, first solo teaching experience. These occasions are important to your students. Knowing that they are important to you as well will create a bond between you and them.

Another simple way to let students know that they are valuable to you is to send birthday cards. Have every student put down their birthday when they first sign up with you. Trade magazines often have an appropriate selection of cards. Or buy them at the drugstore. If you have a word-processing or desktop publishing program, you can make them yourself and print them out on colorful paper. Who gets them? Everyone. Both active students and inactive students, children and adults should receive a personal birthday card with their name on it and the signature of the senior instructor (and maybe the other instructors as well) at the bottom.

Major events in your students' personal life should also be acknowledged. A student or parent in the hospital should receive a card. Deaths or births in the immediate family deserve acknowledgment, as does graduation from high school or college. If you have a word processor, you can print your logo on cards and keep them for occasions such as these. If you have an e-mail account, you can send casual notes this way.

Send mail to children in their own names. They love to get mail, but often don't.

Don't forget postcards. Not only can they save you postage, they are sometimes better than mail in envelopes. If mail is private, it needs an envelope, of course. Bills and personal notes need the privacy an envelope provides. On the other hand, if it is something you wouldn't mind other people seeing, put it on a postcard. Everyone who handles a postcard sees your logo on it. Send "thanks for stopping by" notes on postcards. Announcements of anything to which the public is invited should be on postcards. Birthday cards, sympathy cards, invitations to closed parties? Put them in envelopes. Direct mailing pieces, dates and information for your next tournament? Post cards are your best choice.

Make regular, one-on-one contact with your students. Students who feel like an important part of your school will want to continue being a part of your school. Students who feel good about what they do when they're training with you aren't likely to stop training. Students who feel that you value their presence will continue to grace you with their presence.

Keep Them Successful

Some martial arts define success as dominating the opponent. The one who is still standing when the fight is over is the winner. On a day-to-day basis, this translates into winning sparring matches, accumulating trophies, dominating other students. Winners get the spotlight. Losers and "also rans" are ignored on the sidelines. In an environment concerned mainly with competition, a student can steadily improve, can be twice the martial artist he was six months ago, and can still be considered a loser.

Examine what success looks like at your school. Do you have students off on the edges convinced that they will always be failures because they've lost a few contests?

Build Self-Esteem

So what do you do? Do you tell students that they're doing great even if they aren't? No. Current psychological research shows that self-esteem training that isn't built on a foundation of success can be counterproductive. Simply chanting "you're wonderful, you're won-

> **WHETHER YOU BELIEVE YOU CAN,
> OR WHETHER YOU BELIEVE YOU CAN'T,
> YOU ARE ABSOLUTELY RIGHT.**
> —HENRY FORD

derful" isn't encouragement. Self-esteem must be built on a real foundation, not an imaginary one.

How do you build a solid foundation with your students? You help them set and meet manageable, bite-sized weekly, daily (or minute-by-minute) goals. Help them see what they do today as a part of their longer-term goals. Find where your students' challenges are. For some, a challenge is a slow steady march to a national championship. For others, a challenge is standing still or focusing for five minutes, or even one minute. Find that "place" where they are challenged but not overextended. Create an atmosphere where students succeed repeatedly, regularly. Then help them recognize and celebrate their successes.

Transcend Failure

If they fail, that failure becomes a learning tool. Allow mistakes. Don't make a big deal of them. Think of a young child learning to walk. Walking is a very complex skill. Yet young children learn it readily. Sure they fall, but when they do, they get up and try again. Eventually they learn. Could they make those incredible strides if every time they fell they worried and stressed over the "failure"? Teach your students to get up and focus on the next attempt rather than wallowing in the failure. Teach them how to use the mistake as stepping stones to doing better the next time.

Set Goals

Another reason students lose interest is that they don't see a future in what they do. Students who are just going through the motions will soon tire of the motions. Students need to have goals and priorities. You can't set those goals for them, but you can help

> **FAILURE IS THE OPPORTUNITY TO START FRESH, THIS TIME WITH GREATER KNOWLEDGE AND MORE EXPERIENCE.**

them set their own. Sit down with your students; ask each of them to dream. Ask them to picture where they would like to be, what they would like to be doing in six months, a year, five years. Never say "that's impossible." People have been trying to do the "impossible" since time immemorial. Some succeed in the trying. Let your students build castles in the air. It's your job to help them build foundations under those castles.

The "foundation" you build under their dreams consists of many small reachable goals on their way to doing the impossible. These smaller goals should be something they can achieve in a matter of a week to ten days for some students, in a matter of hours, or even minutes, for others. For some students, a short-term goal may be as seemingly simple as being able to keep their eyes and mind on their opponent through an entire sparring match, not a small accomplishment for someone with attention deficit disorder, for example. Others who come in with great athletic ability may want to be able to jump up and kick the ceiling. No matter what size these short-term goals are, they should be clear enough to you and your students that there is no question when the students have accomplished them. Most of all, these goals should be something that is important to the student, or the student won't put in the work to make them a reality.

Know what's important to your students and what their goals are. Help your students keep their goals in front of them. And keep them in front of you.

Motivational Awards and Programs

Another technique to keep students coming back is a special student-recognition program. This program includes certificates for "student of the month" or "most improved" student. It recognizes individual student achievement in a regular, formal way.

The advantages of a program like this are that it increases motivation in some students. It gives you, the teacher, an opportunity to recognize students who have done well. In addition, students will sometimes bring in their friends or family to see their name on a plaque on the wall, and that's good advertising.

The disadvantages, however, are just as real as the advantages. The motivation won't work for many of your students. Some students are "intrinsically motivated." Some are "extrinsically motivated." Extrinsically motivated students will work for prizes, trophies, special recognition awards. But intrinsically motivated students are pushed to achieve by something inside themselves. For them, "student of the month" awards mean little. Know your students. If trophies and certificates mean little to them, special awards will probably be scant motivation.

Another disadvantage is that you are opening yourself to the possibility of favoritism. Do you have some objective criteria for choosing one student over another? Or is this an honor that will go to everyone eventually? If it is just a rotating certificate, does it mean anything, or is it just a gimmick? Another possible disadvantage, depending on your students and the atmosphere in your school, is that it could foster jealousy or overcompetitiveness among your students.

If, however, you still like the idea after weighing the advantages and disadvantages, put some effort into your awards program. Make it work. Develop several categories: most improved, best effort, highest score in a tournament, best attendance. Offer each of these awards to different age categories. You could have four "most improved" students each month: one from the young children's class, one from the children's, one from the teen's, and one from the adult's. Or put together teams. Some possibilities are the great attitude (GAT) team, instructor's assistants team, the welcoming team. Each team should have not only responsibilities but also privileges. Recognize your assistants with a plaque or certificate annually. Make your special recognition public and sincere. If you're looking for other ideas for awards, check with public school teachers, managers, or motivational experts.

One word of caution: if you start an award or special recognition program, you must keep it up. If you still have May's student of the month award up in August, it sends the message that this award isn't important. Make the plaques or certificates look good. Hang them in a prominent place. Put some thought and effort into them or don't do them at all. If done well, they can be a valuable teaching/motivational tool. Treat them as seriously as you would any of your teaching tools.

Keep Them a Part of the Group

One main reason students join a sports school is for the social contact. They want to feel like part of a team. The school is the place where everyone knows your name, where friends miss you if you don't show up for a few days. An easy way to lose students is to let the social structure of your school break down.

Nip Discipline Problems in the Bud

Occasionally you will have a troublemaker. One of the biggest tricks in handling unruly students is stopping the problematic behavior without poisoning the atmosphere. Reprimands break the momentum of the class. They make some more sensitive students nervous, even if it isn't their behavior being corrected. Yet good discipline is crucial to successful teaching. How do you "artfully" correct discipline problems before they get out of hand?

Sometimes, especially with young children, a behavior can be "starved" out. If the student isn't in immediate danger or isn't dragging the rest of the class into misbehavior, ignore the student. Give him no reinforcement at all. Praise the other students for good behavior. Show the misbehaving student that it's more fun to behave than it is to misbehave. Often misbehavior is just a call for attention. When the student begins to behave correctly again, praise the student for the next thing he does right. Show the student that he gets more attention for being good than for being disruptive or disobedient.

Sometimes, however, you must confront a student. Whenever possible ask for good behavior rather than dressing the student down for bad behavior. If a student is fidgeting and bumping into others in line, remind him, "Please wait quietly with your hands at your sides." Then praise the student when he does so. Notice when drills go well, especially in classes where there has been trouble in the past. Compliment the students on their focus and self-discipline.

If a student is being unsafe or dragging down the atmosphere of the class, correct him immediately. But if you need to address serious misbehavior in detail, do so in private. Overall, the rule is "praise in public, correct in private." A public dressing down is like a red cape waved in front a bull for some students. They will feel that they have to get back at you, and they will do it in public.

It is tempting to focus on troublemakers. Watch yourself, though. Keep mental notes about how you deal with students during each class. Every now and then, count or have someone on the sidelines count the number of times you praise and the number of times you reprimand. You should be reinforcing good behavior noticeably more often than you are correcting bad. Otherwise, the message you send to the student is "misbehavior gets the most attention."

If you do use punishment to correct bad behavior, use it as a last resort. Use it when other alternatives haven't worked or when allowing the behavior to continue will endanger other students or disrupt the class. Especially for children, an effective form of punishment is the "time out." If a student is misbehaving and doesn't correct the misbehavior at your request, you separate him from the rest of the students. The student in "time out" sits on the edge of the training floor, in a chair or on the floor, away from activity. The student stays there until he is willing to stop the problematic behavior. After a few minutes, ask the student if he is willing to comply with class rules. Or tell the student to come in when he is willing to comply. The attitude behind a time out is that you are quarantining unsafe or distracting behavior, not that you are putting the student down for doing something wrong. Be aware, however, that some children feel humiliated by time outs. After they come back into training, monitor them carefully for signs of resentment or temper.

Sometimes, too, you may have to institute a similar quarantine for yourself. Do you have a temper? When something sets you off, are you likely to say or do something you will regret later? If you're in charge of the class, you can't very well put yourself in time out until you cool down, but you can do something similar. First, if the situation that made you angry is unsafe, stop it. Then shift gears. Move to another activity that doesn't require your intense supervision. Call a break. Hand off to your assistant. Work with another student for a while. Don't just sit in the middle of the situation that made you angry. Back off and wait until you have yourself under control before you correct or discipline students.

Think carefully about what you use as punishment. A common form in many martial arts schools is push-ups or other physical exercises. If you use push-ups as part of your training, you may want to examine their use as punishment. If push-ups are punishment, why should students want to do them as a part of their personal training? If they are an important part of training, are they really punishment or just another opportunity to train? Examine what you use as punishment. Make sure it is consistent with the rest of your training.

Stay above Student Society

You are the teacher at your school. You are not one of the crowd. You are responsible for discipline. If something goes wrong, the buck stops with you. For this reason, you cannot afford to be one of the gang. Should you be friendly? Of course. Informal? When appropriate. Buddy-buddy? Not at the expense of your objectivity.

Neither can you afford to play favorites. True, you will have better students and worse students. Some will be more talented, harder working, more regular in their attendance. And let's face it, some people are easier to get along with than others. But your school is not your social circle; it's your business, a service business. You must not work with your "good" students to the exclusion of others. Nor should you neglect them because they manage better on their own than others. Don't ignore your super athletes. Don't make them your social circle either. Concentrate on spreading your attentions evenly and fairly among your students.

Make Contact

Try to make contact with each of your students each day. If all you have is thirty seconds per student, give each of them those thirty seconds as though they were the only person in the world. Be fully present with each student as you talk with them. Sure, you may be interrupted. Emergencies arise. But when at all possible, be focused when talking with each student. Be aware, too, of how much time you spend with each of your students. If you consistently spend more time with one or two, the other students will notice. Ask yourself what message that sends. Is it a message you want to send? Is it a message that encourages teamwork?

Keep students and parents informed of any special events. Let them know about changes in the schedule as soon as possible. If they need to know something, make sure that you, your assistants, or your office manager makes personal contact. Don't just put up posters; call attention to the posters. Talk up special events. Talk to individuals about their participation. Phone or e-mail students if necessary. And don't forget to keep parents in the loop. Make personal, one-to-one contact.

Make the Tough Choices

Sometimes you have a student who will cost you several others. Perhaps that student is habitually unsafe. Perhaps she is a perennial behavior problem. Perhaps she is a bad influence, engaging in drug use or other illegal behavior. Perhaps there is just something about that student that chases others off. Sometimes you have to dismiss one to keep the others. The adage that "martial arts build character" has some truth to it. Occasionally you will get a student who comes in with serious problems and uses the training to turn her life around. But sometimes that student with real problems will cost you. You must decide if you are willing to sacrifice good students, maybe even your business, in the hopes of a single success story. Encouraging a student to leave may be difficult, but sometimes you must sacrifice a part for the greater good of the whole.

Build Community

Do your students have the sense that they are part of something larger than themselves? Are they part of a team, part of a community that cares about their well-being? For some of your students, the martial arts school is their main social network. Others may find a few lasting friends there. Students who feel a part of a community are more stable in their training and more regular in their attendance. You, as a school owner, should be helping build that sense of community.

Newsletters

You should be regularly mailing out a newsletter. Actually, to say that you "should" have a newsletter is not nearly strong enough. You must have a newsletter. A newsletter is sometimes the only way of keeping students emotionally involved in the school as a whole. You, as the instructor, see the whole student body every week. The students only see the individuals in their class and maybe the next class. They often do not realize how many people are involved in the school as a whole. Newsletters give students the sense that they are part of something big and important. When they read that someone has won a tournament or gained special recognition, they can say with pride, "they're from my school."

What should you put in a newsletter? The general rule of thumb is that a newsletter should be part information and part inspiration. Under the heading of information, you might want to include dates and information about upcoming events. Include, too, reports on past events. Your newsletter is the official "bulletin board" where you post notices that your students need to see. Include regular educational features: general information about the school and its history, background information about training equipment or weapons, or biographies of founders and important people in your art or organization. Give students special recognition for shows, tournaments, and promotions. Include anything that will inspire school spirit.

The newsletter is also a great way to help students and parents at your school get better acquainted. Overall, you'll want to include as many names as you can. (And make sure they're spelled correctly.) List birthdays, promotions, and tournament results. Welcome your new students. Include interviews with, or biographies of, instructors and students, especially senior students.

Another thing you should always have is a personal note from the senior instructor that is both informational and inspirational. Here's your chance to share the wisdom, the information, that just doesn't seem to fit into your classes. It's a chance for you to give your views on upcoming or recent special events. Think about what's important to you and your students and say a few words about it. Keep your notes short, less than a page. And keep them largely positive.

Your newsletter doesn't have to be "fancy." It just has to look businesslike and neat, with attention to detail. You can start with your logo and typed text on a couple of sheets of white or pastel 8-1/2" x 11" paper and work up from there. Eventually, especially if you're interested in building your desktop publishing skills, you might want to add pictures, graphics, or fancy layouts. But until then, make sure your typing is neat and your text is readable.

"But," you say, "I could barely manage to pass English when I was in school, and that was . . . we won't say how many years ago." Fair enough. But don't scrap the idea of a newsletter just yet. Maybe you need to find an "editor." Maybe your assistant instructor or office manager would be willing to take on the job of putting together the newsletter. Sometimes a parent, student, or group of students will welcome the task. Maybe you need to hire someone. A lot of people are doing desktop publishing as a first or second job out of their homes. Ask around. Check with your dentist, your pet sitter, anyone you know who has a newsletter. Ask who does theirs. Find out who has a reputation for being reasonably priced and reliable. If you're on a shoestring budget, check the local business and community colleges for desktop publishing classes. Sometimes a student will take on your project at minimum wage or in trade for martial arts classes. If you do have someone else putting together the newsletter, you still need to write a letter to the students each issue. The editor can clean up the spelling and grammar, but you need to make yourself heard in this forum. Make it a rule, as well, that you always have final approval before the newsletter goes to the printer. You decide whether something should be included.

Who should be on your mailing list? Both current and past students. To save postage you can hand out newsletters to current students after class. But be sure to mail the rest before the information in them becomes outdated. Print up a few extras to keep in the office to hand out to potential students. They are a snapshot of your school and why you are so proud of it.

Get-Togethers

Another way to build community is to schedule regular get-togethers. Consider parties, outings, picnics, potluck dinners, training weekends, fund raisers, anything that will get your students together doing something other than what you normally do at your school. You will probably want to plan for four events per year—enough to build community but not so much that they become a drain on your students' free time. Try to achieve a balance in the activities. Some may be for adults, others for children, still others for all ages. Some may require the student to spend a little money to attend (for example, admission to a zoo or amusement park); others may be free (for example, volleyball in the park). Some may be indoor, others outdoor. Some may focus on life inside the school (an annual spruce-up-the-school day); others may focus outward (for example, a fund-raising activity for a local charity). You know your students. What would they enjoy? Get them together to do it a few times each year.

A few of words of caution: First, if you are raising funds for an outside charity, don't make the event mandatory. Some people have very strong views about which charities they wish to support. You don't want to lose a student over something outside your school. Second, make sure you have budgeted the time and the money necessary to publicize special events well in advance. People's schedules are often tight. Give them plenty of advance notice. Build interest over time. Give them an opportunity to fit your event in with all the other things they have in their lives. Third, every event does not have to be for every person if you have enough events. Some people just aren't party people, but they might like a training weekend. Some might not have the money for a trip to an amusement park, but they would enjoy a work party. If you have a special event every three months or so, everyone should find something during the year that they enjoy.

As for organizing these events, you may want to do that yourself, or you may want to delegate it to your resident "party person." Do you have students or parents who love throwing parties? Put them in charge of your next party. Let them know if you can give them a budget. Make sure they report to you before setting their plans in concrete. Then turn them loose. Check in with them every now and then, but allow them the privileges of being in charge.

Keep Them Safe

Another reason students leave martial arts schools is injury or the fear of injury. One of the most fundamental human needs is the need to feel safe. People will go to great lengths to feel safe, even to the point of leaving an activity they enjoy if it makes them feel endangered.

Take a realistic look at your school. Is it a safe one? How many injuries have you had in the recent past? Have any of those injuries been serious? Try to see them through the eyes of your students, especially your new students. What the veterans consider to be normal bumps and bruises can be intimidating to new people. Check to make sure your children and new people aren't being banged around. Check that your senior people aren't unnecessarily jeopardized. If you have had a serious injury or several minor injuries recently, you may have to spend some time reassuring your students. Let them know that you know why the accidents happened and that you have a good idea how to prevent similar accidents in the future. Then do so. Prove to them that you are serious about their safety.

From a liability perspective, you are obligated to give your students the information and physical skills they need to keep themselves safe. If doing a technique incorrectly could cause injury, you need to warn students about that. Then you need to break the correct technique down so they can master the component parts and keep themselves safe and healthy. But quite apart from your legal obligations, you need to warn students of unsafe technique and guide them toward safe technique because it is your role as a teacher. Your students need to trust you to take their safety seriously.

Remember, too, that being safe and feeling safe are two different things. One can be safe and still feel in danger. Be vigilant for signs of anxiety. If you have a timid student, you must not only teach technique, you must also train the student's spirit, an important part of success in the martial arts. A certain amount of risk is inherent in any martial art. A student must develop skills to manage the fear associated with that risk. Teach your students focus. Teach them how to control their nervousness. Teach them the techniques they need to keep themselves safe.

Keep Them Charged Up

Most martial arts schools have a time when students seem to get tired and drop out. That time may be shortly after a major promotion or during a period where promotions are infrequent. It may be at two or three years, when the novelty has worn off. Or it may be just after promotion to brown or black belt. It's important that you know when your school has its biggest retention problem. And it's important to keep your experienced students training through those rough times.

One common time for people to drop out is at the intermediate stage, around the beginning of the second year of training. Their initial awkwardness has passed. So has the novelty of "being a martial artist." Some students at this time enter a stage when they believe they know everything and have nothing left to learn. Others look at the advanced ranks getting ever closer, and they panic. Still others enter a time of directionlessness when training just seems like more of the same thing. The intermediate ranks are a time of change, a time when a student goes from being a new student to being a regular student. They are a time when students need your help to find a direction for their training.

Spend some time with your intermediate students. Make an appointment with them to sit down in your office and talk about the place the martial arts have in their life. Talk about how far they've come. Help them identify goals they have accomplished and help them set new goals. Identify their challenges, fears, boredom. Then help them find a way to stay charged up.

You might want to give them a private lesson or two as a bonus for signing up for their second year. Use that lesson to work on their next challenge, something they're excited about. You might want to get them started mentoring a new student, to start giving back to their school. If they're intimidated by what lies ahead, you might want to ask a more advanced student to help them get ready for their next promotion. Listen to your intermediate students, and find ways to help them recapture their initial excitement and get back on track.

Another time that students drop out is just after they've received their brown or black belt. How do you keep your senior students charged up?

Rank should have its privileges. Chances are good it has some responsibilities—you rely on your senior people at the very least for example and demonstration. Make sure you give out your most advanced techniques, the most difficult and the most effective techniques, only to your advanced people. Let students know that you save some of the "good stuff" for your black belts/senior students. That gives them an incentive to stay with you.

You might also want to design a uniform that shows experience level, rank, or time in grade. That uniform can include patches, colored belts, chevrons, or some other symbolic way to recognize achievement. Consider offering discounts to your senior students or assistant instructors. Or offer them a special class.

You may also want to begin a club for your senior people—the Three-Year Society, the Advanced Students Association, the Assistant Instructors Society. Be careful, however, not to use your advanced students' club only as a money-raising technique. Some schools push senior students to enter a club that means special dues, extra responsibilities, and more work. If your club costs too much (in either time or money), you may find that it doesn't charge your people up; it pushes them away. If your advanced student club is going to succeed, its value must outweigh its costs. If you have an advanced student club, make it mean something.

While you're recognizing your student's achievement, look at your own. Do you have what it takes to train advanced students? Granted you don't need to be an active athlete to teach. Look on the sidelines at the Olympics. Very few professional coaches also compete. Yet you do need to evaluate where your skills are in relation to your students'.

Let's say you have four years of experience when you open your school. That makes you four years ahead of your people if all your initial students are beginners. But if you no longer train actively at your art, where will you be in four years?

The best thing you can do for your senior people is to continue your training, to make sure you continue to have something to teach them. Go to seminars and camps. Find a teacher to teach you. Read books. Watch videos. Continue to learn and keep your skills sharp. Always keep at least one step ahead of your students.

Keep Yourself Charged Up

What are you doing to make sure you yourself aren't burning out? Let's say that after two years your school is thriving, bringing in and keeping students, and making enough money to meet your goals. But let's say that after those two years you yourself are tired, overworked, and miserable. Is your business a success?

You need regular times for yourself. At first, realistically speaking, you will probably not have the time for a two-week vacation. Even a week may be out of your grasp during those early years. That's why you need to make sure to take a weekend, maybe even a long weekend occasionally. Get out of town. Go to a ball game. Spend time with friends or family. Do the things that recharge you. Eat properly. Get enough sleep. Keep yourself healthy and charged up.

Then also keep yourself healthy and charged up as a martial artist. Make sure to budget time and money to attend seminars. Find yourself a training partner who is working at your level, not the level of your students. Get together with other teachers to exchange teaching and training ideas. Your life can get terribly musty if you don't open a window and let some fresh ideas in occasionally.

Keep Them Paying

All school owners eventually have a student take them aside and say, "Sorry, I just can't afford to train anymore." Sometimes the problem is legitimate. A student has lost a job, has had a major financial upset. Other times "I can't afford it" is a smoke screen for something else. It's your job to tell the difference.

If the problem is legitimate, if a student does indeed have a tight financial situation, you may be able to help. Sometimes you can arrange payments over time for special expenses such as seminars, tournaments, special programs, and so on. Rather than have students not attend because they can't afford the lump-sum payment, you may choose to carry some of those costs and have the students pay you back in monthly or weekly payments. In these cases, it's crucial that you agree exactly how much they have to pay you and when the payments are due. Make sure the students can realistically make the payments. Write the schedule down and give them a copy. Then insist they live up to their end of the bargain. Better yet, anticipate expenses before they come due. Encourage the student to set aside money a little at time so when the expense hits, they are ready for it.

There may be a time when a student is deep in debt through no fault of his own. The student would pay if he could, but can't. You want to keep the person as a student, but you know he is too proud to continue to study while owing you money. You may decide in a case like this to cancel that student's debt. If you do so, find the student a temporary job to do around the school. Let the student clean windows or mop the floor. If the student is an experienced teacher, allow him to teach a few classes on a short-term basis to work off the debt. Working to pay the debt allows the student to save face.

For legitimate emergencies, you might want to set up a scholarship fund. The money you put in this fund could come from special fund raisers, or from sales of energy bars or sports drinks at the school. Or you might be able to find a sponsor—a financially secure student who comes to you wanting to help the less fortunate, or an outside sponsor who believes in what you're doing. If you have a scholarship fund and a student does need some temporary help, you can give it to him without cutting into the rent or your salary. Set a limit, however, as to how much time a student can be on scholarship. It should be a temporary leg up, not a permanent endowment.

Whatever you do, don't ever let a student's debt get out of hand. If students owe you money they can't pay, they will avoid you. In other words, ignoring a debt could lead to losing a student. Some students will drop out rather than see you every day knowing they owe you money. You do neither your student nor your school a favor by ignoring late payment.

Keep Your New Students

One of the most important things you can do to keep your new students is to learn their names and use them. Listen when they introduce themselves. Learn not only their name but also their parent's name, their spouse's name. Pronounce their name the way they want it to be pronounced.

Settle your new students into a special beginner's class for the first few months. If you wish to allow them to join your other classes as well, that's OK. But offer them at least one class a week where they learn beginning skills with other beginners. Beginning classes serve more than just a skill-building need. They also serve an emotional and social function. People don't want to be the only one in a group that can't do something. They want to see people who are at their level or a little above succeeding. They want to think, "If they can do it, I can do it."

Most new students, especially adults and juniors, appreciate a class exclusively for beginners. It's a place they can ask questions "all" the other students seem to know the answers to. It's a place where everyone is getting used to the same new customs and traditions, a place where everyone is developing new muscles and balance. In short, beginning classes should be a nonthreatening environment for breaking into something that could be potentially very threatening—learning an entirely new set of physical and mental skills.

The first couple of months are crucial, not only for building the foundation for future skills but also for building new attitudes and habits. Remember: These newest students haven't yet made training with you a habit. Unlike students who have been training with you for years, they can very easily picture a life without you and your art. These new students were living that life mere weeks ago.

Some new students fall into the routine easily and quickly, almost on their own. For most students, it's your job to bring them along. The two most important parts of bringing students along—from being the new kid on the block to being old regulars—are clear communication and the expectation that they will come back.

Clear communication means, quite simply, not taking anything for granted. Why should they know how to put on their uniforms or what safety gear to wear? Why should they know that you expect students who remove equipment from the shelf to put it back when they're finished? Don't insult their intelligence, but be sure they understand the bits and pieces of custom and etiquette that you and your other students manage as easily as breathing. Let them know that you and your students expect them to ask questions. Better yet, assign them an intermediate-level student to make them feel welcome and to answer all the little questions a new student has.

A word about who should teach new students: It's tempting to leave them in the hands of some of your lower-ranking students. After all, the things they are learning aren't that difficult. But teaching a new student is about more than just teaching techniques. It's also about teaching them new habits, teaching them how to fit in, allaying their fears, gaining their trust and respect, giving them a reason to come back. All of that is too complicated to entrust to just anyone. It is very easy to lose a student to poor teaching on their first night in class. Teach the new students yourself. Or put them in the hands of someone you would trust with the life of your business. New students are just that—the future life of your business.

As for the expectation that they will keep coming back, well, that's more about creating an atmosphere at your school where everyone is important right from the beginning. Use phrases like, "on Thursday when you come in, we'll cover . . ." Notice: "when you come in," not "if you come in." Hold your new students to the same requirements you expect of all your students. Help them set attainable goals and require that they spend the same amount of time and effort to achieve those goals as any other student. Requiring any less of them sends the message that they're different, less than full members of your school.

Overall, treat them like what they are: individuals who may be lacking in skill but who are an important part of your school. Make it clear that everyone came in "cold" just like they did. Be aware of the process by which new students become assimilated, and help them through that process step by step. Encourage more than you discourage. Above all, require of them the most important things you require of all your students—a good-faith effort and a willingness to learn.

Watch their attendance closely. If they miss a class, call them immediately to let them know you missed them.

One thing you find out in the first three months is whether a person belongs with you. Some don't. Some don't have even the most basic capacity to learn the art. They don't seem able to work safely with other students. Their learning style is so different from your teaching style that the two of you will never be able to work well together. They thought they could work their new interest into their schedule but they can't. The list of reasons goes on and on. Usually, the student will realize that the arrangement isn't working. You just need to let them leave. Sometimes you must be the one to break it to them. Either way, if possible, you want to be able to part friends. They may never be back, but maybe their brother or sister, their spouse or best friend will. Never burn your bridges.

Win Them Back

Try as you may to hang on to your students, some will drop out. What do you do then? You do what you can to bring them back. It's easier to bring back a former student who has drifted away than it is to bring in a new student. In the former student you know you have someone with an interest. You know who they are and what appeals to them about the art. You will never have that extent of knowledge about a newcomer.

Here's how you court a lapsed student: If a student has not been to class for the past week, give her a call to find out why. Let the student know that you noticed she was gone. Go ahead and leave a message on the student's answering machine if she isn't in. The main purpose of the call is to let the student know you miss her. The next week, if the student still hasn't come in, drop her a note. The week after that, call again. Keep in touch each week for the first four to six weeks. After that, make sure the student still gets your newsletter. Call occasionally. Send a birthday card or holiday greeting each year. If you've added a new class or changed your schedule, let the student know about it.

Unless the student tells you to go away, stay on her mind but not underfoot. Keep in contact for as long as you think the student may be back. Be sure to let the student know when you have special events coming up. Coming back first for a party or special event may be easier than coming directly back for classes.

Remember, the longer students are out, the harder it is for them to come back into class. They may feel inadequate, as if they can't catch up. They may picture everyone they trained with getting ahead of them. A fear of failure may set in. Try to catch your lapsed students as soon as possible.

Welcome Them Back

When students finally do come back, welcome them warmly. This is not the time for recriminations unless you want to lose them again. Simply tell them you missed them and that you're glad they're back. Don't make a big deal about their absence or their return.

Then get on with the business of getting them caught up. They will probably need some individual attention. Offer a special catch-up class. Get a senior student to help them out. Or better yet, give a senior student responsibility for catching them up. If they're looking shaky and you think you might lose them again before they get caught up, you might want to offer them a couple of free private lessons or maybe some personalized attention during an open time in your schedule. Notice, too, when they are working with people they didn't work with before. They may need to be introduced. Most of all make sure they know that you are glad they're back.

Your students are the life blood of your program. To keep your school healthy and profitable, you must keep them motivated, safe, and successful. You must keep them coming back for more.

CHAPTER FOURTEEN
RETAILING:
CREATE A SUCCESSFUL PRO SHOP

Not all of your income has to come from tuition. Some of it can come from retail sales. Running a pro shop is a way to increase your profits while providing your students with merchandise they need.

Whether your shop is a few uniforms on a shelf or a small-scale retail department store, you will find that selling goods requires a different set of skills than selling a service. To make money, you need to keep an inventory large and diverse enough to meet your customers' needs. But you need to do so without tying up the money you need for the rest of your business. How profitable your store becomes depends in large part on how well you run the business. And how well you run the business depends on how much you know about the business of retailing.

Do You Want to Have a Retail Area?

Before you start buying inventory, look at the pros and cons of running a retail operation. The decision whether or not to have a pro shop is essentially one of resources: Where do you want to invest your time, energy, space, and money? Given your situation, can you make a retail investment pay off for you?

The Challenges

If you were to decide against starting your own pro shop, how far would your students have to travel to purchase equipment? If they can easily get reasonably priced gear five or ten minutes from your location, you need to ask yourself why you want to open a shop yourself. Do you plan to offer your students things they can't get at the other shop? Will the convenience of shopping at your school be a significant benefit for your students? Will enough students buy from you to make the investment in time and money worthwhile? If you're content with the products your students get at local shops, and if you're not particularly keen on starting a retail competition, you may decide against opening a pro shop.

A pro shop ties up money. You can't use money invested in inventory to pay the bills or your salary. You could conceivably own thousands of dollars of merchandise and still be cash poor. Before you begin planning for your pro shop, consider whether you want to tie up the cash.

A pro shop is labor intensive. You will need to spend time (yours or an employee's) on ordering, display, marking, taking inventory, record keeping, collecting and paying taxes, and other tasks. Do you have the time for a retail shop? Do you want to work more hours? Do you want to take on the responsibilities of having an employee?

A pro shop takes up space. If you're content with a small operation—a few uniforms and essential gear—you can probably get by with a small wall display. But the question still remains, "Where will you put it?" Seriously consider whether you have the space.

A pro shop means more government paperwork. You may need to collect sales tax for your state and city. You will probably need a retail license from your city. Come tax time, the federal government will be asking questions about profits and value of inventory. In short, opening a pro shop puts you under the jurisdiction of several more government laws and regulations. Before you open your shop, consider whether you have the time and patience to deal with another layer of government requirements.

The Opportunities

Still interested? Good. If you're willing to invest the time, money, and energy, a pro shop can be a valuable addition to your school and your bank account.

It offers an important convenience for your students. No longer will they have to travel to another shop in town. No longer will they have to wait for catalog orders to arrive. They can get everything they need for their training at the same place they train. One-stop shopping is an important benefit that can help bring in and keep students.

HOW TO START A PRO SHOP

1. Decide whom you plan to sell to and what they need.
2. Take care of government requirements.
3. Choose a supplier or two.
4. Develop a preliminary inventory list and budget.
5. Order the merchandise.
6. Price the items.
7. Display and advertise the items effectively.
8. Keep accurate records of sales to help you make wise adjustments to your inventory, pricing, and marketing.
9. Keep accurate records of inventory.

Having a pro shop also creates uniformity within your school. If all your students buy their uniforms from you, they will look alike when they line up in class. This similarity may seem like a small thing, but it is part of building a cohesive school. If one student is wearing a red uniform because he likes the color, another a black one because he thinks it makes him look like a ninja, and still another a white uniform from a style she studied before she trained with you, you have a class whose very appearance reminds them they are thinking in different directions. If they all buy their uniforms from you, it reinforces the idea that they are part of your group.

Furthermore, if your students are all using the same gear, you can be very familiar with their equipment and clothing. You can control the quality of the gear they use. If a students come to class with unsafe or substandard equipment, you can have safe equipment available for their immediate purchase. You can correct a problem with unsafe equipment on the spot.

A pro shop that draws customers from the surrounding community can also draw new students for your school. Inactive martial artists, people who don't train but who are fascinated by martial arts gear, students who are currently training but who are dissatisfied with their current school—all of these people may come to purchase equipment, and may stay to take classes.

Running a pro shop also makes financial sense. You can buy uniforms for yourself and training equipment for your school at wholesale. That discount can save you hundreds of dollars each year, depending on how often you buy new equipment. Even if you only plan to carry a few uniforms for sale, opening a retail shop may make financial sense if you plan to spend a lot of money on training equipment such as mats, heavy bags, or other gear.

The bottom line is that a pro shop can be an additional profit center. Each time your student buys a uniform, you keep part of the retail price. Each time a parent buys a martial arts-related birthday present for a child, you make a profit. This additional income can help you make the money you need from your school, and it can help you keep your tuition affordable. The chart on the previous page provides a list of key steps in starting a pro shop.

Organize Your Shop as a Profit Center

If the purpose of your pro shop is to have a few uniforms in stock for your students' convenience, you may be content just to break even. But if you want to make money from your pro shop, you need to organize it to make money. Profit is not a dirty word. It is what pays your salary and puts food on your table. If you set up and manage your retail area well, it can make a steady profit for you. If you set it up and manage it haphazardly, you could find yourself stuck with thousands of dollars tied up in an operation that mostly gathers dust.

Who Are Your Customers?

Once you've decided you want a profitable pro shop, you need to think about who your customers will be. A retail business, like a service business, must have a target market. If you are selling martial arts-specific merchandise, your target market will obviously be those who practice the martial arts. But beyond that simple description, you also need to decide whether you are marketing to just your students or to others in your area.

Selling to Your Students

If your target market is only your students, a small restricted inventory is all you need. Look at what your students need in their training, and offer it in your pro shop. If you wish, you can also add a few specialty items—T-shirts, items bearing your logo, a few small things for less than ten dollars. But usually, you will not need to offer kendo armor if your students practice wushu. You will not need to offer sparring equipment if students in your school do not spar.

Besides required equipment and specialty items, you may also wish to carry the kind of training equipment you use in class. Some students like to have their own equipment for home practice. Look at what you use in class—focus mitts, kick pads, weapons. How much of it could your students use at home? You can either stock that equipment or offer it on a special order basis.

Selling to Other Schools

If your target market also includes martial artists from other schools, you need to do a little more research. Find out where students from nearby schools buy their equipment. Ask yourself, "If a nearby school has a retail area, why would students from that school buy from me?" In other words, what do you have that their home shop doesn't? If their home shop doesn't have it, do those students really need it? It's tough to market to outside students who can get their equipment at the same place they train.

If you decide you want to try, visit schools in your area to learn what you can offer them. Typically, you can assume that outside students won't buy anything from you that they can get cheaply and easily at their home school. So what you need to learn is what equipment they can't get at their school. Do students use equipment in class they can't get at their school? If your retail space is physically larger, you may want to offer larger items—heavy bags, mats, practice dummies. Or maybe you can offer specialty or novelty items that aren't available anywhere else in town. But, typically, if you are competing with other pro shops, you need to offer something the students need but can't easily get at your competitor's store.

If, however, schools near you don't have retail shops, you are in a much better position to sell to them. Marketing to more than one school means you will need a broader inventory with more selection. Watch some classes at local schools. Talk to the instructors. Do they use the same equipment as you do, or do they prefer different brands or colors? Does their martial arts style require different weapons or safety equipment? Plan to stock your shelves based on what your potential customers need.

One way to bring in business from nearby schools is to offer the school owners discounts on their own purchases if they recommend your shop to their students. For example, offer instructors merchandise at wholesale (a price above your landed costs [costs including freight] but below your retail cost). Or if you really want to bring in business, offer to return a percentage of every purchase to the student's home school. This latter option, of course, involves much more record keeping. But it allows students the feeling that they are supporting their own school. Whatever you decide, talk to local school owners. Ask what their students' need. Ask what services you can offer them. Make them your allies.

Selling to the Public

If you choose to market to the general public—not just to your students and the students from specific nearby schools, but to any athlete in your area who might be interested in the equipment you offer—you will need to stock an even broader inventory. The range of uniform styles and colors will be larger. You may need to carry equipment for several different styles of martial arts. If you plan to market to the general public, you may find that your initial investment, and your day-to-day operating expenses will be higher.

You will have to do a good deal more work to check out the competition and market. To be competitive, you must offer a selection of products that is unique, products your potential customers consider desirable. Some store owners find that what draws customers is a unique item they can't get anywhere else in town. Others find that their customers respond to low prices. Others find they bring the most customers in by offering the best quality in town. In short, if your customer base is larger, your sales volume can be larger. But the time you devote to defining your target market, researching it, and tailoring your service to that market will also be greater.

Getting the Word Out

When selecting a target market, take into account how you will advertise your pro shop to your target market. It is not enough just to put the items on the shelf. Even if you are selling only to your students, you will need to post flyers, mention new products in your newsletter, and display your items so they are visible. If you are marketing to a broader market, you will also need expand your advertising. Check the cost of Yellow Pages ads, local newspaper and radio ads, ads in trade magazines, and Web sites on the Internet. (For more information on getting the word out to your target market, see chapter 8 & 9.)

Take Care of the Red Tape

Before you open your pro shop, make sure you have the appropriate government red tape taken care of. Retail sales mean more government paperwork. Know what that paperwork is before you sell your first item.

Retail Licenses and Sales Tax Numbers

You'll need to apply for a state, city, and if necessary, county resale license. These licenses will provide you with a sales tax number(s). Since the application process differs greatly from state to state, you'll need to research specific requirements for your area. One good source of information is the Smart Start series of books from Oasis Press (Central Point, OR).

Federal Income Tax Requirements

While you're researching government requirements, check the federal government tax requirements for retail businesses. You need to be sure you are keeping the records the IRS requires from the beginning, or you may be unpleasantly surprised at tax time. If you have any questions about record keeping or tax requirements, check with your accountant.

Specifically, however, the IRS will want to know how you cost your inventory. You must answer this question when you set up your business in a particular form and its record-keeping system. It isn't something you can decide at the end of the year.

LIFO vs. FIFO

When you (or your accountant) fill out your tax forms at the end of the year, the IRS will ask you if you are using the LIFO or FIFO method of costing your inventory. LIFO stands for "last in, first out." FIFO stands for "first in, first out." They refer to ways of calculating how much your inventory is worth, in other words, how much money you have invested in the goods you offer for sale.

For example, let's say you have one uniform in stock. You paid $20 for it. You reorder and purchase three more uniforms. The manufacturer's price has gone up to $22 for the same kind of uniform. You now have four uniforms in stock—one you paid $20 for, three you paid $22 for. When you sell your next uniform, do you record the cost for that uniform as $20 or $22? If you're using the FIFO method, the cost of that uniform is $20. If you're using the LIFO method, it's $22.

Why? If you are using the FIFO method, you keep track of what each individual uniform cost you (not what each *kind* of uniform cost, what each uniform cost). You cost the first uniform you purchased first, the second uniform second, and so on. In other words, the value of your inventory is the sum of what you actually paid for each individual item.

By contrast, LIFO looks at what a kind of item cost you the last time you purchased it. All of the particular items of that kind are then valued at the same amount. So you multiply the total number of Brand X, size y uniforms you have on hand by the cost of the last Brand X, size *y* uniform you purchased. The result is the value of your Brand *X*, size *y* inventory.

The advantage of the FIFO method is that it is an accurate representation of what you paid for your inventory. The advantage of the LIFO method is that it is much easier to calculate—you don't have to keep track of several costs, just a single cost per kind of item and how many of those items you have on hand.

If yours is a small pro shop, you will most likely use LIFO, unless you or your accountant has a pressing reason to do otherwise. Consider the decision carefully, however, because the IRS has limitations on the number of times you may switch between the options. The following chart summarizes the advantages of the two approaches:

LIFO OR FIFO?

Advantages of FIFO:
 More profitability
 More accurate value of inventory

Advantages of LIFO:
 Lower taxes
 Greater cash flow
 Simplicity

How Much Working Capital Do You Need for Inventory?

The amount of money you need for inventory is determined by: (1) your target market, and (2) the size of inventory you need to meet their needs. If your target market consists only of your students, and if those students need little more than uniforms and sparring equipment, your inventory can be small. If you have agreed to sell to five other schools, each with unique needs, you will need to invest a good deal more in your initial inventory.

On the other hand, at least at first, you will probably need to look at the problem backwards: the amount of money you have to spend may be the biggest factor in determining the size of your shop. If you dream of having the largest martial arts retail shop in town, but you are opening it with a $2,000 loan from your Aunt Roberta, you need to scale back your plans, at least in the beginning. Remember: the money you use to buy inventory is unavailable to you unless you sell your stock and don't reinvest in replacement merchandise. At first, you need to balance investment in inventory with your need to keep cash available for monthly expenses.

> ### RULE OF THUMB FOR INVENTORY
>
> Mandatory inventory:
> 70% basic equipment
>
> Peripheral inventory:
> 15% T-shirts or other logo-wear
> 10% seasonal items or
>   nonessential equipment
> 5% pickup items

Developing a Preliminary Inventory List

To estimate how much money you will need for inventory, put together a preliminary inventory list. Start by listing the items you want to sell. Browse catalogs, visit other shops, ask yourself what you yourself have occasionally needed but have been unable to find.

You need to select your inventory based on what will create business for your shop. Basic equipment, things your students will need for everyday training, should be the majority of your inventory. This basic inventory can include things like uniforms, mandatory safety equipment, and regularly used weapons. T-shirts, sweat pants, gym bags, or

> ### DEVELOPING A PRELIMINARY INVENTORY LIST
>
> 1. List the products you wish to carry.
> 2. Divide the list into blocks—essential, desirable, optional, pure luxury.
> 3. Decide how many of each product to carry.
> 4. Get a wholesale price list and a list of freight costs, and record costs for each item in your list.
> 5. For each product, multiply the wholesale cost by the number of items you wish to carry.
> 6. Add the total costs per product.
> 7. Eliminate nonessential blocks as necessary to make your inventory conform to your budget.

other items with your logo on them give your students a way to show school pride while getting your logo out into public. Seasonal or peripheral items—things like national tournament T-shirts, Christmas gifts, or books—create interest for your pro shop. If you bring in new seasonal items regularly, students will stop by regularly to see what's new. Pick up little things that sell for less than ten or twenty dollars to make it easy for customers to buy on impulse. You will probably want to stock a few key chains, patches, or posters just because they're fun for your customers to buy.

Estimating Costs

Once you have a preliminary inventory list, look at the items one by one and find out what it will cost you to stock that item. For example, consider uniforms. Let's say the first kind of uniform you want to stock comes in eight sizes. How many of each size will you want to stock? Consider how often you will be reordering. If your supplier can get you your order overnight, you may only want to carry a one-week supply. If it takes them a month to get you your order, you will probably want to carry a two-month supply. Let's say you plan to reorder every six weeks. How many new uniforms will you need in that time? How many new students will come in needing uniforms? How many existing students will want to replace their old uniforms? If you don't want to tie up a lot of money in inventory and if you can restock quickly, you can probably get by with two uniforms in each size, "one to show and one to go," plus a few additional uniforms in the most popular sizes.

Remember: This is just a preliminary inventory list. After you've been doing business for a year or two, your inventory may look very different. For now, however, just estimate what kind of inventory you want to carry.

Put together your inventory list in blocks. One block should contain essential items. Another should contain desirable items; still another, items you might want to carry but could easily do without; and a fourth, luxury items. If you are operating on a small budget, you will have most of your inventory devoted to essentials, the basic equipment every student needs. If you have more to spend, you can increase the number of optional items you offer. If you build your preliminary inventory in blocks, you can scale back on the size of your inventory simply by cutting an inessential block of items. The above chart lists the steps needed to develop an inventory list.

Don't just guess at wholesale costs. Get real prices from your supplier—prices for the items and prices for shipping. Multiply the cost per uniform by the number of uniforms you want to stock. Add up the landed costs for that particular product. Then go down the list and repeat the process for each item you wish to buy for your inventory.

Planning and Record Keeping

Without detailed planning and careful record keeping, making money from your pro shop is still possible. Accidents happen. What is not possible without careful records is: (1) knowing just how much money you've made, (2) diagnosing and fixing any problems that might develop in your shop, (3) duplicating your success consistently.

Getting the Right Products from the Right Place

Every industry has several main suppliers from whom retailers buy the bulk of their inventory. The martial arts business is no exception. You probably already have some well-formed opinions on brands of equipment. You may, however, find that a little research can turn up some pleasant surprises. You may find that another manufacturer has solved a problem you've put up with in your "usual" brand for years. Or you may find that another manufacturer has equally good quality for a lower price. Unless you have some sound reasons for staying with a specific supplier, do a little research to see who's out there. Check the trade magazines, ask other retailers, compare notes with other teachers in your local or national organization, look around at tournaments. You may find another supplier can offer you better equipment and a better deal.

Choosing a Supplier

Choosing a supplier is a little like choosing a brand of equipment for your own use. You need to like the "the feel" of the merchandise. It should be worth the price you pay for it. In choosing a main supplier, however, you need to look not just at the equipment but also at the business that sells the equipment. Look at four things in particular:

1. Availability of inventory: Does this supplier have what you need when you need it? Look at what equipment your students use in their training. If you can't get that equipment from the supplier, little else matters.

2. Pricing: Consider wholesale costs, shipping and handling costs, and import costs if the supplier is out of the country, then look at volume discounts. Suppliers often offer discounts based on the size of your order, for example 10 percent off wholesale for a $1,000 purchase, 15 percent off for $1,500, and so on. If you use one main supplier and batch orders, you may qualify for the larger discounts. These discounts will allow you either to offer lower prices to your students or to add to your profits. After you've factored in freight and other costs and deducted the volume discount, ask yourself whether you can sell items purchased from this supplier at an affordable, competitive retail price. If not, you might want to consider another supplier.

3. Customer service: What are this supplier's policies regarding returns? If they send you a defective item will they replace it? Are they prompt in filling orders? Are the orders complete and accurate? Do they keep enough items in stock, or do they have waiting lists for the most popular items? Suppliers will generally post their customer service policies in writing for you to examine. Beyond policy, information on how they really do business may not be so easy to discover. Check with other retail shop owners. Ask them about their experiences with various suppliers.

4. Quality of merchandise: Your reputation is on the line every time you sell a uniform, an article of clothing, a piece of equipment. If the uniform you just sold to a student falls apart the first time he washes it, that reflects on you. If your customers are dissatisfied with the quality of the merchandise you sell, they will take their business elsewhere.

If your merchandise lasts too long, they may be satisfied but not buy anything else from you for years.

On this point, however, you need to find a balance. Find a supplier that carries the quality that serves your students' needs but that is also profitable from a retail point of view. For a retail business to be successful, it needs to turn inventory quickly. In other words, it needs to sell inventory as quickly as possible after it is purchased. If your shop sells only "buy one to last a lifetime" goods, you may find yourself out of business after your customers have purchased their "one." Ideally, you want your products to wear well enough that your customers will be back for another just like it when the first wears out.

How do you know if a supplier's quality meets your needs? You order a sample. Order one of a given item in your size. Try it yourself. If it meets your needs, you may decide to offer it to your customers. After you've been selling an item for a while, you can ask your students' opinions. Let them tell you if a product meets their needs.

Opening an Account

Once you've chosen a supplier, it's time to open an account with them. With most suppliers, opening an account is an easy process. All you need is a business letterhead and a valid state resale license. Write them a letter and tell them you are an instructor with a pro shop in your school. Sometimes a supplier will also ask for references, but usually only if you are getting credit terms from them. Catalogs usually include a telephone number you can call for more information on opening an account.

Maintaining Accounts with More Than One Supplier

How many suppliers should you do business with? More than one. Not only does doing business with multiple suppliers allow you to offer a wider range of merchandise, it also protects you if you can no longer rely on your main supplier. Sometimes a supplier's quality will go down, or their prices will go up. They could be shut down by a strike or go out of business. Having accounts with more than one supplier will mean you can continue to offer merchandise to your customers even if your primary supplier shuts down.

Although you need to have accounts with more than one supplier, you should do most of your business with a single supplier. Doing so allows you to take advantage of volume discounts and specials. It also simplifies your inventory. Imagine keeping track of seven uniforms in any given size, each made by a different manufacturer, each having to be appropriately priced. How do you keep accounts open while doing business with a main supplier? Buy the bulk of your inventory from your main supplier. Then choose a specific kind of inventory, sparring gear only or T-shirts only, and order that inventory from your second supplier.

The Basics of Pricing, Costs, and Profits

Before you order merchandise, you should already know how much you will sell it for and what your profit margin will be. In order for your retail program to be successful, you must offer good-quality merchandise at competitive prices. That's easy to say. To find that "competitive price," however, you need both skill and instinct. Pricing mostly involves paying attention to detail and adjusting your inventory and marketing to increase sales and profitability. Retailing skills are built on some basic, fundamental knowledge and a lot of practice.

A book of this kind can give you some basic principles of retailing. If, however, you want to go beyond carrying a few pieces of equipment for your students' convenience, you will need to educate yourself on some of the finer points. The basics of retailing are simple and can be learned in a very short time. The nuances, the "art" of retail, can take a lifetime to master.

Markup

Markup is the difference between the landed cost of an item (what an item cost you including the cost of the item, shipping, import fees, and any handling costs) and retail price (what you sell it for). It is expressed as a percentage of the retail price. When it is expressed in dollars, it is typically called gross profit. For example, if an item cost you $8 landed cost, and you are selling it for $16 retail, the gross profit on that item is $8, and the markup is 50 percent of the retail cost. The chart on the following page shows calculations for selling price and gross profit.

From your gross profit, you pay operating expenses—wages/salaries, taxes, advertising, rent, utilities. What is left over is your net profit. What is a decent markup? Anywhere from 35 to 50 percent.

How much you mark up a product depends on several factors. Balancing those factors is where you use your skill as a merchant. You need to develop a feel for what price your customers will pay for something. You also need to know what your competition is doing. Who in your immediate area is selling the same or a similar product? What do they charge for it? Your competition is not only other pro shops but also the discount sports stores and, to some degree, catalogs. If you go into head-to-head competition with other shops in your area, that is to say, if you offer the same items they do, your markup is determined in large part by what your competition is charging. If you offer different merchandise—different brands or unique items—your markup is based on what your customers will pay.

One of the other criteria in markup is perceived value, how much your customer thinks an item is worth. For example, let's say you have two uniforms. One is well made of durable material. The other is flimsy and will shrink the first time your customer washes it. It doesn't matter if your landed cost for the two uniforms is the same, you will not be able to charge as much for the second as you do for the first. You have two choices: either you don't carry them both, or you make less profit on the inferior uniform. If you have a limited budget, it's best to carry only the item with the higher perceived value.

Sometimes you might want to mark up items a specific percentage— 35 to 50 percent. Other times, you might want to look at not what percentage you are marking up an item, but rather what your gross profit is in dollars. For example, let's say you have an item that costs $5 landed cost. You mark it up 50 percent for a retail price of $10. Your profit on each item is $5. On the other hand, let's say you have a more expensive item, an item that costs you $150. A 50 percent markup would bring the retail cost of that item to $300, which may be more than the item will sell for. In a case like this, you may want to figure the markup on gross dollars rather than on percentage. If you price the item at $200, you may be able to sell it and make a $50 gross profit. Granted you are making only a 25 percent markup, but on the other hand, you would have to sell ten of the small item to make the same profit you would with one of the large item.

In other words, sometimes retailers figure markup in percentages and sometimes in dollars. Why does that matter to you? Because markup is as much art as it is arithmetic. You could mark everything up a standard percentage and wonder why no one is buying certain items. Or you could take the easy way out and charge manufacturer's suggested

---

CALCULATING SELLING PRICE AND GROSS PROFIT

	Landed cost
Divided by	100 − desired markup percentage
Multiplied by	100
Equals	**Selling Price**

	Selling Price
Minus	Landed cost
Equals	**Gross profit**

example:
      landed costs = $8
      desired markup percentage = 50%

      8 / (100 − 50) = .16
      .16 X 100 = $16 (selling price)
      16 − 8 = $8 (gross profit)

retail price on everything. But to make more money faster, you need to manage your own markup. For higher-priced items, and items you sell a large number of, a lower markup can still be very profitable. A 30 percent markup on an item that sells is better than a 50 percent markup on an item that sits on the shelf. You need to balance making a profit for yourself with making sure your prices are not too high for your market. A rigid percentage approach to markup can result in your not making as much as you could on some items and not selling as many as you could of others.

Brand Names and Blind Items

Walk through any mall, watch any professional or college sport, talk to any teenager, and you will see how much brand-name athletic equipment has permeated modern culture. The American consumer is very brand conscious. You may even be very brand conscious. As a retailer, however, you will find that brand names look very different than they did when you were looking at them as a consumer.

In your pro shop, you will probably want to stock brand-name items. They have the obvious advantage of brand recognition. In other words, the manufacturer advertises their products, and you reap the benefits. A great deal for you, right? Yes and no. Here's where the shift in focus—from consumer to retailer—comes into play. Brand-name items have the disadvantage of being able to be shopped around. Customers will compare your prices with your competition's. If you carry a brand-name item for $30, and the megasports store down the street carries the very same item for $22, not only won't you sell yours, but you can also get the reputation for having high prices. It doesn't matter that the large sports store is probably getting a large volume discount. Your customers don't see things like volume discounts; all they see is the retail price. Your students may pay a dollar or two, maybe even more, for the convenience of shopping at their school. They may tolerate slightly higher prices in the name of school loyalty. But if they have to pay a lot more at your shop, they will take their business elsewhere. Your customers, who are used to noticing brand names, are also used to noticing who has the best deals on brand names.

So what do you do? You use your brand-name items to establish your shop as a place where the customer can get a good deal. You institute price-matching guarantees (more on that later in the chapter). You let your competition dictate your prices on brand-name items. And you make sure you have not only brand-name items but also blind items.

A "blind item" is an item that cannot be shopped around. It is an equal or better value than a similar brand-name item. Anything your customers can't get at your competitor's store and can't get by mail order can be a blind item. Custom-made goods can be blind items. Good-quality generic goods can also be blind items. The selling price can be a little higher than brand names if the perceived quality is a lot higher. But the cost of blind items for you is not necessarily higher. In fact, it is sometimes lower. Sometimes blind items cost you less because the manufacturer spends less money on advertising. You can pass some of that saving on to the customer, while keeping some of it as profit. You've heard the commercials, "Same quality as designer labels but at a lower price." That's an advertisement for a blind item.

In short, blind items benefit a retailer in two ways. First, when pricing blind items, you don't have to compete with other stores. You don't have to set your prices in tune with theirs to keep from looking like you're gouging the consumer. That means you can charge a higher markup and keep a higher percentage of the selling price. Second, the perceived value of blind items should be higher. Customers should believe they are getting a good deal. So your shop gets the reputation for being a place that carries good-quality merchandise at reasonable prices.

Ideally, you will have a balance of blind items and brand name items. The only way to tell just what that balance looks like in your shop is to experiment and see what your customers want—what they will perceive as a good value and what they will ignore.

Turnover

A crucial piece of information you'll need to manage your pro shop effectively is the turnover rate for your inventory. Your turnover rate, the speed at which you turn (or sell and replace) your inventory, is a ratio that shows how often you sell your entire supply of a specific product in a year. The following charts illustrate how to calculate your turnover rate and return on investment.

Why is it important to know your turnover rate? Knowing your turnover rate helps you get maximum profit from your investment. Let's say you sell sixty pairs of gloves per year. On average, that's five pairs of gloves per month. If you carry an average inventory of ten pairs, you are carrying a two-month supply. If you can reorder gloves from your supplier in ten days, you may need to carry only a month's supply, five pairs instead of ten. You sell just as many. You're making the same profit. But you're tying up less money in inventory. You've increased the rate of return on your investment, while freeing up money that can be used to pay bills, expand your shop, or buy new equipment for your school.

In other words, if you can increase your turnover rate on an item, you increase your return-on-investment ratio. The money you invest in your pro shop works harder for you. How do you increase your turnover rate? By either increasing sales or decreasing the average size of your inventory.

You should be using your turnover rate as a guide to set the minimum quantities of each item you carry regularly in your shop. If you can abide by a strict policy of ordering to a minimum stock and reordering as soon as necessary, you can control how many dollars you tie up in your pro shop and increase your profitability on each item.

Does that mean you should always keep just one or two of every item, reordering every time you sell an item? Not necessarily. You do need to have enough depth to your inventory to meet customer demand. There is an old saying, "You can't sell from an empty wagon." You should also try to take advantage of your suppliers' volume discounts whenever possible. How do you balance these seemingly contradictory demands? By keeping careful records. Careful long-term sales records can help you get a very good picture of what customer demand is for any given item. Armed with that information, you can then group and time your orders to take advantage of volume discounts. To increase the profitability of your shop, you need to develop

TURNOVER VS. RETURN ON INVESTMENT

A turnover rate comparison for bag gloves:

Landed cost: $20

Selling price: $33
Gross profit per pair: $13

Number sold per year:
60 pair
Gross profit per year: $780

If you keep an average inventory of 20:
Turnover rate is 60 ÷ 20 = 3:1.
Investment is 20 x $20 (landed cost) = $400.
$780 (gross profit) ÷ $400 (investment) = $1.95
You make $1.95 annually for every dollar you've invested.

If you keep an average inventory of 5:
Turnover rate is 60 ÷ 5 = 12:1.
Investment is 5 x $20 (landed cost) = $100.
$780 (gross profit) ÷ $100 (investment) = $7.80
You make $7.80 annually for every dollar you've invested.

**A HIGHER TURNOVER RATE MEANS
A GREATER RETURN ON YOUR INVESTMENT.**

a feel for the quantity and timing of orders based on turnover rates and long-term sales records.

Your turnover rate can also alert you to problems in your inventory. Check the turnover rate for your shop as a whole. A good turnover rate is around 5:1. If yours is lower than that, or lower than it was last month or last year, you probably have one of two problems. Either you have too much inventory on hand or, more likely, you have items that aren't selling, items that need to be marked down to sell immediately. Also check your turnover rate for specific items. Doing so helps you adjust your minimum quantities for an item. A low turnover rate tells you when you need to mark down an item to get it moving so you can convert it to cash. It also can give you an idea of which items are good investments for you and which aren't.

Get into the habit of aggressively turning your inventory. An item that sits on a shelf ties up working capital you could be using for something else. Owning a shop full of items that aren't selling is like having

```
┌─────────────────────────────────────────────────┐
│            CALCULATING TURNOVER RATE              │
│                     Annual sales of an item       │
│      Divided by     Average inventory             │
│      Equals         Rate of turnover              │
│                                                   │
│      example:                                     │
│      You sell 60 pairs of bag gloves each year.   │
│      You maintain an average inventory of 10 pairs.│
│      Your rate of turnover is 60 / 10, or 6:1.    │
└─────────────────────────────────────────────────┘
```

a fortune in a locked box for which you have no key. Your landlord, the electric company, and the bank don't care if you have the best-stocked pro shop in the western hemisphere. They care if your check clears when it comes time to pay them. If you turn your inventory quickly, you are more likely to have the profit in your hands, not tied up on your shelves, when you need it.

Furthermore, if an item sits on a shelf for too long, it gathers dust, literally and figuratively. Sometimes styles change. Sometimes your customers change—what last year's customers loved, this year's wouldn't use on a bet. Your inventory needs to be fresh, needs to address the needs of the customers who walk through your doors today.

You should turn seasonal and peripheral items especially fast. By turning your peripheral inventory quickly, you create excitement in your shop. You give customers a reason to come through your doors regularly to see what's new.

Overhead

Is your retail shop profitable? To answer that question you must look at much more than whether you are selling your merchandise for more than you paid for it. The real cost of your merchandise is not just the cost on the invoice.

How much is your retail space costing you to rent, light, heat, and maintain? What is it costing you to take credit cards? How much is your retail staff costing you? What is your own labor worth? These expenses are called overhead. If your retail space is going to be profitable, you must make enough money to pay not only for replacement merchandise but also these overhead costs.

CALCULATING PRO SHOP OVERHEAD	
	Square feet devoted to your pro shop
Divided by	Total square feet in your school
Equals	Percentage of school devoted to pro shop
	Percentage of school devoted to pro shop
Multiplied by	Total fixed expenses for your school
Equals	Overhead costs for your pro shop space
	Employees wages
Multiplied by	Percentage of employee's time devoted to retail
Equals	Employee wages for retail work
	Overhead costs for your pro shop space
Plus	Employee wages for retail work
Plus	Credit card charges
Plus	Cost of advertising your retail business
Plus	Other costs of doing retail business
Equals	Your pro shop overhead

How much is your overhead costing you? A simple way of figuring that out is to calculate overhead as a percentage of your total school expenses. Figure out how much your entire space costs you to rent and maintain. Include not just rent and electric but triple net, insurance, taxes, all fixed expenses. Then figure out what percentage of your space your pro shop occupies. Multiply your total overhead costs by that percentage. To that total, add any other costs of doing business associated only with your shop: credit card fees, additional accounting fees, employee wages or commissions and taxes, any costs you wouldn't be paying if you didn't have the shop. The total is your cost of pro shop overhead. The chart above illustrates how to calculate your pro shop overhead.

If your markup doesn't cover overhead, you're not making a profit. If you don't make a profit, you're just trading dollars with your students. Another way of looking at it is this: After you've paid your overhead bills, how much money are you making? If you put the cost of your inventory in a savings account instead of in inventory, how much would you make in interest? If your investment is making you less profit than you would get from a savings account, you need to reevaluate your pro shop. Perhaps you need to alter your pricing policy. Or perhaps you need to look at your pro shop's place in your school's overall profit picture.

Tracking Inventory

Keeping accurate records is an important part of increasing the profitability of your shop. There are several ways to keep track of your inventory. Whichever way you choose, you need to keep track of two things: the items themselves and the dollars they represent. More specifically, you need to know (1) what items you have purchased, what you have sold, and what remains in your inventory; (2) when it is time to reorder an item and how many you need to reorder; (3) how much profit you have made on any given sale and on all your sales for a particular period; (4) what your inventory is worth; and (5) what sales taxes are due, to whom, and when. More detailed records can tell you which of your items are the best sellers, whether you have seasonal trends in your retail business, and which items just don't sell.

In short, an effective retail operation is built on accurate records and the ability to analyze and act on them. A computer is a valuable tool for both keeping records and generating reports that make analysis much easier. However, a computer is only as useful as the data entered into it. Whether or not you choose to use a computer, you need to understand the basic principles of managing inventory, so you can generate retail profits consistently, not just by accident.

A Nonautomated Inventory System

You can keep a basic nonautomated inventory system in a box of index cards on your desk. Create a card for each item in your inventory (each size, if an item has multiple sizes). On each card write the brand, stock number, landed cost, retail cost, and minimum quantity. When you take in new merchandise, you add the number of items you've received to the appropriate cards. When you sell an item, you subtract that item from the total on the card.

Your inventory cards are a record of exactly what you have in inventory at any given time. If you want to know whether you need to reorder elbow protectors, you don't need to go count how many you have on your shelf then try to guess whether that will be enough for the next month. You should be able to go to your card, find out how many you have, look at how many you have sold, and make the correct decision easily.

Recording Sales

At the time of sale you need to be focused on customer service, not on your paperwork. Nonetheless, when you sell an item, you need to record what item has been sold, how much it sold for, and how much sales tax was paid. Your form for recording this information needs to be quick and simple but detailed enough to allow you to transfer the information you need into your financial journal and inventory records later.

With a little modification, you can use the same custom receipts you use when you take in tuition payments. (See chapter 11 for more information.) Or you can purchase standard NCR receipts. On each receipt will be the basic information about the product—the item, brand, size, and selling price. If your state or city requires you to collect sales tax, you should have a space for that as well. Think about what you will need for your financial records and for your inventory records, then make sure that information gets recorded every time you make a sale.

Later when business is slow, or after hours, you can copy the information into the appropriate records. The financial information is transferred to your daily journal. The inventory information is transferred to your inventory cards. Keeping your cards up to date ensures that any time you need information about reordering, profits, or how quickly you are turning your inventory, you can go through your cards and compile a summary.

Another way of handling these inventory records is to computerize them. You enter information at the time of sale. The computer prints out a receipt and automatically records the information in the appropriate database. The advantage of investing in a computer system is that it will generate retail summary sheets and statistics on command. A computer can save you hours of recopying and calculating. Whether you want a computer system for your retail business, however, is a matter of money and how well you get along with computers.

Getting an Overview of Your Inventory

On a regular schedule, every second Tuesday of the month, for example, make time to look at your inventory. Assess what is selling well and what isn't. Look at what you need to reorder. If you are managing your inventory with the aid of a computer, you can track this information electronically. If you aren't automated, you will need to pull information from your index cards and record the totals on a sheet like this:

Monthly Inventory as of (date)								
Item	Size	Landed Cost	Selling Price (retail)	Beginning Inventory	Minimum Inventory	Received This Month	Sold This Month	Ending Balance
Uniforms	3							
	4							
	5							
	6							
T-shirts	S							
	M							
	L							
	XL							

Landed cost is what the item cost you—the supplier's price plus freight, duty, import fees, and so on. The selling price is just that, the retail price you normally sell the item for. The beginning inventory is how many of the item you had last time you filled out this work sheet. The minimum inventory is the minimum number of any given item you want to keep in stock. See the section on turning your inventory to learn how to calculate this number. Received is the number of items you took in. Typically, this number is the number of each item you received from your supplier. If, however, you have had returns, they are also factored into this number. Sold refers to the number of items you've sold since your last count. Ending balance is the number of items you have in stock. Ending balance is calculated as your beginning inventory plus inventory you've received minus inventory you've sold.

List all the items in your inventory in the first column. You can keep track of all of a particular product (for example, uniforms) together. Or you can break the category into size, style, or type. If you have a different landed cost or selling price for different sizes or styles of the same category or item, or if you're using the FIFO method of costing your inventory, give those sizes or styles their own lines. If you reorder different sizes or styles at different rates, give each their own line. Also, if you want to see if one size or style is selling better than another, make sure you have appropriate breakdowns. Once you've filled in each row with an item from your inventory, go down the rows and fill in each column for every item. Take the information you need from your inventory cards.

From this work sheet, you can also tell how much money you have invested in your shop and how much you are making from it. You can also learn how well your inventory is selling.

Which items are selling well and which are not selling at all? You can tell this information at a glance by scanning down the sold column. If an item is selling poorly, you can then look over at the landed cost column and the selling price column to see how much you can mark the item down to get it moving.

From the work sheet you can also determine how much money you have invested in inventory. Multiply the landed cost for an item by the number of those items you have in stock (your "ending balance"), as shown in the formula below:

MONEY INVESTED IN INVENTORY	
	Landed cost
Multiplied by	Ending balance
Equals	Money invested in inventory
Used for:	keeping your inventory the desired size; tax calculation

Do for each item in your stock (in other words, for each row in the work sheet). Then, add the results to get the total amount your current inventory is worth. You will need this number to fill out your tax forms for the IRS.

Your "money invested in inventory" figure is also crucial for calculating your "open-to-buy" figure. Open to buy refers to the amount of money you have available to reinvest in inventory. For example, if you calculate that you have $4,500 invested in inventory, and you want your total inventory to stay under $5,000, you have an open to buy of $500. The next time you order merchandise, you want the value of that order to be $500 or less. Knowing your open-to-buy figure when you place orders helps you from tying up in inventory money that you will need for something else.

Beyond looking at your open to buy for your inventory as a whole, it's also wise to look at it for individual categories of items. So, for example, let's say you sell $400 (landed cost) of uniforms and $100 of T-shirts. You know you will need to replace those uniforms and T-shirts to meet future demand. If you take that $500 open to buy and sink it into a couple of heavy bags, you won't have the financial resources to replace the uniforms and T-shirts you sold. In other words, if you are satisfied that your current inventory has the diversity to meets the demands of your customers, your open to buy for any given item will be the total landed costs for the number of that item you have sold since your last order. The following chart illustrates the open to buy calculation:

OPEN TO BUY	
	Desired maximum value of inventory
Minus	Money currently invested in inventory
Equals	Open to buy
———————— or ————————	
	Landed costs
Multiplied by	Items sold
Equals	Open to buy
Used for: deciding how much money you have to spend on your next order.	

To calculate how much profit you've made on any given item, multiply your landed cost by the number of items sold. Then subtract the result from the selling price multiplied by the number of items sold, as shown below:

PROFIT FOR AN ITEM	
	Selling price (items sold)
Minus	Landed cost x items sold
Equals	Profit from an item

Used for: deciding whether to continue to carry a particular item

To calculate your gross profits for the shop, for each item multiply your landed cost by the number of items sold. Subtract the total from your gross receipts. Gross receipts, a dollar amount from your financial records, should be the same figure as number sold multiplied by selling price. If it is not the same, you have experienced shrinkage; or, to put it more plainly, someone has stolen merchandise from you. The chart below illustrates the formula for calculating gross profit:

GROSS PROFIT FOR THE SHOP	
	Gross receipts
Minus	Number sold x landed cost
Equals	Gross profit

Used for: seeing how many dollars are available for overhead and profit; when transferred to your profit and loss statement, it becomes part of your overall profit calculation

Taking Inventory

Every quarter, count your inventory. You must take inventory at the end of the year for tax purposes. You should do it quarterly to verify what you have in stock. Go through everything and make sure your actual physical inventory matches your computer or on-paper inventory. If you are taking inventory yourself and you're confident of your ability to make an accurate count, you can simply go through your inventory, count the physical items, and compare them with the quantities on your inventory work sheet. If you want a more objective count, or if you are having an employee do the count, use a blind inventory method. In other words, make up a work sheet with the items listed in the first column, but without any quantities. Do the manual count for the entire work sheet. Then compare the results with your records.

Taking inventory is your chance to see if anything has been misplaced, stolen, or lost in the shuffle of items and records. You definitely want to know this information at tax time. If an item has been stolen, you will want to take it as a loss rather than as a part of your inventory. But you should take inventory quarterly to help you see any problems in shoplifting or inadequate record keeping before they get too far out of hand.

Theft is a serious problem, especially for a small pro shop. When someone steals something from you, you lose not only the profit you would have made from that item but also the profit from other sales until you have recouped the cost of the stolen item. Even a small item can cost you a lot. If you have a problem with shrinkage, take inventory monthly. Knowing what is missing can help you detect who's taking it so you can solve the problem.

Each time you inventory, do a thorough dusting. Move things around to make the display look fresh and interesting. Put your hands on each item and get a qualitative, not just quantitative, feel for what you have in your store.

Creating an Effective Display

Even if you have devoted a small area of your school to your shop, proper display is essential to keep your sales level high.

To decide how to lay out your pro shop, your best bet is to see how the experts have done a similar space. Visit sporting goods stores. Check out country club, golf course, and hotel pro shops. Make notes. Draw sketches. Take pictures. Use the ideas that appeal to you and tailor them to accent your merchandise.

Getting Fixtures

Where do you get display cases, racks, hangers, the things you need to set up your retail space? You could, of course, buy them new. Or you could save a great deal of money buying them at fixture sales.

A fixture sale is a retail store's final sale. When a store is going out of business, it first sells all its inventory and then sells its fixtures— clothes racks, display cases, security cameras, cash registers, and other fixtures. Watch your local newspaper for going-out-of-business sales. Go in during the regular retail sale and talk to the manager. Ask when the fixture sale is, and let them know you are interested in certain fixtures if the price is right.

Another way of finding inexpensive fixtures is to watch for things that are being discarded. Check behind grocery stores and other retail stores in your neighborhood. Often distributors will send special display furniture to retail outlets to promote their product. Once the product has gone out of vogue, the retailer has little use for the display. You, however, can make good use of these castoffs. A little paint or a little sanding can turn a throwaway into a very serviceable piece of equipment. If you see a rack discarded behind a store and you wish to use it, always check with the store manager before you take it. In some states it is illegal to take certain containers, for example milk crates, that are being thrown away. And you don't want a manager to come into your shop and find a rack they left behind their store for someone else to pick up. Check before you bring in your truck.

If you're looking for desks or counters, look for banks or other professional businesses that are doing remodeling. Often you can buy their old furniture at greatly reduced cost. Check, too, with carpet dealers. Sometimes they will have carpet remnants at reduced cost. Even if the pieces are too small for your floor, you may be able to use them to line shelves. Laminating companies also may have castoffs you can use. Sometimes they will have countertops or cabinets that were the wrong size or color for a job. If the color fits with your shop's image, you may be able to purchase a counter at a greatly reduced price.

With a little creativity, you can work a lot of second hand equipment into your shop. Of course, you will want to monitor quality. You may need to do some fix-up. You may need to invest in some paint. But if you choose a bright color scheme for your shop, a little spray paint and some creativity can turn castoffs into a professional-looking shop.

Laying Out a Shop

What you are looking for is a bright, active look. Many martial arts schools have bland color schemes—black, white, and maybe a little red. You might want to consider silver, bright primary colors (red, yellow, and blue), maybe even fluorescent or neon colors.

Be sure you also have room for people. Walk between the displays yourself. Get a few friends to join you in your shop. Do you still have elbow room?

Make sure prices are clearly marked on every item. Make sure everything is openly displayed. Make sure your customers can get to the merchandise they need without digging through huge piles.

Look at your shop as it relates to your marketing identity. Does it contribute to your image? Does it appeal to your target market? If your shop is dirty and cluttered, that image will reflect negatively on your school. If it is clean, well lit, and easy to shop in, it will reflect positively on your school as a whole.

Once you have a layout, don't assume your work is done forever. Change your display occasionally, or people will learn to ignore your shop. You might want to keep the uniforms and basic equipment in one unchanging place but change the featured items monthly. Do you need to sell a slower item? Use your display to highlight it. Do you use signs on the windows to feature specific merchandise or to advertise sales? Change those signs often enough to make sure they do their job. Signs that remain in place for too long are often mistaken for wallpaper.

And please dust. Often. Would you buy new merchandise that looks like something out of an archeological dig? Enough said.

Day-to-Day Management

When you first set up your pro shop, set up a routine as well. Set aside a specific time each month to look over the inventory and make reordering decisions. Add the advertising to your overall advertising schedule. Do your bookkeeping on a set schedule. Running a pro shop requires time and effort. If you expend that time and effort efficiently, you can maximize your profits with minimal effort.

Ordering

When it comes time to order merchandise, you shouldn't find any surprises. Ordering inventory for your pro shop is quite similar to placing personal catalog orders.

Before you start selecting items from the catalog, however, check your open to buy. See how much money you have to spend on this order and for what items.

Most companies will take orders by phone or mail. Some will also accept fax and e-mail orders. Whichever way you choose, be sure to keep a record of your order on file, so you can check it against the merchandise when it arrives.

As for payment, most companies ship C.O.D. If you prefer not having to drop everything to write a check when the shipment arrives, talk to your supplier about establishing a billing account. Or you might prefer to pay by credit card. If you pay using your personal credit card, however, be sure to keep good records. You want to make sure reimbursement doesn't get confused with salary or loans.

Receiving

When you get new stock in, make a careful record of it. Compare your copy of the order to the packing slip, and note any discrepancies. Then count the items that have come in. Make sure everything on the packing slip is in the boxes. Then, price the merchandise for sale, stock the shelves, and record the new items in your inventory records.

Advertising

It is not enough to put your merchandise on the shelves and wait for business to come through your doors. When was the last time you purchased something from a store you knew nothing about? If you have something to sell, you need to let your target market know. The ideas discussed in chapter 9 can bring in not only new students for your classes but also new customers for your shop. The basic principles of advertising work for both the service and retail sides of your business.

A few advertising techniques, however, have been proven to work particularly well for retail. These techniques integrate pricing policy with advertising.

Loss Leaders

Loss leaders are products you advertise at an attractively low price to bring business into your store. Whether because your landed cost on them is low or because your markup is low, or both, you offer these items at a low price.

For example, let's say you offer two kinds of uniforms, a good quality one and a lesser quality one. You might use the lesser quality one as your advertised loss leader. Customers come in because of your advertised low price on the lesser-quality item, but decide they are willing to pay extra for the better quality one next to it. Or they come in, buy the low-cost item, but then decide they need another piece of equipment you have displayed. Loss leaders have one central goal: to bring people through your door.

To take maximum advantage of your loss leaders, look at how you are displaying your inventory. What do you especially want to sell? What do you especially need to sell? Put those items in an eye-catching display next to your advertised loss leaders.

Note, however, loss leaders are not bait and switch. Bait and switch is the practice of advertising something you don't have or don't plan to sell at the advertised price, only to offer something you do have at a higher price once the customer comes through your door. Bait and switch tactics are unethical. They are also illegal. Loss leaders, on the other hand, are a savvy pricing strategy that can help you generate business. The difference between the two is that for an item to be a loss leader, you must have the item in stock and you must be willing to sell it at the advertised price.

For a loss leader to work, you must not only offer the items at a lower-than-normal price, you must also advertise them at that price.

Put an advertisement in front of your target market. Make the sale a limited-time offer. Decide before you place the advertisement whether your offer will be good only for the items you have in stock or whether you will give rain checks. Consider the effect on your reputation if you advertise widely, bring in lots of people wanting to take advantage of your "great deal," but then you run out of the item an hour into the sale. For a loss leader to generate satisfied customers, you must do your advertising and inventory homework. Have enough of the item on hand to satisfy demand. If you want to limit the quantity any one person can buy, or if you want to limit the time you are making the offer, make sure to state that in your ad.

Pickup Items

Pickup items are another strategy for generating an atmosphere where buying is easy. Pickup items are little things that sell for less than ten dollars. They can include key chains, patches and stickers, small toys, posters, and other small items. Typically these small items should make up about 5 percent of your inventory. Pickup items are easy to buy on impulse because of their low price, and maybe your customer, while buying the pickup item, will see a larger item they want to purchase. Pickup items help your customers get into the habit of shopping with you.

Special Sales

Some school owners periodically offer special sales, where they sell, at a reduced price, the equipment they have used in class. These sales allow students who are unable to afford new merchandise to purchase their own home training equipment. At the same time they allow you to refresh the training equipment in your school periodically. You make a profit on equipment that otherwise would have been only an expense. And if you put the used equipment on sale periodically and advertise each time you do, you can use these sales to bring in business for other items in your shop.

For this sales strategy to work, however, you need to make sure the used equipment you sell is still in good condition. You need to sell it at enough of a reduction to make it an attractive offer for the customer. And you need to make sure the customer knows the equipment is used and that you are selling it "as is" without any guarantee.

Whether or not this sales strategy works for you depends on whether the equipment you use in class is likely to be useful in a home training situation. It also depends on whether your students are likely to purchase it. Does using it in class make them want one for their home use? Or do they figure they can use it at school and don't need to bother to purchase one for home? Only you can make that judgment about your students and customers.

Sales and Customer Service

Sales is a matter of connecting the right person with the right product. Listen to your customers. Find out what they need. Then meet that need if you can. At its heart, sales is customer service.

When you think about customer service, consider how many of your customers will also be your students. Your sales will only grow if you gain a reputation for being fair and for having a good customer service policy.

Returns

Have a return policy. Why? Consider it from the customer's point of view. Let's say you buy a shirt at a retail store. You bring it home, wash it, and it falls apart before you even have a chance to wear it. You bring it back to the store and ask for your money back. The store manager declines curtly. Would you shop there again? Now imagine that the customer is your student, and you are the store manager. Now imagine looking that student in the eye next time she takes one of your classes—if she does indeed come back to class.

Take returns. If you find you get a lot of returns of a particular item, then you need to change your supplier for that item to meet the needs of your customers.

Special Catalog Orders

Besides the inventory you choose to keep in your pro shop, you can also elect to special order merchandise for your customers. In your pro shop, keep a selection of catalogs from the companies with whom you have an account. If someone wants something from one of the catalogs, you can take half the money up front and half when the merchandise comes in. Or, if the item is something extremely unusual, you might want to ask for the total price before you order it. Tell the customer that the next time you place an order with that manufacturer, you will include his item in the order. Give the customer an estimate of when you expect to receive the item. Then of course, try to order it as quickly as possible.

Why would you want to do special catalog orders? First, it allows you to offer merchandise without having to keep it in stock. You don't have to tie up money in inventory. And you don't have to find floor space for bulky or unusual items you may not sell for months or even years. If, however, you special order an item for a customer, you can batch it with a regular order, get your volume discount, and make a little money. On top of that, you can save your customers the hassle of having to place the order themselves. The customers don't have to pay freight. They don't have to be home when it's delivered. They don't have to send it back to the company if it doesn't fit right. And they can support their local school.

Price-Matching Guarantees

Here's the situation: You have a brand-name pair of bag gloves for sale. Your price is the manufacturer's suggested retail price, $60. The discount sports store down the street has the same gloves for sale at $45. You have a choice. Do you want to stick to your original price and risk not selling the gloves, or do you want to go down to $45? If you have a policy that you will always come down to your competitor's prices, that's a price-matching guarantee.

Here's how a price-matching guarantee works: If a customer comes to you with a competitor's regular price or advertised sale price, you agree to match that price. You might want to take their word for it, or, if you don't know the person, you may offer to hold the item for them at the discounted price while you give your competitor a call.

You need to decide if you want that guarantee to be up-front or retroactive. If it's up-front, all the customer needs to do is bring in an ad, and you will match the price on the exact item. If the guarantee is retroactive, a customer who purchased equipment from you in the last month or two months (or more—your choice) comes to you with their receipt and an ad for the identical piece of equipment at a lower price. You refund the difference. Or you refund the difference plus 10 percent, again your choice. Unless the price is a competitor's short-term sale price, you should change your price on that item across the board.

Why would you want to have a price-matching guarantee? Beyond the simple fact that it will help you sell more merchandise, it also is a way to have your customers scout your competition for you. But more than that, it's a part of the personal business you have chosen to run. Yours is unlike a furniture store, where your customer may be in every ten years to buy a new sofa. Your customers will be in regularly for equipment. If you're selling to your students, they will also be in two to five times a week for training. By pricing your products competitively, you are building loyalty not just for your retail business but for your school.

Layaway Programs

Another program you may also wish to institute is a layaway program. Customers can pick out an item, and you will hold it for them until they can pay it off. If you have such a program, you will need to establish a payment schedule: how much the customers will pay and when. Get it in writing. Then keep a computer record or a card in your accounts receivable file that records their payments. Make sure both you and they know when they will be able to pick up the item— when it is half paid, three-quarters paid, fully paid.

Be aware that a layaway program is different from financing. In a layaway program you are not charging more than the cost of the merchandise; you are only spreading out the payments. The minute you start charging interest or finance charges, you are under the jurisdiction of the truth in lending laws, and you must comply with government regulations.

Markdowns

Markdowns are sometimes necessary if you overbuy, if you aren't selling an item quickly enough, or if you have too much money tied up in inventory. Shopworn merchandise can sometimes be sold at a reduced price. Markdowns can also help you sell seasonal merchandise—the tournament T-shirts you can't get rid of at $20 might sell at $10. In short, marking down items is a way to turn your inventory at a satisfactory pace.

A rule of thumb: Staple items, items you know you can sell steadily if not quickly, should remain at full retail price. But seasonal items must move quickly, or they may not move at all. If an item isn't selling, reduce the price. Sell it and spend the money buying something that will sell.

Keep a specific area in your pro shop for markdowns and sale items. Use them to bring customers in regularly looking for "great deals."

Reordering

Timing your reordering is a matter of balancing the desire to keep a minimum stock on the shelves and the desire to take advantage of your supplier's volume discounts.

Your inventory work sheet is your main tool for deciding when to reorder. When your ending balance (that is, the number of items in your current inventory) dips below your minimum inventory number, it's time to reorder. (See the section on turning your inventory to learn how to calculate your minimum inventory.) Subtract your ending balance from your minimum inventory to see the minimum number you need to order, as shown in the formula below:

MINIMUM ORDER	
	Ending balance
Minus	Minimum inventory
Equals	Minimum order

You will probably not want to order fewer than your minimum order number, but you may want to order more. You may wish to order more to take advantage of your supplier's volume discounts. You may order more of an item because of seasonal variations in demand. You may also wish to batch orders to save on freight. But don't get carried away in your desire to get the best volume discount. Always check your open to buy before placing an order. If you aren't careful about keeping within your inventory budget, you may find yourself with $2,000 worth of chest protectors when what you need is rent money.

Starting Small and Building

If you're starting a pro shop on a tight budget but have dreams of building one of the largest shops in town, how do you go about it? You need to build your inventory in blocks—essential, desirable, optional, pure luxury. Your initial inventory should consist of the essential items. You then plow all your profits back into the store for a fixed period—six months, nine months, a year. Reinvest them next into the "desirable" block of items, then the "optional." Gradually build through the list.

Remember though, a successful pro shop is not necessarily a large one. A successful pro shop is one that makes money by meeting its customers' needs. Even if you believe the bumper sticker "the one who

---

BASIC DAY-TO-DAY OPERATION OF A PRO SHOP

1. Ordering: Get your merchandise from the supplier.
2. Pricing: Decide on your retail price.
3. Receiving: Take items in, count them, put prices on them, and record them.
4. Display: Set merchandise out in an attractive and compelling way.
5. Advertising: Let your customers know what you have to offer.
6. Sales: Help the customer buy products they will be happy with.
7. Record keeping: Track both items and dollars.
8. Inventory: Keep track of what you have on your shelves.
9. Reordering: Know when, what, and how many to order to maximize both profits and customer service.

OPERATING A SUCCESSFUL MARTIAL ARTS SCHOOL

dies with the most toys wins," that philosophy is not the best one for building a retail shop. A small shop that turns its small inventory quickly is more successful than a shop with a huge inventory that sits for months. Keep records of what sells and what doesn't—know the turnover rate for every item in your shop. Turn your inventory aggressively. Based on your turnover rate and the volume discounts your supplier offers, determine what your minimum inventory is for each given item. Don't tie up capital in unnecessarily large quantities of items. Keep a minimum inventory and invest the money you have left over in new items.

Set goals: How much money are you willing to have in inventory? What return do you want on that investment? Set a specific point when you begin to send your profit to your own bottom line rather than reinvesting it in the shop.

Buying is not just an essential activity, it is also an emotional activity. When customers purchase an item, they are not just meeting a need, they are expressing their tastes and individualism. A good retailer, therefore, gets in touch with the pulse of the customer. As a retailer, you need to make it easy for your customers to buy. Make it easy for them to pick up something and purchase it. You need to know what's most important to your clientele—quality, price, image. In retail, as in any other art, practiced skills form the foundation for instinct and intuition.

CHAPTER FIFTEEN:
TROUBLESHOOT PROBLEMS

The first symptom you may notice is that your salary is shrinking. After you've paid the bills, you have very little to pay yourself. Or you find that paying the bills is becoming ever more difficult. Or you may have just received your second notice from the electric company and the checkbook is empty. Your business has problems.

Here's the reality: Students drop out. Others get behind on their payments. Growth rates can far too easily sink into negative numbers. Your books can slide into the red. As a business owner, if you don't catch problems early, you can lose your business.

To keep your attendance and income stable you need to do three things regularly: (1) check your goals, (2) compile and review relevant statistics, and (3) pinpoint and solve problems as they occur.

Step One: Check Your Goals

Go back to your financial goals. These goals give you a yardstick to judge whether you're beginning to have a problem. What is your main financial goal? Is it to make enough money to keep up with the operating expenses of your school? Is it to make more money than you did at your last job? Is it to take in more money than any other school owner in town? Do you have a well-thought-through goal? If you don't, set one. Then determine how much money you have to deposit in the bank each month, each week, each day to make that goal a reality. How many paying students do you need? How much merchandise will you have to sell? If you don't have a goal, you will have no idea whether your growth rate is acceptable.

Your goals are not only the yardstick by which you measure your business; they also give you an incentive to keep building your business. Let's say you need fifty students to meet your financial goal. You decide you want to have those fifty students by the end of the year. Keep that goal in front of you. Break it down into daily and weekly amounts. Keep records to see whether you are making progress. Keep a running tally on your desk blotter. Or put up a bulletin board in a private area and keep records of how many new students you have signed up this month, this week. You will find that watching yourself inch up on your goal, inching up on your financial security, is a great motivator.

Step Two: Compile and Review Relevant Statistics

If you don't keep statistics, you have to rely on your instincts to tell you when you're meeting your goals and when you have a problem. Although those instincts may serve you well in your martial art, chances are good they will be too little warning too late if your business is in trouble.

What Growth Rate Do You Need?

If you haven't already, calculate what your break-even point is. Then calculate your target enrollment, the number of students necessary to make your school what you want it to be. (The information on these calculations is in chapter 2.) Subtract the number of students you have now from your target enrollment. Decide when you want to be at target

```
┌─────────────────────────────────────────────────────────┐
│            CALCULATING YOUR DESIRED GROWTH RATE           │
│                                                           │
│  Number of students needed:        200                    │
│  Less number of current students:  − 100                  │
│                                                           │
│                                    100 students           │
│  Divided by the time frame:        ÷   10 months          │
│  Desired growth rate:              10 students/month      │
│                                                           │
└─────────────────────────────────────────────────────────┘
```

enrollment. Then divide the remainder by the number of months in that time frame. The resulting number is your desired growth rate.

In other words, in the above example, you must increase your school's total enrollment by ten students every month to reach target enrollment in ten months. The desired growth rate is ten students per month.

Calculate Your Enrollment Goal

Your desired growth rate is not, however, the number of students you need to sign up each month. To figure out this number, your enrollment goal, you must also factor in your drop-out rate.

Look at your drop-out statistics for the last year. If you don't have statistics for the last year, make estimates. (And you'll have to set up a system for recording drop-out rates to help you monitor your school's health in the future.) How may students have you lost in the last year? ("Lost" in this context means students who are no longer paying their monthly tuition.) Take that number and divide by twelve (months).

CALCULATING YOUR ENROLLMENT GOAL	
Your desired growth rate	10/month
Plus your drop-out rate:	+15/month
Enrollment goal:	25/month

Let's say you typically lose about fifteen students per month. These fifteen represent your drop-out rate. Whether this rate is acceptable depends on your goals. Add your drop-out rate to your desired growth rate. The number you get is your enrollment goal, the number of new students you must sign up each month.

Can you meet that goal? Can you sign up that many students? If not, you have two choices: curb your drop-out rate, or settle for a slower growth rate.

Minimum Required Statistics

In order to monitor the health of your school, you must know who's coming in, who's leaving, who's paying, and who's not. You must know whether you are gaining or losing ground toward your goals.

MINIMUM REQUIRED STATISTICS

Target Enrollment Statistics:
- Estimated monthly operating expenses
- Average monthly per-student income
- Break even
  - In dollars
  - In number of students
- Number of current students
- Desired growth rate

Drop-Out Statistics:
- Attendance for each class
- Drop-out rate
  - Broken down by month
  - Broken down by student level
  - Short-term drop-outs (haven't attended for two weeks, or are temporarily doing another sport)
  - Long-term drop-outs (haven't paid for two months or have moved away)

Drop-In Statistics:
- Number of prospective students who call
- Number of prospective students who come through your door

Closing Statistics:
- Number of new students signed up
- Percentage of callers who signed up
- Percentage of walk-in visitors signed up

Payment Problems/Cash Flow:
- Record of student payments (who paid, how many students paid, how much money you took in)

Other:
- Day-by-day record: what you did in classes
- Record of tournaments, testing, seminars, and when they were held, how many participated, how many paid
- Record of any changes you made to the schedule or routine; when you made them

The only way to know these things is to keep records. You ought to be looking at your records at least twice a month. In the middle of each month, scan your statistics. See if you have any large problems you need to address immediately. At the end of each month, dig in and chart the statistics. Pinpoint problems that need to be fixed. Analyze your records as though your life depended on it. In fact, your business life does. At left is a sample summary of the minimum statistics you need.

Each of these statistics tells you something vital about the health of your business. They will help you troubleshoot any problems you may have.

Step Three: Pinpoint and Solve Problems

You've been keeping detailed sign-up and drop-out records. You know your numbers aren't what they need to be, but you aren't sure why. Chances are good you have at least one of five problems: (1) a

```
┌─────────────────────────────────────────────────────┐
│  R        DROP-OUT PROBLEMS                          │
│   X                                                 │
│           The symptoms: You sign up lots of new     │
│           students but still aren't making your     │
│           enrollment goal.                          │
│           The diagnosis: Too many students are      │
│           dropping out.                             │
│           The treatment: Look for drop-out          │
│           patterns. Learn when and why students     │
│           drop out. Adjust your program to keep     │
│           students training.                        │
└─────────────────────────────────────────────────────┘
```

drop-out/attendance problem, (2) a drop-in problem, (3) a problem with closing, (4) a payment problem, or (5) an income-per-student problem.

Drop-Out and Attendance Problems

Let's say you've calculated your break-even point and determined your drop-out rate. From these statistics you've calculated your enrollment goal. For the last several months you've been trying to meet that goal, but you're having problems. You're signing up students, but you're still having trouble meeting your goal because of your high drop-out rate. You realize that unless you don't hold on to your current students, you're unlikely to realize your goals.

When Do They Leave?

Is there a pattern to when students leave? Keep notes on what you do in classes and look at them side by side with your drop-out statistics. When do students drop out? When you're preparing people for tests? When you've just finished a test? When you're doing a lot of strength-building exercises or calisthenics? When you're in the middle of competition season? When you're in the off-season? Do you have specific activities that seem to cause a mass exodus? Can you do without these activities? Can you do something to make them less burdensome? Compare the problem activities to your marketing identity. Are people leaving because they're not getting what they signed up for? Is your day-to-day school the school you advertise, the school you present to potential students? Does your walk match your talk?

Keep records also about when in the training program students leave. Do most of the drop-outs never make it past their first three months? Do you lose them when they get to the intermediate or advanced ranks? Do you lose many of your students just after they get their black belt? Is there a particular hurdle that few students seem able to jump?

One karate school owner, for example, noticed many of his women students dropped out just before or just after getting their brown belt. He intended his school be a place for young, single adults to meet. He advertised to young singles, tailored his classes to them. Losing three-quarters of his women at brown belt was, therefore, unacceptable. He began to look at the brown belt tests. He and his assistant instructors conducted them separately and differently from the previous colored belt test. As he watched his assistant instructors, all men, running candidates through their paces, what he saw was a male-bonding ritual. There were occasional raucous jokes, displays of upper-body strength, and heavy competition—things that weren't essential to the testing, but that had become something of a tradition. Many of the men were having a great time. Many of the women looked miserable. He changed the tests and over time stabilized the problem.

If you find that you lose your largest numbers of students during a particular time of training, look at chapter 13. It can give you hints on how to hang on to your beginning, intermediate, and advanced students.

Seasonal Fluctuations

If you analyze your drop-out statistics over two or three years, you'll probably notice seasonal fluctuations in your attendance and income. Martial arts schools, like most small businesses, have natural cycles. Some months regularly bring in larger numbers of students. Others always seem to have small classes and low income. Sometimes you will be able to detect easily what causes your fluctuations. If you live in an icy climate, chances are you will be bringing in fewer students during those months when the roads are bad. If your studio is across the street from a college campus where many of your students study, don't be surprised if summers are a bit slow. One karate instructor always looked forward to times when the local TV station ran *The Karate Kid* because it always brought in new business. All kinds of factors can affect your enrollment.

Seasonal fluctuations are inevitable. Even if you don't know what causes them, if you know when they occur, you can anticipate and plan for them. Let's say summers have always been slow for you. In the spring, or even in the late winter, begin to plan to fill the empty spaces on your training floor. More to the point, you will need to fill the empty spaces in your bank account. At the very least you need to save enough money during the "up" times, so you'll have money to pay operating expenses and yourself during the "down" times.

Better yet, instead of using seasonal fluctuations as an excuse, use them as an opportunity to try something new. Consider a day camp for children who are out of school. Offer special programs for college students who are home for the summer. Hold special tournaments or seminars. Or maybe take some time during down times to plan for the up times. Put together your advertising plan. Try some new drills. Make contact with students you haven't seen for a long while. Or maybe just use down times as a vacation for you. Ideally, you don't want down times to get you down. You want to come through them recharged and ready to build again.

"Hidden" Problems

If you're sure you have a drop-out problem, and if looking for a seasonal explanation has turned up nothing, you may need to dig a little deeper. People drop out for a reason. If your drop outs' reasons have something to do with you, your teaching, or your schedule, you need to know that. How do you get that information?

One way is to check in with your "intelligence" sources. Your office manager is often a valuable source of information. His is the friendly face your students see every day. Chances are good your students tell him things. Without asking him to betray confidences, ask him to report to you if he hears of any dissatisfaction. He should be your early warning system of any "rumblings in the ranks." Senior students can also be a help. They sometimes hear things instructors are insulated from. Parents of some of your longstanding students can also be helpful. Often in sitting and watching classes with other parents, they feel the "pulse" of those parents in a way you can't. Listen to your people. Ask them to come to you if they sense any dissatisfaction.

Make sure when they do that you accept their information graciously. Reassure them you do want to hear even the negative and upsetting things. Assure them you will preserve their anonymity if that's what they want. Then, behave as though you want to hear what they have to say. Listen. Thank them for their comments. Think about what they've said, and act on it if you need to. If you have a tendency to "kill the messenger," you will always be the last to hear bad news.

Another possibility is to get opinions from a fellow teacher or from a mentor. Have her come in, watch you in action, and give you an honest response. Ask for specific feedback as well as general impressions. If you suspect you have problems in a particular area, ask her to watch that area. If you're not sure where your problems may be, ask that person to evaluate your overall strengths and weaknesses.

If you want this kind of formal evaluation, ask it from a peer or a mentor, not from a student, even a senior student. Your student may avoid giving you bad news for fear of being disloyal to you. Or the student may not see your blind spots any more than you do, especially if he has been studying with you for a long time. Even if you trust a student to give you an insightful, honest opinion, you should never put a student in the place of having to sit in judgement of his teacher's teaching. Occasional observations are fine. A formal, serious evaluation could put too much stress on the relationship. Find an outside advisor who can be objective and honest, one whom you respect.

If you want student opinions, consider putting up a suggestion box. Put up a locked box where students can drop anonymous suggestions and complaints. Not only does this give students the chance to say things they wouldn't say directly to you for fear of hurting your feelings, but it also gives you a chance to read, think, hit a heavy bag in private. It gives you a chance to analyze and digest the information before facing your students. It gives you a chance to plan positive action.

If you need information on something specific, consider circulating a survey. A survey can help you gain information on your students' (and parents') opinion of your classes, your policies, your image, your schedule, whatever you need information on. Think carefully about what you need to know. It is less than courteous to ask your students to fill out a long survey when you aren't sure how you plan to use the resulting information.

An alternative to surveys is interviews. Have someone you trust, someone your students trust, conduct them personally. If you want information on a specific area, make sure to tell your interviewer that. But ask the interviewer to get general impressions, as well. Sometimes problems can show up in completely unexpected locations.

When the results of the interviews come back, you will, of course, have to practice a bit of detachment. It's perhaps harder to hear bad news face to face than it is to hear it from an impersonal survey. But if you're serious about staying in business, you must be willing to face the truth. If your interviewer brings back bad news, don't take your anger or hurt out on her. Insist on brutal honesty. Then listen. Resist the knee jerk reaction to justify yourself. Thank the interviewer.

Once the interviewer has gone, ponder what she has said. Again, resist the temptation to justify the way you've always done things, even to yourself. The purpose of the information in front of you is not personal validation. The purpose is to pinpoint specific things you are doing right and specific things you need to fix. Having the painful opportunity to solve a specific problem is better than watching your business sink without knowing why you're going down.

If you seriously listen to your students, your employees, and your advisor, you may find you have some unexpected strengths and gaps in your abilities. Running a small business requires such a wide range of skills that it would be very surprising if you didn't have both strong spots and weak spots. You might find that you are a good business person but only a fair teacher. Or you might find you're great with senior students but not so good with beginners. Or your adults love your classes, but the children are afraid of you. Can you change? Can you find people, classes, organizations, books, seminars to help you shore up your weak areas? If not, can you delegate? To be a successful small business owner, you must be a creative problem solver. Think of your students' needs. Can you find a creative way to meet them?

DROP-IN PROBLEMS

The symptoms: You don't have much of a drop-out problem, but you still aren't able to make your enrollment goals.

The diagnosis: You have a drop-in problem.

The treatment:
1. If no one is calling or dropping by, boost your advertising.
2. If people are calling but not dropping by, work on your phone skills.
3. If they are coming by but not signing up, work on your sign-up and closing skills

Drop-In Problems

Maybe a drop-out problem is not your main difficulty. Maybe you're hanging on to most of your current students. Yet you still aren't meeting your enrollment goal. One possible reason is a "drop-in" problem.

How many new people have come through your doors in the last month to ask about beginning to study with you? Let's say you need twenty-five new students each month to meet your enrollment goal. If only five prospective students are coming through your doors each month, you have a drop-in problem.

How many people have called asking about classes? If you signed up every caller, would you meet your goals? Or are very few people even calling? If people are neither calling nor coming through your doors, maybe your potential students don't know you're in business. You need to get your name and image before your target market. You need to increase the effectiveness of your advertising program. (chapters 7 through 9 provided details on how to do so.)

How many callers stop by to check out your school? If you have plenty of initial callers but very few come by for a visit, you may need to brush up your phone skills. (Check chapter 10 for more information.)

Maybe the problem is your location. How is the walk-by traffic past your space? Reread chapter 4 to assess whether your location is working for you or against you. Granted you can't do much about a bad location in the short term. But if you have drop-in problems, location may be something you will want to look at next time your lease is up. In the meantime, you may need to improve your advertising so you can survive long enough to move to a better location.

A martial arts school cannot survive without a steady influx of new students. If you don't have new people walking through your door every week, analyze your numbers to find out why. Then set specific goals to help you solve the problem.

Closing Problems

Let's say you have thirty-five prospective students come through your doors each month. Of those thirty-five, only four sign up—not nearly enough to make your enrollment goal. If that's so, you have closing problems.

Go back to chapter 10. Have you educated yourself and your staff on closing techniques? Are you showing visitors around your school? Does the look of your school match your desired image? Do you present your image and your main benefits in a clear, concise, persuasive way? Do you know how to ask a person to join your school as a student? Spend some time practicing with your staff.

As part of your introductory sales offer, do you offer a free trial lesson or a trial week (or month) of classes at a reduced rate? If you do,

---

CLOSING PROBLEMS

The symptoms: You have plenty of people coming by to check out your school, but very few of them sign up.

The diagnosis: You have closing problems.

The treatment:
1. Work on your sales and closing skills.
2. If students sign up but don't last any more than a class or two, look at whether your introductory and beginning classes are consistent with the marketing image you present to prospective students. Check too whether your program is tailored to your target market.

---

look at the number of students taking the trial lesson versus the number who sign up for regular classes. Are you losing students during the trial period? Even if you don't offer trial lessons, look at your new students. What percentage of your new students last more than a month? If more than 25 percent of your students drop out in a month or less, look carefully at your beginning classes and introductory lessons. Do they fit with your marketing identity? Are they lessons that appeal to your target market? Are they fun? Do they give the student a chance to learn something useful? If your free introductory lessons are chasing off students, they aren't "free" for you; they're costing you a lot of money.

PAYMENT PROBLEMS

The symptoms: Your projections and financial records are in order. You've been making your enrollment goals. But you still don't have enough money to pay the bills.

The diagnosis: You have a problem collecting student payments.
The treatment: 1. Make sure you have good enough records to tell when a student is even a few days behind on payment.
2. Remind students when it's time to pay their bill.
3. Mail written bills with a specific due date.
4. Hire a billing company.

Payment Problems

According to your records, you should have enough students to meet your financial goals. But somehow you never seem to have the money to pay the bills.

First check to make sure you haven't underestimated either the amount or the timing of your expenses. Go back to your cash flow and accounts receivable work sheets (chapter 11). Look at your actual expenses over the last few months. Revise your projections if you need to. If your expenses are higher than you projected, you need to adjust your "students needed to break even" number.

If your projections and estimates are good, check your bookkeeping. Have you accounted for all your expenditures? Some people record "all" the money going out—all of it except maybe petty cash, and the little stuff like office and cleaning supplies, and of course the heavy bag they were going to record but forgot. If your bookkeeping isn't completely accurate, don't be surprised if you think you have money but don't.

Let's say you've checked your projections and estimates. They're accurate. So are your financial records. You're meeting enrollment goals. But you still can't pay the bills. Then your problem is with payment. In other words, you need to look at your accounts receivable and check on how many students are behind on tuition. Make sure everyone is paying their bill. Check to see if their additional payments—for equipment, seminars, and tournaments—are up to date. Check how many scholarships or freebies you are giving.

If your problem is a payment problem, a couple of simple principles will help you solve it. First, you need to have a systematic method of tracking student payments. If a student is a week behind, would you know? You should. Helping a student who is a week behind catch up is easier than helping a student who is two months behind. You must deal with payment problems early before they become unmanageable for the student. Good school management software can be your most valuable help in tracking student payments. If, however, you aren't running a computer-automated business, check chapter 11 for the basics of a manual system for tracking

---

How to Speed Up Your Collections

1. Send invoices immediately.
2. Charge late fees.
3. Give discounts for early payment.
4. Take credit cards.
5. Encourage automatic credit card payment.
6. Encourage electronic funds transfer.
7. Don't be timid about asking students to pay their bills.

---

student payment. Whatever system you use, record student payments promptly, then check your accounts receivable at least twice a month.

As discussed in chapter 11, some students will drop by the business office like clockwork to pay their monthly tuition. Others will need a reminder when they drop by for class but will pay regularly if reminded. For still others, you may need to institute other ways of making payment. Consider beginning a direct deposit or automatic credit card payment program. See if a student wants to pay by mail. If so, mail them a bill with a specific due date. For some people a debt doesn't seem "real" unless a notice comes through the mail. If you have students like that, you need to make your tuition bill as "real" as their phone bill, their electric bill, their credit card bills. (For more information on billing, see chapter 11.)

If collecting money each month becomes too much of a problem, or if it's a job you hate, you might want to hire a billing company. Trade magazines often contain ads for companies who specialize in handling the billing for martial arts schools. These companies bill your students based on the information you send them. They collect tuition, pursue past due accounts, and sometimes provide you with additional training to help you make your business more successful. If you're considering hiring a billing company, shop around. See which have a selection of services that can meet your needs.

Before you hire a billing company, however, make sure you know what they charge. Learn if they charge a flat fee per student or a percentage of what they take in for you. Factor their fee into your break-even estimates to see how it will affect your profitability. Then ask them for a copy of their student contact letters to make sure you approve of their content and tone. The billing company will be representing you, so you need to make sure they treat your students in a way that is consistent with your image.

Per-Student Income Problems

Another scenario: let's say your business seems healthy. You're meeting your enrollment goals. You have plenty of students in each class. Your school may even be a bit crowded. Your students pay their tuition on time. You should have enough money to meet your financial goals, right? But when you look at your books, the money just isn't

PER-STUDENT INCOME PROBLEMS

The symptoms: You're meeting your enrollment goals. Your students are paying their tuition on time. But you are still not making enough money to meet your obligations.

The diagnosis: Your per-student income is too low.

The treatment: 1. Advertise your current seminars, tournaments, pro shop to bring in more business.
2. Find additional sources of income: seminars, a retail area, programs for schools, businesses, and so on.
3. Raise your tuition (after careful planning).

there. If these are the symptoms, the most likely diagnosis is that your per-student income is too low.

Look again at your per-student income projections. (See chapter 2 for more information.) Are students spending as much as you expected on retail purchases? If your retail income is steady, are you taking in the income you expected from seminars and tournaments? If you aren't, maybe you aren't offering a good value for your customer's money. Or maybe you need to do more advertising. (Look at chapters 7, 8, and 9 for ideas on how to advertise a tournament or seminar.)

Raising Tuition

If, however, your additional income isn't the problem, or if you don't think you can raise it any further, that leaves two alternatives. Either you have to lower your expenses, or you have to raise your tuition.

How do you raise tuition rates? Unless you are in a major financial bind, you don't—at least you don't for your existing students. Every time you raise your rates, you will lose some students. If you change their payments, students who have been paying their bills faithfully for months will reexamine whether what you offer is worth the money. Some who may have been a little restless for other reasons may use the tuition increase as their opportunity to leave.

If you must raise tuition, taking a few precautions can help you do so in a way that causes the minimum damage to your existing student base:

(1) The least disruptive way to raise rates is to raise them for new students only (those who haven't yet signed up with you at the time of the increase). Keep existing students' rates the same. Granted, this approach doesn't get you the extra money you need immediately, but it does keep the drop-out rate among your current students to a minimum. If you raise tuition for everyone, the resulting drop-out problem could leave you taking in less than you did before the increase.

(2) If you do need to raise tuition rates for everyone, try to raise them less for existing students than for new students. For example, you may raise tuition five dollars a month for existing students, ten for new students.

(3) Give students something new in exchange for tuition increases —an extra class, a new and better kind of instruction, some thing they see as a new benefit.

(4) If you announce a raise in tuition, make sure you are giving the best classes of your life. Create an atmosphere where your students couldn't imagine leaving.

(5) When students ask why you are increasing rates, tell them honestly. Most people understand things like the rent being raised or the electricity bill going up. Granted, some may still choose to leave. After all, they have bills to pay, too, and those bills sometimes mean they have to do without luxuries, like your program. Other students, however, may be willing, or even happy, to make sure their school stays open despite an increase in bills—yours and theirs.

If you tell them you're raising rates to keep up with school expenses, don't show up to school the next day in a brand-new sports car. Most students don't begrudge their teacher a fair wage. But if they think you see them as nothing more than just a source of income, they will resent it. If they think their tuition payment is more important to you than they are, they will leave.

Holding Pattern?

Maybe you aren't ready to raise tuition. Maybe a higher tuition isn't consistent with your image. Maybe a raise in tuition would price you out of your target market. Then it may be time to ask yourself a crucial question: Are you content with your school as it is? If your primary motivation in wanting the extra income is to meet a goal, maybe you need to reevaluate that goal.

Let's say you've been holding steady at 110 students for the last three years. You're paying the bills, making a little money yourself. You have a good advertising program, good sign-up skills. You are bringing in students, but students seem to leave just as fast. You've asked peers and mentors, people you trust, to look at your classes, and they see no problems. You're in a holding pattern. Why? Maybe you've reached the limits of your school, the limits of the actual physical space. When you reach beyond those 110 students, people start feeling cramped, start having to wait too long for their turn with the equipment. They're physically uncomfortable, so they start dropping out.

The obvious solution then is your getting a larger space, right? Not necessarily. Expanding may not be the ideal solution it seems. A larger facility means more overhead. You could be teaching more students, putting more time into your school, and still be bringing home less money. Before you expand, you need to calculate how many students you will need to meet your financial goals in the new facility. Will you need help to teach that many students? What will that help cost you? You could find yourself with twice as many students and the same problems you have now. If you don't plan your resources carefully, you could hit the maximum capacity of your new space before you start clearing the money you make now. A larger school does not necessarily mean more money. It does, however, mean more financial responsibility.

Another question you have to address is the limits of your own comfort. Maybe it's comfortable for you to keep up with the training schedule and personal quirks of 100 students. But maybe when you push beyond that, you find yourself training strangers, a situation you don't like. Do you want to be the manager of a large school with a multiperson staff? Or do you want to be closely involved in the lives and training of a small number of students? What makes you happy? Consider the answer carefully before you go looking for a larger space. Growth is not necessarily the best thing to happen to either a martial arts school or a martial arts instructor.

Let's say you like your small school. Does that mean you are going to have to revise your financial goals? Maybe. Maybe not.

If you're happy where you are, there's no reason to change. Of course, you still have to pay close attention to your statistics and bring in enough new students to cover the loss of old students through natural attrition. If you don't, you'll find you're no longer in a holding pattern but in a nosedive.

As for your financial goals, don't forget that tuition from your regular students doesn't have to be your only source of income. Have you considered doing camps, seminars, private lessons? Have you considered renting out your space to another teacher during the times you aren't running classes? Have you considered starting a program in your local school? How about a fitness program for a local business? Look around—you may find that several paths lead to your financial goals.

How do you decide if your school is a healthy one or a troubled one? It is a process involving hardheaded realism. Sit down with the books. Are you paying the bills? Are you paying yourself a salary you can live with? If you can't pay the bills or are having to keep a second job you hate, you have a problem. Gather your statistics and analyze them as though your business life depended on it. The nature of the problem lies within the numbers. The solution to the problem lies within your creativity as a teacher, martial artist, and business owner. Remember the dreams you had when you opened your school, then dare to dream a few new ones. Go through your goals and break them down into specific tasks. Decide when you want to do these tasks. Put each task into your calendar. Then get to work. Start building your future today

Terms used elsewhere in the glossary are italicized.

1099 report—A report submitted to the Internal Revenue Service (IRS). It reports payments made to someone other than a regular employee for work done. It is submitted in January for the previous tax year.

accounts payable—The money your business owes to others, your short-term business debts to others.

accounts receivable—The money other people owe your business.

accrual accounting—A way of keeping financial records. It accounts for revenue when it is earned, not necessarily when it is received. Similarly, it accounts for expenses when they are incurred, not necessarily when they are paid. It contrasts with *cash accounting*.

accumulated depreciation—The sum of all of the *depreciation* from all of your items.

accumulated earnings—The monies left in the business as working capital; the profits that remain in the business, that are not distributed to the owners or spent on other things.

acid test ratio—The acid test ratio consists of liquid assets divided by current liabilities. It measures how much money your business has immediately available. A ratio of 2:1 is considered good.

active listening—Listening intently to what is being said, restating what you have heard and understood, asking for confirmation, and then using that information to ask another question. The purpose of active listening during the sign-up process is to give you the information you need to match a specific feature-benefit to what a prospective student needs/wants/desires.

actual cash value—An insurance term. It is a calculation of how much your personal property is worth. Replacement cost minus *depreciation* equals actual cash value.

ADA (Americans with Disabilities Act)—An act passed by the United States Congress in 1994 to provide accommodations and access to people with various disabilities. The Department of Justice, Civil Rights Division, offers guidelines to help businesses comply with the mandatory provisions of the act. Small businesses are required to provide "reasonable" accommodation.

addendum—An addition to a lease or other contract. It is a legal document by which the parties making the contract agree to modify or add to the terms of the contract.

amortization—Spreading the repayment of a loan over time, repaying the loan in several equal monthly payments that include principal and interest.

annual report—A compilation of a company's financial documents from a particular year. It contains a *profit and loss statement, balance sheet,* and *cash flow statement* for the year. It also includes financial comparisons for several years. Any changes in operating procedure, financing and debt changes, or marketing that had a significant financial impact (either positive or negative) can also be included in an annual report.

appreciate—An accounting term meaning to increase in value over a period of time.

arbitration—A method of resolving disputes that does not involve the court system. The two disputing parties agree to abide by the decision of a third party, who hears both sides of the argument and decides.

assets—Anything owned by the business that could be sold for cash. See also *fixed assets, current assets, tangible assets,* and *intangible assets.*

assignment—Transfer of any property, real or personal. Leases and contracts can be assigned provided assignment is allowed by the contract.

audit trail—Written records of all of a business's monetary transactions, that is, of all the money coming into and going out of a business. It is the "paper trail" a CPA needs to do an audit.

balance sheet—A statement showing the financial status of a business. It reports the total *assets, liabilities,* and *equity* of the business. In short, it is a statement of what you owe and what you own at a given point in time.

balloon payment loan—A loan that contains a final payment that is much larger than the preceding monthly payments. Part of the loan amount is amortized over monthly payments. At the end of the loan period, the remainder of the loan must be paid in full with one large payment.

barter—An exchange in which only goods and services are traded; no money changes hands in the transaction.

benefits—How *features* tap into the basic needs and motivations of your students. Benefits are the specific things a student/customer believes your school can do for them.

blind item—A product whose value cannot be exactly compared to a similar brand name item. It offers a seemingly equal or better value, and so allows the retailer to make a bigger profit on the item. Custom-made items or good-quality generic items can be blind items.

bodily injury liability insurance—If a physical injury happens to someone you are responsible for, bodily injury liability insurance protects you against losses as the result of lawsuits or other judgments.

bookkeeper—Someone who enters data into the financial records.

bottom line—The last line on your *profit and loss statement*. It is the money left after all your expenses and costs have been paid. If the bottom line is a positive number, it is also called net income, earnings, or *profit*. If the bottom line is a negative number, it is called a deficit or loss.

break-even point—The volume of business needed to pay all your expenses. Any money taken in beyond the break even point is *profit*.

broker—See *insurance broker*.

business interruption insurance—If you are no longer able to conduct business due to fire, theft, or vandalism, this insurance will compensate you for lost revenue. It will pay key employees, including yourself, and also pay rent and major fixed expenses for a limited time.

business license—A permit issued by a state or local government agency that allows a business to operate legally within the boundaries of the issuing agency.

business personal property insurance—See *personal property insurance*.

business plan—A report that includes a business's mission statement; financial, marketing, and operating plans and projections; key personnel resumes; and strategies for the future. It is the foundation for both loan applications and for strategic planning.

CAM (common area maintenance)—Expenses incurred in maintaining the areas that merchants in a complex share, for example, parking lots, signs, landscaping, and so on.

capital—The money the owners of a business have invested in that business. The term can also be used as another word for "money" or "cash."

capitalization—The long-term financing of a business.

card deck—A pack of postcards from various businesses. The pack is distributed together, but the cards are mailed back to the individual businesses, requesting a product or information.

cash accounting—A way of keeping financial records that accounts for revenue when it is received, not when it is earned. Similarly, expenses are accounted for when they are paid, not when they are incurred. Also called "cash method," it contrasts with *accrual accounting.*

cash budget—A system for planning and controlling projected cash flowing into and out of your business. It includes beginning cash, cash receipts, cash payments, and ending cash as well as total expenses paid out over a specific period.

cash flow statement/projection—Cash flow focuses on when money comes into your business and when it goes out. In its simplest form, a cash flow statement is a record of when during the month/year you bring in income and when you pay bills. A cash flow projection is your best guess, based on past information, of when you will be getting money in, and when you need to pay it out.

certificate of occupancy—A statement issued by the city or county government that states a building is up to code and may be occupied for business.

certified financial statements—Financial statements, such as *balance sheets, profit and loss statements,* and *depreciation* schedules that have been prepared by a *certified public accountant.* To produce a certified financial statement, a CPA audits your books and traces the path of every dollar that comes in and out of the business. Although for bank purposes it is considered the most accurate financial statement, it is also the most expensive.

certified public accountant (CPA)—An accountant who has the training and licensing to audit the books of a business and produce a certified financial record. CPAs can also prepare unaudited financial statements from figures provided by the business and give financial planning advice.

Chapter-S corporation—See *S corporation.*

closing—The process by which you take a prospective customer from interest to a completed transaction.

collateral—*Assets* pledged by a borrower to secure a loan.

commencement date—The date a contract takes effect.

common area—Places, structures, and equipment that the tenants and customers of a building share. They can include parking lots, elevators, stairs, sidewalks, courtyards, and corridors leading to tenant spaces.

common stock—A term used by C-type and S-type corporations. Common stock is the way the owners (shareholders) of the company maintain ownership and how their percentage of ownership is determined versus that of fellow shareholders. Usually the maximum number and value of stock shares are specified at the time of incorporation. Common stockholders have voting rights and elect the board of directors.

cooperative advertising—Underwriting of all or part of an advertisement by a sponsor. It is also sometimes used as another term for *cooperative mailing*.

cooperative mailing—Advertising in which several businesses package and distribute advertisements together. Examples of cooperative mailing includes *card decks*, stuffers, and inserts.

corporation—A legal business entity that exists separately from its owners. It is formed when the appropriate papers are filed with the IRS and the state in which the company does business. The owners of a corporation are known as stockholders. Those who guide its course are called a board of directors. Personal assets of the stockholders are not subject to debts and claims against the business. Corporations can take several different legal forms including C corporation, *S corporation*, and others.

cosigner for a loan—Two or more people who sign the same loan document and are equally responsible for the payments and other responsibilities of that loan. The loan is approved based on the combined strength of the individuals' financial statements.

cost—What you pay for an item. Contrasts with *price*, which is what you sell the item for.

cost of goods sold—The amount of money you, the retailer, spend for the products you sell. It includes wholesale cost, shipping and handling costs, duty on imported items, and in some cases the sales commission paid. To calculate cost of goods sold, take the manufacturer's cost, subtract any volume discounts given you by the manufacturer, then add any service charges, freight, or other costs. It is also called "cost of sales." In some cases it is the same as *landed cost*.

cost of living clause—A clause in a lease or contract that ties the cost of rent or other expenses to the state of the economy. Cost of living clauses tie rent increases at the end of year to a cost of living index, such as the consumer price index for a specific large city, state, or nation.

CPA—See *certified public accountant*.

credit line—See *line of credit*.

creditor—A person or institution who has lent money to you or your business or who otherwise has a claim on your business's assets.

crime insurance—Insurance coverage that reimburses you for losses resulting from employee dishonesty.

current assets—Cash on hand and items that a company intends to sell during the normal course of business. They are things that could be sold or redeemed for cash within a one-year period. *Accounts receivable*, short-term certificates of deposit, short-term loans you have made to someone else, and inventory are all current assets.

current liability—Any loan or debt that must be paid in a year or less.

current portion of loans—The payments on a loan that are due within a year. The current portion of a loan is a *current liability*. The remainder of the loan is a *long-term liability*.

current ratio—*Current assets* divided by *current liabilities* equals current ratio. Current ratio tells you (or a bank or investor) what proportion of your total assets you could convert to cash within a short period of time.

In other words, it is a measure of how liquid you are. Current ratio is one ratio the bank will use to assess the health of your business. A ratio of 2:1 is considered good.

day book—See *journal.*

deductible—The amount of any insured loss that you must pay. The balance is paid by the insurance company. Usually the insured must pay the deductible before the insurance company pays for the rest of the loss.

default—Failure to fulfill any obligation or requirement in a lease or contract. The term is used, for example, to refer to a situation in which a debtor has failed to make prescribed payments on a loan in a timely matter. It is also used to refer to a situation in which either party in a lease has failed to comply with any of the conditions listed in the contract.

delay in commencement—A clause in a lease contract that says that if the landlord cannot give you the space within a specified period of time, you can cancel the contract.

demographics—Social and economic information about people living in a specific area. It often includes information on age, gender, education, income, and so on. Demographic information is important in choosing a location for your business and in planning effective advertising.

depreciation—The gradual reduction in value of tangible fixed assets. As an object gets older and natural wear and tear reduces its value, the object is said to depreciate. Depreciation is listed on a balance sheet because it represents a recapture expense. For tax purposes, depreciation is calculated on a specific schedule over a specific time period, usually according to the IRS's estimate of the life of the product (usually five or seven years). The methods for calculating depreciation are the *straight-line* and the accelerated methods. See also *accumulated depreciation.*

direct marketing—Advertising, promoting, or selling to people whose name, address, and perhaps lifestyle or buying habits are known to you.

discretionary expense—Things you spend money on that are neither required (fixed) nor based on volume (variable). Optional training equipment or decorations are discretionary expenses.

disposable income—The amount of money a consumer has to spend on inessential items. The money left over after the rent/mortgage, food, transportation, and utilities are paid.

double-entry bookkeeping—A system of bookkeeping that enters each transaction twice, once as a credit and once as a debit. Its advantage over single-entry bookkeeping is an increase in accuracy and a better audit trail.

draw—See *owner's draw*.

EIN—See *employer identification number*.

employer identification number (EIN)—A mandatory, thirteen-digit number assigned to a business by the Internal Revenue Service. In many ways, it functions like the business's social security number.

equity—The net worth of a business. It is calculated by subtracting all the business's liabilities from all its assets. The term can also refer to the owner's or investor's share of what a business is worth.

evergreen loan—See *revolving line of credit*.

expense—A business cost. See *fixed expenses, discretionary expenses,* and *variable expenses*.

face value—The amount of money that a debtor must pay as stated in a loan contract.

features—The objective resources you have to offer a student. Features include equipment, physical space, resources, staff members available to teach or help with customer service, and your own training and skills.

FICA (Federal Insurance Contribution Act)—Social Security and Medicare taxes that are withheld from an employee's paycheck and matched by the business. FICA is remitted to the Internal Revenue System on a scheduled basis.

FIFO (first in—first out)—A way of costing your inventory for tax purposes. See also *LIFO*.

financial statements—A collection of statements including a *profit and loss statement*, a *cash flow statement*, and a *balance sheet*. Together they give a picture of the health of a business.

fixed assets—The material things you own but don't plan to sell to a customer. Office and training equipment are fixed assets.

fixed expenses—The monthly costs of doing business that do not fluctuate with an increase or decrease in business. For example, rent is a fixed expense, as are utilities. Fixed expenses are also called "fixed cost." They contrast with *discretionary* and *variable expenses*.

FUTA (Federal Unemployment Tax Act)—A percentage of payroll paid annually to the federal government to provide for unemployment insurance.

general partnership—A partnership in which all partners participate in the day-to-day operation of the business. Any of the partners can act as an agent of the partnership to conduct business. Profits and losses are treated as personal income, and all partners are personally responsible for any debts and claims against the business.

gross income—Income from all sources before adjustments and deductions. The IRS requires businesses and individuals to report gross income on their tax returns.

gross profit—Gross receipts minus the *cost of goods sold*. It is your profit before subtracting *overhead* costs and taxes. See also *gross volume*.

gross volume—The total amount of money you take in from a retail operation before subtracting the cost of merchandise and other expenses. See also *gross profit*.

guarantee—See *personal guarantee.*

guarantor—A person who promises to pay someone else's debt if that person can't or won't fulfill the contractual obligation to do so. In most business loans, the owner of the business is required to guaranty the loan personally. Business loans can, however, be guaranteed by someone other than the owner.

guaranty of a lease—Sometimes spelled "guarantee." The guarantor agrees to pay the amount of the lease out of personal funds if the lessor is unable to make the payments. Some lease guarantees require a lump-sum payment instead of monthly payments if the lease goes into default.

HVAC (heating, ventilation, air conditioning)—A general term designating the central heating/cooling system of a building.

image—What people see (or what you want people to see) when they look at you or your school. It is the reflection of the choices you make for your business, the way your business looks and feels, and reflects your values and ideals.

income statement—See *profit and loss statement.*

independent insurance agent—See *insurance broker.*

insurance broker—Also called an independent insurance agent. An insurance broker is someone who is licensed to sell insurance. A broker legally represents the client and may sell insurance from many insurance companies. An insurance agent, by contrast, is sometimes (though not always) a representative of a single insurance company.

intangible assets—Assets that aren't either current assets or fixed assets. They are things that can't be seen or touched. Intangible assets include patents, copyrights, trademarks, and the "goodwill" of the name of your business.

interest—Payment to a lender for borrowed money. Interest is typically calculated as a percentage of the balance due. It is an expense on your P&L, in contrast to *principal*, payment of which decreases liability.

inventory—The products a business keeps on hand to sell.

inventory turnover—The rate at which you sell your inventory and replace it with other inventory. Annual sales of an item divided by average inventory of that item equals the rate of turnover.

inventory valuation—Costing your inventory. See *LIFO* and *FIFO*.

invoice—An itemized description of merchandise sent or services rendered. It also shows the recipient and the cost.

IRS (Internal Revenue Service)—The branch of the United States Treasury Department that is responsible for administering federal tax law.

journal—A chronological (day-by-day) record of financial transactions. It lists debits and credits with a short description of each transaction. Information from the journal is used to put together financial statements.

landed cost—The invoice cost of an item plus any freight, taxes, import charges, handling charges, or any other cost of getting the item into inventory.

layaway program—A program that lets a customer pick out an item and reserve it until they are able to pay the whole price. The customer picks out an item, pays a down payment, and then makes periodic arranged payments. The merchant holds the item for the customer, turning it over to the customer when payments are finished.

lease—A legal contract between someone who wishes to rent a space and the owner of a property. There are several kinds of leases including flat lease, step lease, net lease, *triple-net lease*, *cost-of-living* lease, and percentage lease.

leasehold improvements—Repairs, improvements, or permanent additions or attachments made to a leased facility as agreed to in the lease. See also *tenant improvements*.

lessee—The tenant, the person who is responsible for paying rent and meeting other contractual obligations in exchange for the right to occupy a space.

lessor—The landlord. The owner of a property; the one who leases that property to the occupant.

liability—Any claim on the assets of a person or corporation; something (financial or otherwise) you are responsible for.

liability insurance—An insurance policy that protects you against financial losses due to a negligent act or failure to act. See also *bodily injury liability insurance*.

LIFO (last in, first out)—A way of costing your inventory for tax purposes.

limited liability company—A legal form of business similar to a partnership or sole proprietorship. In a limited liability company, however, the owners are not personally liable for business debts. Profits and losses are treated as personal income.

limited partnership—A partnership that has both general partners and limited partners. Only general partners have the authority to conduct business. Limited partners are uninvolved in the day-to-day operation of the business and are liable for debts against the partnership only to the limit of their investment.

line of credit—A loan that gives you access to a specific amount of money should you need it sometime in the future. A line of credit charges you interest only on the money you actually borrow and only for the period of time you have borrowed it. See also *seasonal line of credit* and *revolving line of credit*.

liquid assets—Assets that can be readily turned into cash.

logo—The name of your business rendered in a distinctive graphic image. Like the slogan, it captures something about your business and conveys it in an immediate, visceral way.

long-term liability—Any loan or debt that does not have to be paid in a year or less.

loss leaders—Products you advertise at an attractively low price to bring business into your store. Sometimes you can offer them at a low price because your landed cost on them is low, sometimes because your markup is low, sometimes both. Often they are bottom-of-the-line items or items of lesser quality than the rest of your line. The main purpose of a loss leader is not to make money but to bring in people to see your entire line of inventory.

markdown—Reducing the price of an item to sell it faster. Markdowns are sometimes necessary if you overbuy and have too much money tied up in inventory. They can help you sell seasonal or shopworn merchandise. And they can keep you competitive if your competition has lowered their prices.

marketing—The process of placing goods or services in the market-place. It includes market research and advertising.

marketing identity—A statement that combines feature-benefit combinations with image to create a picture of your school/business. A marketing identity defines who you are and sets you apart from your competition. Its purpose is to attract students/customers.

markup—The difference between the *landed cost* of an item (what an item cost you including shipping, import duties, and any handling costs) and *retail price* (what you sell it for). It is figured as a percentage of the retail price. For example, if an item costs you $8 landed cost, and you are selling it for $16 retail price, the markup on that item is $8, or 50 percent of the retail cost. Markup is usually expressed as a percentage. When it is expressed in dollars, it is usually referred to as gross profit.

From the markup, you pay operating expenses—wages/salaries, advertising, rent, and utilities. From the markup you also get your profit.

mass marketing—Marketing to a large number of people at once. Newspaper, radio, and television advertisements and general mailings are mass marketing. It contrasts with *direct marketing*.

medical liability insurance—Insurance that protects your business from financial loss due to claims of bodily injury connected with the business.

minimum inventory—The minimum number of any given item that you want to keep in stock. Minimum inventory is calculated by looking at how fast an item turns and how quickly you can get replacement stock from the supplier to replace those you have sold.

negative cash flow—A situation in which cash outflow is greater than cash inflow. In other words, you have negative cash flow if you are spending more than you are making.

net income—See *profit*.

net net net—See *triple net lease*.

net worth—The amount by which an individual's or company's *assets* exceed *liabilities*. Assets minus liabilities equals net worth.

nondisturbance—A clause in the lease that states that so long as the lease is not in default, the landlord will not unreasonably disturb you or your space. Not all leases have nondisturbance clauses.

NSF checks—Nonsufficient funds checks. These are returned by the bank when the check writer's account does not contain enough money for the bank to pay them. They are also known as "bounced checks."

operating expenses—Normal costs incurred as a result of doing business.

overhead—All expenses needed to operate the business except labor.

partnership—A business owned by two or more people. There are several kinds of partnerships. See also *general partnership* and *limited partnership*.

pass through—Expenses billed to the tenant as a cost of occupying a rented space (beyond rent, rental taxes, and triple net). For example, an outside company (or the government) bills the landlord for services rendered for the benefit of the tenant. The landlord passes those costs on directly to the tenant.

payroll taxes—Federal and state taxes that must be paid to the government on a scheduled basis. Payroll taxes include matching *FICA*, *FUTA*, and SUTA. On a financial statement, withholding taxes are a *liability* but not an *expense*.

personal financial statement—A document that contains a summary of your personal assets, liabilities, income, and expenses. Lenders will want it. Landlords may want it.

personal guarantee—When a lender asks a business owner to secure a business loan using personal assets. See also *guaranty of a lease*.

personal property—Desks, files, office supplies, paintings, and wall hangings. Those things that you would remove from your present business location when you moved to another.

personal property insurance—Insurance that protects the contents of your space—your equipment, furniture, tenant improvements, anything you keep at your business—should you be the victim of theft, vandalism, fire, or similar disaster. Like renters' insurance that apartment dwellers have on the contents of the apartment, personal property insurance covers replacement of the things you keep inside your building, not the building itself.

plateau-level bargaining—A kind of negotiation that expects you to put everything on the table during the negotiations. You and your landlord sit down and put your requests and your concessions on the table. You negotiate to an agreement. At that moment you are done; no further changes should be made to the contract after you have arrived at a final agreement.

P.O.P. materials—"Point of purchase" items. They are objects purposely put in a place where business is transacted. Their purpose is to reinforce the attitude that a particular financial transaction is a prudent decision. They may include photos, trophies, posters advertising the benefits of your school, anything that conveys a part of your marketing image in a quick, effective way.

posting—The act of entering financial data into a financial record.

price—What you sell a item for. Contrasts with *cost*, which is what you pay for an item.

price-matching guarantees—A company policy that states you will sell the same products at the same or lower prices than your competitor.

pricing strategy—The rationale behind the price you put on your goods and services.

principal—(1) The owner or one of the owners of a business; (2) the original amount of a loan.

profit—The last line on your *profit and loss statement*. It is the money left after all your expenses and costs have been paid. Also called income, earnings, and the *bottom line*.

profit and loss forecast—A projection of how many dollars you will receive and how many you will spend during some future period of time. It is used by lenders and by business owners for financial planning.

profit and loss statement—A statement of the money you have taken in and paid out. It adds all income from all sources and deducts all expenses paid during a specific period (a month, a year, or some other specific period). The balance, whether positive (*profit*) or negative (loss), tells you how your business is doing financially.

property insurance—Insurance that covers damage to the building in which you do business.

proprietorship—See *sole proprietorship*.

ratios—A comparison of one number to another. It is calculated by dividing one number into another. Part of managing a business involves calculating specific ratios. These ratios are based on numbers taken from a balance sheet or *profit and loss statement*. They reflect a business's financial health (and can help prove that health to a lender if necessary). See *return on investment, acid test ratio,* and *current ratio.*

release statement—A document that releases you from responsibility should a student be injured on your premises during one of your classes or at any function sponsored by your organization. It should be signed by any student who wishes to train with you even for a single class.

retail business—A business that exists to sell goods to the consumer. It contrasts with a *service business.*

retail income—Money coming in as payment for a product (that is, tangible things, goods sold). It contrasts with *service income*, which is money coming in as payment for time and effort (that is, intangible things, services rendered).

retail price—The price that the final consumer pays for an item.

return on investment (ROI)—A ratio that measures profitability by dividing net profit by total assets. It is typically expressed as a percentage. The lowest acceptable ROI is around 1 to 3 percent; 5 to 10 percent is a good ROI.

revolving line of credit—An agreement with the bank to borrow money as your business needs it. You pay back the amount borrowed as you are able, and pay interest only on the amount you have borrowed. A typical purpose of a revolving line of credit is to help you meet your growth needs over the course of a year or more. Typically this kind of loan requires collateral. See also *seasonal line of credit.*

S corporation—A legal form of incorporation that has the legal advantages of a corporation but is taxed like a partnership.

SBA (Small Business Administration)—An agency of the federal government whose purpose is to foster small business growth.

SCORE (the Service Corps of Retired Executives)—A group of experienced volunteers who work with the SBA to provide free counseling on most facets of starting and managing a small business.

seasonal line of credit—A specific amount of money that is kept available for you by a lender. You borrow what you need and pay interest only on what you borrow. Generally, you will need to pay these loans back within a year. See also *revolving line of credit*.

secured loan—A debt backed by collateral.

security deposit—Money paid up front by the tenant and held by the landlord against possible damage to the property (other than that caused by normal wear and tear). If at the end of the leasing period the property is undamaged, the security deposit is returned to the tenant. For the tenant, a security deposit is considered an *asset*. It is not, however, a *current asset* unless it will be returned within the year.

self-employment tax—Taxes paid by self-employed individuals for Medicare and Social Security.

selling price—See *retail price*.

service business—Any business that operates to provide a service, not goods to its customer. It contrasts with *retail business*.

service income—Money coming in as payment for time and effort, that is, intangible things, services rendered. It contrasts with *retail income*, which is payment for a product, a tangible thing (that is, goods sold). In many states service income is not subject to sales tax.

SE taxes—See *self-employment tax*.

short-term financing—A loan or line of credit that must be paid back in a year or less.

single-entry bookkeeping—A way of keeping financial records that requires each financial transaction be entered once. It contrasts with *double-entry bookkeeping.*

slogan—A short statement, eight words or less, whose purpose is to link a central facet of your image with the name of your business.

sole proprietorship—A business owned, financed, and operated by a single individual or married couple. Profits and losses are treated as personal income. The individual is personally liable for any debts and claims against the business.

solvency—The ability of a business to meets its financial obligations.

spreadsheet—A working paper on which numbers are arranged in columns and rows.

start-up capital—The money needed to cover the expenses associated with beginning a business. The money needed to cover the costs incurred before the business begins making money.

straight-line depreciation—The most common method of depreciation. It divides the purchase price of an asset into equal parts (five or seven parts, depending on the anticipated life to the item). Doing so allows you on your taxes to deduct the cost of the item over a period of time. You spread the cost of that equipment over the P&Ls of the next five to seven years. See also *depreciation* and *accumulated depreciation.*

Subchapter S corporation—See *S corporation.*

subletting—An arrangement in which the lessee leases the space to another person. For example, X, the landlord, leases a space to Y for five years. Y then leases that space to Z for four of those years. Some leases prohibit subletting.

subrogation—See waiver of subrogation.

tangible assets—Material things (things that you can see or feel) that you own. Tangible assets include *current* and *fixed assets*.

target enrollment—The number of paying students you will need to break even, pay your salary, and support any additional projects you would like to have.

target market—The people to whom you aim your services. A description of target market usually includes age, gender, marital status, disposable income, location of residence, and other social and economic factors.

tenant—The lessee, the one who is given the right to occupy a space in exchange for rent.

tenant improvements—Often called "TIs." Improvements to a building or the land it's on to make the space meet the needs of the tenant. The costs of TIs may be born by the tenant or the landlord, depending on what is specified in the lease. See also *leasehold improvements*.

traffic pattern—The flow of movement inside or outside your school, the places people commonly walk to get between the different areas in your school.

transaction privilege tax—Sales tax.

triple net lease—The most common form of commercial lease. In a triple net lease the stated rent excludes insurance, common maintenance expenses, and real estate taxes. You as the tenant pay these cost as additional expenses over the rental fee.

turnover—See *inventory turnover*.

unemployment insurance—Insurance that enables your employees to collect a portion of their salary if they are laid off or fired without good reason. Premiums for unemployment insurance are calculated as a percentage of payroll. Both the state and federal government offer unemployment insurance benefits.

use tax license—Sales tax license.

variable expenses—Costs of doing business that vary depending on how much business you do or the choices you make for your business. Sales commissions are a variable expense.

W-2 form—The IRS Wage and Tax Statement. It is a form that the employer files with the IRS and State Tax Authority at the end of the year. Copies of the W-2 are given to the employee to account for the year's wages and withholding.

W-3 form—The transmittal form an employer uses to send the W-2s to the IRS.

W-4 forms—The IRS Employee Withholding Allowance Certificate. The employee fills out this form for the employer, stating his or her name, address, Social Security number and number of deductions. Its purpose is to tell the employer how much income tax to withhold.

walk-away pack—The packet of information that prospective students take with them after an initial visit. It might include your brochure, a price list, a schedule, or information about special offers. It should definitely include anything you want students to remember when they are assessing your competition

workers' compensation insurance—Insurance that covers employee injury and loss of wages resulting from accidents on the job. Most states require that any business with more than a certain number of employees have workers' compensation insurance.

awards and programs, 185–86

B

bait and switch, 236

balance sheets, 157–58, 167–69, 265

balloon payment loan, 265

banks

    choosing, 28–29

    credit card services from, 71–72

    loans from, 20

barter, 136, 265

basic needs, 7–8

beginner's classes, 199

benefits

    analysis of, 7–9

    definition, 265

    matching needs to, 121–23, 131–32

billing companies, 257

bills (accounts payable), 158–59, 263

birthday cards, 182

blind items, 221, 265

bodily injury liability insurance, 265

bookkeepers, 265

bookkeeping and accounting, 156

    double-entry, 271

    single-entry, 282

    See also financial records

bootstrapping, 19

bottom line, 164–67, 266

brand-name recognition, 220–21

break-even point, 15–19, 266

brochures, 59, 82–84

broker (insurance broker), 273

buildings. *See* locations

burnout, 197

business cards, 59, 82

Business Information Centers, 30

business interruption insurance, 60, 266

business licenses, 57, 266

business loans. *See* loans

business names

    choosing, 9–11

    registering, 59

business offices, 53, 108–9

business personal property insurance, 278

business plans

    break-even point calculations, 15–19

    definition, 266

    evaluating, 36–37

    information in, 36

    layer approach, 34–36

    monthly expenses estimate, 15–16

    per-student income and expenses estimate, 16–18

    reasons for writing, 33–34

    start-up costs estimate, 13–14

business registration, 57

business structure options, 31–33

C

C Corporations, 32

caller information sheets, 123–26

CAM (common area mainte-
nance), 44–45, 266
cancellation provisions, 69
capital, 266
capitalization, 266
card decks, 266
cash accounting, 267
cash budget, 267
cash drawers/boxes, 148–49
cash flow statements, 267
catalog orders, 235, 239
certificate of occupancy, 57, 267
certified financial statements, 267
certified public accountant (CPA),
267
checking account registers,
160–61, 162, 163
checks, from students, 147
children, 4, 125, 174–75, 188
See also students
city requirements, 57
closing, definition, 267
closing techniques, 132–35,
254–55
collateral, 24, 267
collections. *See* student payments
commencement date, 268
commercial loans, 20
common area, 268
common area maintenance
(CAM), 44–45, 266
common stock, 268
community, building a sense of,
190–94
competing martial arts schools
choosing a location and, 40

setting fees and, 65–66
computer software
accounts receivable, 153–54
attendance tracking, 144–47
custom-made, 146
financial records, 170
consistency, 176–77
contracts. *See* leases; student contracts
cooperative advertising, 268
cooperative mailings, 268
corporations, 32, 268
correction (criticism) of students,
179–81
cosigners, 22, 268
cost, 268
cost of goods sold, 268
cost of living clause, 268
costs
inventory methods, 210–11
landed, 228, 274
leasing, 43–45, 51
start-up, 13–14
county requirements, 57
coupon books and packages,
97–98
CPA (certified public accountant),
267
credit card brokers, 72
credit cards, 71–72, 147–48
credit line (line of credit), 19, 275,
280, 281
credit reports, 23
creditor, 269
crime insurance, 269

criticism (correction) of students, 179–81
current assets, 269
current liability, 269
current portion of loans, 269
current ratio, 169, 269–70
customer service, 238–41
customers
    pro-shop, 207–9
    See also phone contacts; walk-in customers

D
daily balance sheets, 157–58
deductibles, 270
default, 270
delay in commencement, 270
demographics, 3, 38–40, 270
depreciation, 270
direct mail campaigns, 98–99
direct marketing
    definition, 103, 270
    leads clubs, 105–6
    low-cost ideas for, 104
    neighborhood, 103–5
    point of purchase materials, 108–9
    service clubs, 105–6
    student referrals, 106–7
    walk-away packets, 110, 284
discipline problems, 187–89
discretionary (optional) expenses, 18, 271
dismissal, student, 190
display and layout, pro shops, 232–34

disposable income, 271
double-entry bookkeeping, 271
dressing rooms, 52
drop-in problems, 253–54
drop-outs
    identifying reasons for, 250–52
    numbers of, 247
    preventing
        among intermediate students, 195–96
        among new students, 199–201
        among senior students, 196–97
        avoiding teacher burnout, 197
        building sense of community, 190–94
        ensuring feelings of success, 183–86
        focusing on student needs, 178–83
        good discipline, 187–89
        maintaining interest, 173–77
        personal contact, 181–82, 183, 189–90, 201–2
        by playing, 177
        promoting safety, 194
        solving student financial problems, 197–98
        by working, 177–78
    seasonal, 249–50
    and training levels, 248–49
    winning back, 201–2

financial records
accounts payable, 158–59
accounts receivable, 150–54
annual reports, 264
balance sheets, 157–58, 167–69
checking account registers,
160–61, 162, 163
collections, 148–50, 158
computer programs, 170
journal, 161–63
minimum requirements, 155,
170
petty cash, tracking, 156
profit and loss statement
(P&L), 164–67
ratios, 167, 169
receipts, 157–58, 159–60
See also student payments
financial statements, 272
financing plans, 66–67
first aid, 70, 75–76
first impressions, 126–28
fixed assets, 272
fixed expenses, 272
fixtures, pro shop, 233–34
floorplans, 51–54
flyers, 84–89
checklist for, 86
event, 84–87
feature, 87
principles of design, 87–89
freedom of information laws, 143
fun, importance of, 177
fund raisers, 193
furnishings, 38, 233–34

FUTA (Federal Unemployment
Tax Act), 63, 272

G
general journal, 161–63
general liability insurance, 61
general partnerships, 31, 272
get-togethers, 193–94
goals
school, 244–47, 260
student, 184–85
government loans, 20–22
government requirements
for employees, 73
IRS, 57–58, 155, 170, 210, 274
licenses and certificates, 56–59
for pro shops, 209–11
grand opening rates, 67
graphic artists, 80–81
gross income, 272
gross profit, 272
gross volume, 272
growth and expansion, 260–61
growth rate, 245–46
guarantor, 273
guaranty of a lease, 273

H
Handicapped Assistance Loan
Program, 21
heating, 43, 273
HVAC (heating, ventilation, air
conditioning), 43, 54, 273

I
identity. *See* marketing identity

price-matching guarantees,
239–40
profit from, 206, 219–20,
225–26, 231
pros and cons of, 203–6
retail licenses for, 209
returns, 238
sales tax, 165, 209
size of, 242–43
special catalog orders, 239
special sales, 237–38
steps in starting, 205
suppliers, 214–17
theft, 232
tracking inventory, 226–32
turnover rate, 221–24
working capital needed, 211–14
profit, 279
profit and loss forecast, 279
profit and loss statement (P&L),
164–67, 279
property insurance, 45, 60, 280
proprietorships. *See* sole proprietorships
prospective students
children, 125
closing problems, 254–55
closing techniques, 132–35
contracts (agreements), 68–71,
136–37
drop-in problems, 253–54
employees and, 139–41
first impressions of, 126–28
follow up, 138–39
phone calls from, 117–26

schedules and fees, explanation
of, 135–36
school tour, 130–32
treatment of, 128–30
walk-away packets, 110, 284
walk-in customers, 126–32
punishment, use of, 180, 188–89

R
ratios, 167, 169, 280
real estate agents, 39, 41, 46
real estate attorneys, 46, 50
real estate taxes, 44
receipts
balancing, 156–58
custom forms, 149
pro shop, 227–28
saving, 159–60
student payment, 149–50
record keeping
for minimum required statistics, 246–47
pro shop, 226–32
See also financial records; student records
referrals, 106–7
release statements, 69–71, 280
rental tax, 44
repetition, 175–76
retail business, 280
retail income, 280
retail licenses, 57
retail price, 280
return on investment (ROI), 167,
169, 221–24, 280
revolving line of credit, 19, 280

NOTES

NOTES

NOTES